Law, Time and Historical Injustices

This book provides a critical assessment of how judges reason in the adjudication of historical injustices.

The practice of adjudication in historical cases of injustice require that, in determining collective responsibility, judges impart meaning to past injuries. This book analyses the narrative mechanisms through which this meaning is produced. Focusing on three areas of adjudication—racial discrimination, post-colonial extractivism and the climate crisis—the book's analysis focuses on the issue of time. It considers the interplay of how historical injustice adjudication is shaped by temporal presuppositions and how it enacts a particular idea of temporality. As experiences of injustice are narrated, the book demonstrates how some of those experiences are included and others are excluded within the process of adjudication. Drawing on legal theory, legal epistemology and the philosophy of time, the book thus offers an instructive, and provocative, account of how collective responsibility is determined in cases of historical injustice.

This book will appeal to scholars working in the fields of legal theory, legal reasoning, socio-legal studies, comparative jurisprudence and transitional justice.

Harison Citrawan is a researcher at the Research Center for Law under the Indonesian National Research and Innovation Agency.

Law, Time and Historical Injustices

A Critical Analysis of Intuitive Judicial Reasoning

Harison Citrawan

Routledge
Taylor & Francis Group
a GlassHouse Book

First published 2025
by Routledge
4 Park Square, Milton Park, Abingdon, Oxon OX14 4RN

and by Routledge
605 Third Avenue, New York, NY 10158

Routledge is an imprint of the Taylor & Francis Group, an informa business

A GlassHouse book

British Library Cataloguing-in-Publication Data
A catalogue record for this book is available from the British Library

Library of Congress Cataloging-in-Publication Data
Names: Citrawan, Harison, author.
Title: Law, time, and historical injustices : a critical analysis of intuitive judicial reasoning / Harison Citrawan.
Description: Abingdon, Oxon [UK] ; New York, NY : Routledge, 2025. | Includes bibliographical references and index.
Identifiers: LCCN 2024037132 (print) | LCCN 2024037133 (ebook) | ISBN 9781032855592 (hardback) | ISBN 9781032855615 (paperback) | ISBN 9781003518693 (ebook)
Subjects: LCSH: Law—Methodology. | Reparations for historical injustices. | Restorative justice. | Judicial process. | Transitional justice. | Race discrimination—Law and legislation.
Classification: LCC KZ6785 .C58 2025 (print) | LCC KZ6785 (ebook) | DDC 347/.05—dc23/eng/20240813
LC record available at https://lccn.loc.gov/2024037132
LC ebook record available at https://lccn.loc.gov/2024037133

ISBN: 978-1-032-85559-2 (hbk)
ISBN: 978-1-032-85561-5 (pbk)
ISBN: 978-1-003-51869-3 (ebk)

DOI: 10.4324/9781003518693

Typeset in Sabon
by Apex CoVantage, LLC

Dedicated to my wife, Susan, and our two wonderful children, Hagia and Hegel—who lend me time to think about time

Contents

Acknowledgments

The journey of writing this book has involved many individuals, organizations and institutions. This book began as a dissertation at Penn State Dickinson Law, and I would like to thank Professor William Butler, my research supervisor, who has shared ideas, critiques and challenging questions throughout the writing process. My deepest gratitude goes to professors Sara Gerke and William Ewald for their valuable time to read, comment and assess the quality of this work. I am particularly indebted to the Fulbright Program, i.e., IIE and Fulbright-AMINEF Indonesia, for the financial assistance and valuable experience during my doctoral fellowship.

Many thanks go to the Penn State Dickinson Law community, especially to Professor Danielle Conway and Dr. Anthony Ogden, for their relentless help, guidance and assistance, and to Brent Newton for an exciting research opportunity. At home, I extend my gratitude to the Ministry of Law and Human Rights of Indonesia and Research Center for Law at the National Research and Innovation Agency. Warm thanks to Professor Sigit Riyanto, Dr. Sri Puguh Budi Utami, Dr. Patricia Rinwigati and Mr. Aman Riyadi for their timely recommendations. I also thank my reading group—Dewi, Angga and Adis—for their constant support and long-night discussions, and Ganesh, Sabrina, Novzel, Mas Arief and Aji Utomo for the conversations about time and memory.

Parts of this book have benefitted from discussions and conversations in the following 2022–2024 events: Joint Socio-Legal Conference (Brawijaya), Socio-Legal Studies Association Conference (York), Transitional Justice in the United States Manuscript Workshop (WashU), Annual YCC Global Conference American Society of Comparative Law (Northeastern), Legal Research Discussion (BRIN), SJD Colloquium (Dickinson), SJD Roundtable (Georgetown), JSEALab Dissertation Workshop (Wisconsin) and Methodologies for Imagining an Alternative Politics of (Human) Rights (LSE). Some initial ideas for this study also came up from chats with colleagues and friends in Carlisle: Mireille, Mahkhsar, Lyubo, Ale and Doug.

Thanks are due to Dr. Colin Perin and Naomi Round Cahalin at Routledge for their superb editorial assistance, and to my mentor and colleague,

Professor Raff Donelson, from whom this work acquires many aspirations. Much gratitude also goes to my parents and in-laws for their unwavering support and prayers. Finally, I dedicate this book to my wife, Susan, and our two wonderful children, Hagia and Hegel—for lending me time to think about time.

Cases (alphabetical order)

Hoge Raad [Supreme Court] Dec. 12, 2019, The State of the Netherlands v. Urgenda Foundation., Case No. 19/00135 (Neth.)

In re African-Am. Slave Descendants Litig., 375 F. Supp 2d. 721, 726 (N.D. Ill. 2005)

In re African-American Slave Descendants Lit., 471 F.3d 754, 762 (7th Cir. 2006).

Korematsu v. United States BT—US, 323 214 (1944).

Mahkamah Agung [Supreme Court] Apr. 10, 2017, Nurhidayah et al. v. PT. Aetra Air Jakarta et.al (31K/Pdt/2017) (Indon.)

Mahkamah Agung [Supreme Court] Nov. 30, 2018, Nurhidayah et al. v. PT. Aetra Air Jakarta et.al (Case Review 841 PK/Pdt/2018) (Indon.)

Mahkamah Konstitusi [Consitional Court] Feb, 18, 2013, 85/PUU-XI/2013 (Indon.)

Michigan v. Lucas BT—US, 500 145 (1991).

Obergefell v. Hodges, 575 U.S. 994, 135 S. Ct. 2071, 191 L. Ed. 2d 953 (2015).

PN Jakarta Pusat [Central Jakarta District Court] Mar. 24, 2015, Nurhidayah et al. v. PT. Aetra Air Jakarta et.al (527/Pdt.G/2012/PN JKT.PST) (Indon.)

PT DKI Jakarta [Jakarta High Court] Jan. 12, 2016, Nurhidayah et al. v. PT. Aetra Air Jakarta et.al (588/PDT/2015/PT DKI). (Indon.)

Rechtbank Den Haag [The Hague District Court] June 24, 2015, Urgenda v The Netherlands, Case No. C/09/456689 (Neth.)

Hoge Raad [Supreme Court] December 20, 2019, Urgenda v The Netherlands, Case No. 19/00135 (Neth.)

Rechtbank Den Haag [The Hague District Court] May 26, 2021, Milieudefensie et al. v. Royal Dutch Shell., Case No. C/09/571932/Ha Za 19–379 (Neth.)

Regents of the Univ. of Cal. v. Bakke, 438 U.S. 265, 292 (1978)

Tables

Introduction

Judge's cognitive dilemma

In historical injustice cases, judges are more often than not required to decide whether they should grant reparation for wrongdoings that once happened in a distant past, to draw the disputed past by using a broader stroke to include a wider context of the wrongdoings or even to eliminate the past and narrow down the wrongdoings from the lens of the present as though the past never existed and does not persist. This situation reflects what we call judge's cognitive dilemma. It is understood as the judges' epistemic capacity to include (or exclude) some experiences of injustice in their reasoning process in order to justify collective legal responsibility. Bearing these dilemmas in mind, a legal *case* has at a glance turned into a series of historical *events* in which the judges' articulation of law is as much contested as their recollection of historical facts. Since legal adjudication is always situated within the judges' epistemic condition, we may want to ask why and how this navigating process actually happens. Isn't it just common sense that guides the judges in navigating the dilemmas? Or, instead, by actually navigating the dilemma, are judges persistently showing a peculiar mode of thinking?

In a 2004 civil case in the United States, the District Court of Illinois was awkwardly positioned to examine and rectify the country's distant past of centuries ago. In this *African American Slave Descendants* civil suit, a claim for historical reparation was filed by a class of citizens against several financial companies that allegedly profited from and were involved in slavery.[1] The District Court, however, decided to reject the claim. This rejection seemingly reflects a common sense that the court is unable to fully contemplate the alleged wrongdoings over such a long time span. Interestingly, four principles are expressed by the District Court to justify the decision, namely that (1) there was no specific connection between the Plaintiffs and the Defendants, (2) the Court is restricted by prudential limitations that prohibit it from giving an answer to such a broad inquiry of social importance, (3) the issue of slavery reparation falls outside of judicial authority, and (4) the reparation

1 In re African-American Slave Descendants Litig., 375 F. Supp 2d. 721, 726 (N.D. Ill. 2005)

DOI: 10.4324/9781003518693-1

claim was untimely submitted.[2] Similar to many other historical reparation claims elsewhere, it seems fair to say that the four principles are basically part of the court's attempt to navigate their cognitive dilemma in establishing collective legal responsibility in legal claims involving a range of narratives that impart meaning to past injuries.[3]

Implicit in *African American Slave Descendants Litigation* are three categories of judges' cognitive dilemmas. The first is related to the dilemma of agency. This agential dilemma primarily deals with the ways in which judges consider factual patterns of historical wrongs that may involve a broad category of social and public importance and why they are prohibited from giving an answer to such an inquiry. As is the case in many legal inquiries involving the collectiveness of persistent and structural injustices, legal inquiries may end up in anonymity. In this sense, Arendt's expression 'when all are guilty, no one is' can be interpreted as a sign to indicate the judges' epistemic capacity in applying the rule against collective guilt.[4] It seems that judges are not adequately equipped with proper methods of reasoning, especially when it comes to concerns about collective responsibility for past wrongdoings. It would seemingly be awkward to have them respond to questions about who the wrongdoers and the victims are in today's pressing matters of societal discrimination, post-colonial legacies or even the climate crisis, to name a few. In these matters, law traditionally requires one's claim to be individuated and well-identified (i.e., in terms of who, what and when of a case), or else the claim will be considered as a mere dubious petition. But at the same time, legal decision-makers are insistent on not turning a blind eye to the complex array of the so-called epistemic injustices; that is, any instances involving some riveting terms such as the community's passive inaction, the victim's unspeakable truth and suffering,[5] the enhanced vulnerability to victimization,[6] the banality of evil[7] and many other exigencies against which law and legal adjudication appear to be silent, let alone acting responsively.[8]

2 Ibid., 780–81

3 *See* generally Eric A. Posner and Adrian Vermeule, "Reparations for Slavery and Other Historical Injustices," *Columbia Law Review* 103 (2003): 689; Naomi Roht-Arriaza, "Reparations Decisions and Dilemmas," *Hastings International and Comparative Law Review* 27 (2003): 157; Sonja Klinsky and Jasmina Brankovic, *The Global Climate Regime and Transitional Justice* (New York: Routledge, 2018).

4 Hannah Arendt, *Responsibility and Judgment* (New York: Schocken, 2003).

5 Priscilla B. Hayner, *Unspeakable Truths: Transitional Justice and the Challenge of Truth Commissions*, 2nd ed. (New York & London: Routledge, 2011).

6 Mark J. Osiel, *Mass Atrocity, Collective Memory and the Law* (Routledge, 2017).

7 James Waller, *Confronting Evil: Engaging Our Responsibility to Prevent Genocide* (New York: Oxford University Press, 2016).

8 Miranda Fricker, *Epistemic Injustice: Power and the Ethics of Knowing* (Oxford: Oxford University Press, 2007); Rachel McKinnon, "Epistemic Injustice," *Philosophy Compass* 11, no. 8 (2016): 437–46; Sinéad Ring, "On Delay and Duration: Law's Temporal Orders in Historical

In these contexts, the dilemma of agency entails the need to a reconsideration and reexamination of the agential role of judges in construing factual patterns and providing answers to any (legal) inquiries of social importance.

The second dilemma is related to the objectification of legal responsibility practices, which neglects society's epistemic interdependence. This cognitive dilemma asserts that judicial practices in historical injustice adjudication have been limited when the courts are required to attribute collective legal responsibility in today's epistemic interdependence. Looking at *African American Slave Descendants Litigation*, for instance, the inquiry into (collective) legal responsibility—which is traditionally structured by harm, injury and risks—impels the judges to infer responsibility from a quantitative measurement based on the principle of proximity.[9] At this point, the cognitive dilemma is that the proximity principle has predominantly framed legal cases narrowly into its *spatial* aspect. That is, this principle insists on objective, predictable and even repeatable laws of responsibility for the purpose of future cases. As a result, the *temporal* dimension of a case is left unexamined. It is important here to note that we are not trying to suggest that judges are (or should be) abandoning the temporal aspect of a case. Instead, it is suggestive that in justifying legal responsibility, judges have been treating time as an *external* object, and they do this through containment and fragmentation of time. Consequently, legal responsibility practices have been virtually underwritten by temporal objectification. These practices tend to risk the qualitative, interdependent and experiential features of harm, injury and risks undervalued, especially in the methods of legal reasoning. To give us a practical instance, one may find in tort cases that the objectification of legal responsibility encounters three kinds of limitation, in a sense that such objectified responsibility practices somehow fail to embrace society's epistemic interdependence, such as, borrowing from Wright, (1) the no-worse-off limitation, understood as "when the harm would have occurred anyway in the absence of any tortious conduct or condition"; (2) the superseding cause limitation, which is "when there was a superseding cause of the harm"; and (3) the risk playout limitation, seen as a kind of situation "when the harm did not occur as part of the realization and playing out of one of the foreseeable risks that made the person's conduct tortious, before the hazards created by the realization of that risk had dissipated."[10] Taking these limitations into account, the problem in the (spatialized-objectified) proximity principle necessitates

Child Sexual Abuse Cases," in *Law and Time*, ed. Siân M. Beynon-Jones and Emily Grabham (London: Routledge, 2019), 93–107.

9 John C. P. Goldberg, "Rethinking Injury and Proximate Cause," *San Diego Law Review* 40, no. 4 (2003): 1315.

10 Richard W. Wright, "The Grounds and Extent of Legal Responsibility," *San Diego Law Review* 40 (2003): 1427.

legal decision-makers re-orienting legal responsibility practice to the extent that such practice can further reinforce society's epistemic interdependence.[11]

The third cognitive dilemma is related to the law's image of linearity and predictability. In this context, in order for the legal decision-makers to express a lawful relation in historical injustice cases, they traditionally perceive the law through the grounds of rules-determinacy. Supported by many legal theories, it has been set out that the rules-determinacy is underpinned by the image of linearity and predictability. In this sense, *linearity* perceives the idea of lawfulness as being generated and transferred from a basic belief that took place within a slice of time. It is from such transferable basic beliefs that judges confer the justification of forms of lawful relation in legal disputes[12]—or, in our case, the justification of collective responsibility in historical injustice adjudications. Meanwhile, *predictability* maintains that any judicial reactions to legal events are logically formulaic, especially in light of exigencies for future cases.[13] Suggested by contemporary critiques of law, the law's images of linearity and predictability have put judicial creativity and inventiveness outside of the law. That is, some oft-used labels such as judicial activism, judicial environmentalism, progressive judgment, landmark decisions and so on, are identified as irregular or uncommon practices in adjudicative exercises. We may now arrive at the view that such linearity and predictability—or one may say 'legal foundationalism'—alienate and even suppress legal decision-makers' creativity and inventiveness in finding justifying reasons and, accordingly, in expressing the law. To put the issue into the context of historical injustices, we may say that the legal foundationalism has set judges down in a dilemma of capturing the multiplicity of witnessing experiences,[14] the continuity and persistence of violence[15] or even the afterlife of judgment.[16]

11 As an example in climate change litigation discourse, *See* Petra Minnerop and Friederike Otto, "Climate Change and Causation: Joining Law and Climate Science on the Basis of Formal Logic," *Buffalo Environmental Law Journal* 27, no. 1 (2019): 49.

12 Courtney M. Cox, "The Uncertain Judge," *University of Chicago Law Review* 90, no. 3 (2023): 739–811.

13 For the predictive power of law, see Rostam Josef Neuwirth, "Future Law, the Power of Prediction, and the Disappearance of Time," *Law, Technology and Humans* 4, no. 2 (2022): 38–59.

14 Benjamin Thorne, "An Atrocity Archive: Sensory Expression of Past-Present-Future," *Law and Humanities* 15, no. 2 (2021): 272–78.

15 Zinaida Miller, "The Injustices of Time: Rights, Race, Redistribution, and Responsibility," *Columbia Human Rights Law Review* 52 (2020): 647–737; Yuvraj Joshi, "Racial Transition," *Washington University Law Review* 98 (2020): 1181.

16 Marci Shore, "Germany Has Confronted Its Past. Now It Must Confront the Present," *Foreign Policy*, August 2022; Nevenka Tromp, "In Search for Truth at Mass Atrocities Trials: Will Judges and Lawyers Have the Last Word," *Journal of Comparative Law* 13, no. 1 (2018): 61–82.

The ineptitude of historical injustice adjudication practices to establish or attribute collective legal responsibility is grounded upon the three judicial cognitive dilemmas. This view insists that societies need to resort to some alternative policies capable of navigating the multiplicity of experiences related to past injustices. As a common discourse, any inquiries into historical injustices have been emerging due to the widespread phenomenon of reparative claims toward past wrongdoings in myriad settings, be it reparations of colonial violence, climate catastrophe, persistent racism and so on.[17] In order to establish collective responsibility practices, the corresponding policies may include institutional building, legal and policy formulation, administrative arrangements, international collaborations and many others.[18]

While we must admit court's institutional limitations in dealing with historical injustice complexities, this book would view that the three cognitive dilemmas (of agency, objectivity and linearity) are part of the judges' epistemic capacity to *express* the reality of injustice and the law.[19] Thus, the dilemmas could become our entry point to further investigate how and the extent to which judges *can* actually justify collective responsibility in historical injustice cases. In other words, we are expected to delineate an alternative epistemology of historical injustice adjudication. Specifically later in the case-studies, our focus will be on historical injustice adjudication within the realm of civil litigation, since these phenomena can illustrate a prosaic and regular depiction of how judges think about duty, moral right and responsibility—that is to say, this type of cases demonstrates everyday libertarianism.[20] That said, the kind of inquiry that we are pursuing in this study is a practical activity that engages with some empirical phenomena while simultaneously being attentive to a variety of temporal orientations and justifications of legal judgment.[21]

17 Elazar Barkan, *The Guilt of Nations: Restitution and Negotiating Historical Injustices* (New York & London: W.W. Norton & Company, 2000); Elazar Barkan, "Historical Reconciliation: Redress, Rights and Politics," *Journal of International Affairs* (2006): 1–15.

18 Peter J. Dixon, "Reparations and the Politics of Recognition," *Contested Justice* (2015): 326–51, https://doi.org/10.1017/cbo9781139924528.016; Larissa Van den Herik, "Addressing 'Colonial Crimes' through Reparations? Adjudicating Dutch Atrocities Committed in Indonesia," *Journal of International Criminal Justice* 10, no. 3 (2012): 693–705, https://doi.org/10.1093/jicj/mqs033; Anthony J. Sebok, "Two Concepts of Injustice in Restitution for Slavery," *Boston University Law Review* 84 (2004): 1405.

19 Joseph Raz, "On the Autonomy of Legal Reasoning," *Ratio Juris* 6, no. 1 (1993): 1–15. See further Chapter 6 on the conceptualization of historical injustice as a temporal legal inquiry. Admittedly, this form of problematization appears proximate to the competing ways in explaining reality and consciousness in the field of philosophy of mind.

20 Steven Schaus, "A Simple Model of Torts and Moral Wrongs," *Notre Dame Law Review* 97 (2021): 1029; Liam Murphy, "The Artificial Morality of Private Law: The Persistence of an Illusion," *University of Toronto Law Journal* 70, no. 4 (2020): 453–88, https://doi.org/10.3138/utlj.2019-0103.

21 Maksymilian Del Mar, *Artefacts of Legal Inquiry: The Value of Imagination in Adjudication* (Bloomsbury Publishing, 2020).

Importantly, this book submits that the judge's cognitive dilemmas are fundamentally temporal, meaning that these dilemmas are underpinned by the kind of temporalities enacted through the process of judicial reasoning. Temporalities here are not necessarily clock times but rather lived experiences.[22] Temporalities are, as Chowdhury reflects, multiple and variegated, and hence they are not a homogenous and uniformed entity.[23] Importantly, temporalities are co-produced and structured at personal, agential and societal levels.[24] Within this understanding of temporalities, we can later find an interplay between how judicial reasoning is *actually* shaped by any given temporal presuppositions and how it *virtually* enacts temporal ordering.[25] Such an interplay contributes to the inclusion and exclusion of experiences of injustice essential to collective responsibility justification.

The temporal approach, therefore, implies that the judge's cognitive dilemmas need to be essentially framed as a ballast to further generate a critical examination against the homogeneity and generality of law. This approach might somehow suspend our academic enterprise to desire for change in law, moving instead to "telling stories . . . beyond the familiar problem-solving script."[26] Particularly, it insists on a reexamination of the limits of interpretation and rationality in law in which the traditional features of law maintain legal decision-makers to narrowly reduce legal responsibility practice into a matter of *measuring* quantitative harm and blameworthiness. In a larger context of historical injustice adjudication, the cognitive dilemmas pave the way for an examination of the judge's method of justification that is capable of (1) recognizing and working *with* the complex reality and experiences of injustice and (2) re-orienting the law of responsibility toward the multiplicity and heterogeneity of time. Ultimately, this critical examination will be

22 Sarah Sharma, *In the Meantime: Temporality and Cultural Politics* (Durham & London: Duke University Press, 2014), 8.

23 Tanzil Chowdhury, *Time, Temporality and Legal Judgment* (Oxon & New York: Routledge, 2020).

24 Ibid. Temporalities, quoting from Sharma, are "like continually broken clocks, they must be reset again and again. They are expected to recalibrate and fit into a larger temporal order. Temporalities do not experience a uniform time but rather a time particular to the labor that produces them. Their experience of time depends on where they are positioned within a larger economy of temporal worth." In this sense, as the argument continues, "the temporal subject's living day, as part of its livelihood, includes technologies of the self-contrived for synchronizing to the time of others or having others synchronize to them. The meaning of these subjects' own times and experiences of time is in large part structured and controlled by both the institutional arrangements they inhabit and the time of others—other temporalities." 8.

25 Siân Maeve Beynon-Jones and Emily Grabham, "Introduction," in *Law and Time*, ed. Siân Maeve Beynon-Jones and Emily Grabham (Oxon & New York: Routledge, 2019), 1–28.

26 Eliana Cusato, Rebecca Mignot-Mahdavi, Sofia Stolk, and Renske Vos, "In Praise of Multiplicity: Suspending the Desire to Change the World," *Leiden Journal of International Law* (2023): 2.

productive for us in grappling with an alternative epistemology of historical injustice adjudication.

Untangling the dilemma

Against this background, our primary mission is to untangle the judge's dilemmas. This book revolves around a central investigation of the ways in which we could construct an epistemology of historical injustice adjudication through the frame of temporalities. To allow us to grapple with this general inquiry, two follow-up sub-questions are provided:

(1) if judicial adjudication is a *process* of creating forms of lawful relationship, what mode of thinking do the judges apply in selecting justifying reasons for collective responsibility in historical injustice adjudication?
(2) if temporalities are *inherent* in legal reasoning, how should judges understand legal inquiry and collective responsibility in historical injustice adjudication?

Suffice it to say that in this book we aim to investigate the ethics of judicial reasoning in its social context and how it lends support to an alternative epistemology of historical injustice adjudications. To achieve that end, sub-question (1) tries to understand the mode of thinking and techniques used by the judges in selecting justifying reasons for collective responsibility. It specifically addresses the methodological aspect of how judges enter into the multiplicity of past injustice experiences. Following that analysis, sub-question (2) deals primarily with the epistemological dimension of historical injustice. It seeks to draw an alternative framework for what and how judges know about historical injustice through the lens of legal temporalities. As briefly mentioned earlier, temporalities play a fundamental role in conceptualizing the judges' reasoning process that guides them in finding and selecting any justifying reasons. A discussion about temporalities brings to the fore the significance of *judicial intuition* in guiding judges to infer their conclusion from the multiplicity of experiences of injustice. In this regard, we will later submit that judicial intuition is valuable for judges in selecting justifying reasons insofar as it allows them to signal creative and experimental legal inquiries into the multiplicity of experiences of injustice. As a result, legal techniques and concepts employed by the judges, as part of their reasoning procedure, are *processed* virtually through intuition, which is seen as an immediate method that conflates the modalities of time (i.e., the past, present and future of injustice). This proposition will be fundamental in building an (alternative) epistemology of historical injustice adjudication.

This book's central argument is that historical injustice adjudication is essentially built upon an interplay between how judicial reasoning is shaped by any given temporal presuppositions and how such reasoning enacts temporal ordering. At the core of this epistemological claim is an investigation into the internal structure of judicial reasoning from which this study suggests later that judge's legal reasoning consists of three essential elements of: plurality of *schemes* of intelligibility, epistemic *expression* of rules and facts and justification of *outcomes* in a form of lawful relation.[27] As will be analyzed throughout this study, each of these elements propounds that temporalities play a fundamental role in conceptualizing judges' reasoning process, guiding them in finding and selecting any justifying reasons.

At the moment, relevant to the said argument about temporalities in legal reasoning is Neil MacCormick's observation which holds that a legal reasoner ought to be able to think 'chronically' (i.e., in analytical time) in order to act in an 'experiential' (i.e., perspectival or real-time) frame. In that case, as MacCormick asserted,

> [w]e are able to act in 'perspective time', that is, real time, only to the extent that we can also envisage our activity in analytical time. The momentary 'now' of the specious present in real time belongs in the broader specious present of an activity or project. But this depends on our being able to comprehend activities and projects as coherent series or congeries of actions or acts linked together under some purpose or value or normative framework. Such a comprehension of activities and projects involves an ability to envisage them in the 'before-simultaneously-after' schema of analytical time.[28]

Following MacCormick's assertions, we can understand that analytical and perspectival time operate within legal narratives, which are tied to coherence. Viewing from a legal epistemological perspective, a case, therefore, should be framed as a series of unfolding narratives in which temporalities structure the plot of a legal claim, assess the proof of evidence, and enact an indictment.[29] It is in these structuring processes that we can identify the judge's cognitive dilemma, while at the same time, in this context, we must also assume that

> [c]ourts of law can never enter into the raw history of the facts and events they decide upon. They have access to them only after the events, perhaps

27 Del Mar Maksymilian, "The Spatio-Temporality of Objectification in Legal Theory: Concepts of Legality between Theory and Practice," *Problema: Anuario de Filosofía y Teoría Del Derecho*, no. 2 (2008): 127–55; Del Mar, *Artefacts of Legal Inquiry: The Value of Imagination in Adjudication*; Geoffrey Samuel, *Epistemology and Method in Law* (London & New York: Routledge, 2016).

28 Neil MacCormick, *Rhetoric and the Rule of Law: A Theory of Legal Reasoning* (Oxford: Oxford University Press, 2005), 216.

29 Bartosz Brożek, *The Legal Mind: A New Introduction to Legal Epistemology* (Cambridge: Cambridge University Press, 2020), chap. 4.

> long after them, only through narrative accounts of things that are said to have happened. Cases as they proceed through time develop narratives about past time constructed so as to be relevant to law then in force, and also in such a way as to invoke the powers of convicting and imposing punishments currently vested in the court.[30]

That being said, the judge's cognitive dilemmas hinge upon the narrative accounts of a case. In this book, the dilemma will be comparatively situated within three narratives of: transitory character of racial discrimination, trauma of post-colonial extractivist relationships and uncertainty of climate crisis. The three narrative accounts, certainly amongst many other contemporary predicaments, are seen as an appropriate depiction of the judge's epistemic capacity to *express* the reality of injustice and the law.[31] As is the case, the judicial cognitive dilemmas reflected in these narratives have long been the subject of contention and disagreement, in terms of legal practice, policies and even theories.[32] In these narratives, judges are, as we have suggested, "caught up" in the interplay between how their reasoning is shaped by any temporal presuppositions and how their reasoning enacts some sorts of temporal ordering.

Suffice it to say at the moment that we need to investigate the ways judges include (and exclude) some experiences of injustice within their reasoning process in justifying collective responsibility. One must note that collective responsibility in this study should not be grasped simply as an outcome of a case. Instead, collective responsibility should be regarded as the way a society lives up to the law rather than a fixed, given object decided by their authority. In other words, understanding how a society *creates* their collective responsibility practice requires an examination of how judges enact *legal qualifications* in legal cases, and, as we will explore in the case-study narratives, how this enactment of legal qualifications represents a judicial *action*, that is, a process that *creates* the legal reality of injustice.[33]

30 MacCormick, *Rhetoric and the Rule of Law: A Theory of Legal Reasoning*, 221.

31 See Emmanuel Renault, *The Experience of Injustice: A Theory of Recognition* (New York: Columbia University Press, 2019). Renault's theoretical observation on injustice is valuable at this point, asserting that there is a sort of general connection between how a society *describes* injustice and how it *justifies* injustice.

32 Elizabeth Fisher, Eloise Scotford, and Emily Barritt, "The Legally Disruptive Nature of Climate Change," *The Modern Law Review* 80, no. 2 (2017): 173–201; Renisa Mawani, "Law as Temporality: Colonial Politics and Indian Settlers," *UC Irvine Law Review* 4, no. 1 (2014): 65–95; Ariela Gross, "When Is the Time of Slavery-The History of Slavery in Contemporary Legal and Political Argument," *California Law Review* 96 (2008): 283.

33 Patrick Nerhot, "The Law and Its Reality," in *Law, Interpretation and Reality: Essays in Epistemology, Hermeneutics and Jurisprudence*, ed. Patrick Nerhot (Dordrecht: Springer, 1990), 50–69.

Suggested by emerging studies about creativity and inventiveness in judicial decision-making,[34] this study puts emphasis on the role of cases for jurisprudence in such a way that, as Mussawir has correctly put it, "not because they [cases] involve serious issues, major problems, big concepts, but because they highlight *a possibly minor technical problem of juristic invention*, a problem that raises the creative instincts of legal thought."[35] Cases, in that sense, are a sort of archetype from which theories of legal reasoning take to be central to explain.[36] At the heart of the inquiry into cases is a question of the procedural dimensions of legal judgment: that is, the ways in which legal decision-makers access knowledge in order to find justifying reasons. It is a question not only about adjudicative judgment as a *representation* of law but also as an *expression* undertaken by judges in exercising law's jurisdiction (i.e., jurisdiction in this sense is not only seen as a technical form of authority for declaring the law, but it *is* the expression of the authority of the law). It is an expression of relationship between subject (*persona*)—in which who can make and have the right (e.g., slave descendant, citizens lacking access to water or communities affected by climate crises)—and matter (*res*)—in which some objects (e.g., portions of ancestor's debt, water resources historical mismanagement or spatiotemporal climate safety) are worthy of elaboration as a matter of law by legal decision-makers. Epistemologically this judicial expression, following Nerhot,

> is not a pure and simple application of the rules it refers to, but an assessment of the situations presented by the parties. This is, quite obviously, within the framework that these rules set forth, and in that sense the decision is bound up with facts, but, and this is an important point, the latter cannot be regarded as either a fragment of reality or even as the manifestation of something underlying it. The object of the human sciences in general and of legal science in particular is *a representation covering a diversity of experience with a view to "putting it in order" and thus providing and organizing a rational knowledge of reality*.[37]

34 Brożek, *The Legal Mind: A New Introduction to Legal Epistemology*; Bartosz Brożek, "Legal Interpretation: Towards a New Paradigm?" *Teoria Polityki*, no. 4 (2020): 79–92; Bartosz Brożek, Michał Furman, Marek Jakubiec, and Bartłomiej Kucharzyk, "The Black Box Problem Revisited. Real and Imaginary Challenges for Automated Legal Decision Making," *Artificial Intelligence and Law* (2023): 1–14; Marek Jakubiec, "Between Legal Philosophy and Cognitive Science: The Tension Problem," *Ratio Juris* 35, no. 2 (2022): 223–39.

35 Edward Mussawir, *Jurisdiction in Deleuze: The Expression and Representation of Law* (London: Routledge, 2011), 77. (emphasis added)

36 Frederick Schauer, "The Jurisprudence of Reasons," *Michigan Law Review* 85, no. 5/6 (1987): 847–70. Some major American legal theorists' works indicate the way they present their theories or perspectives by embarking from particular interesting case(s).

37 Nerhot, "The Law and Its Reality," 57. (emphasis added)

Employing the law-as-process perspective, this work seeks to investigate the ethics of judicial reasoning in its social context and how it lends support to an alternative epistemology of historical injustice adjudications.[38] In this sense, borrowing from Mussawir, we are interested in a kind of "sketching the styles of living that are required of us in order to be placed in the vicinity of the text and its system of judgment."[39] Our interest is thus not necessarily concerned with the judgment and its conditions, but rather with the techniques and procedures undertaken by the courts in *localizing* and *institutionalizing* the performance of creative judgment. It focuses not exclusively on the matter of legal judgments themselves—i.e., the outcome of decisions—but on the process and method of *creating* forms of law and lawful relations.[40] It grapples mainly with investigating cognitive activities and dilemmas encountered by legal decision-makers in cases involving the multiplicity of injustice experiences,[41] rather than finding a single comprehensive model of the legal decision-making process.[42] By investigating the process of enacting collective responsibility in historical injustice adjudication, if we succeed, we will be able to obtain a better understanding of the *active* feature of judicial decision, which is fundamental to the creative and transformative judicial practice.

Situating temporalities *in* legal reasoning

To clearly situate the study's examination of the relationship between legal reasoning, time and historical injustice, it is important to briefly survey our current understanding of the matter in legal scholarship in general. Evidently, much ink has been spilled regarding the issue of law and time, particularly during the recent temporal turn in sociolegal studies.[43] At the moment, it

38 See James MacLean, *Rethinking Law as Process: Creativity, Novelty, Change* (Oxon & New York: Routledge, 2012); Margaret Davies, *Law Unlimited: Materialism, Pluralism, and Legal Theory* (New York: Routledge, 2017), https://doi.org/10.4324/9781315775913.

39 Mussawir, *Jurisdiction in Deleuze: The Expression and Representation of Law*, 14.

40 Lawrence B. Solum, "Outcome Reasons and Process Reasons in Normative Constitutional Theory," *University of Pennsylvania Law Review* 172, no. 4 (2024): 913–88.

41 Anthony G. Amsterdam and Jerome S. Bruner, *Minding the Law* (Cambridge, MA: Harvard University Press, 2009).

42 Cox, "The Uncertain Judge"; Del Mar, *Artefacts of Legal Inquiry: The Value of Imagination in Adjudication*; Cass R. Sunstein, *Legal Reasoning and Political Conflict* (Oxford University Press, 2018).

43 See generally Beynon-Jones and Grabham, "Introduction"; Carol J. Greenhouse, "Time's Up, Timed Out: Reflections on Social Time and Legal Pluralism," *The Journal of Legal Pluralism and Unofficial Law* 46, no. 1 (2014): 141–53; Franz von Benda-Beckmann and Keebet von Benda-Beckmann, "Places That Come and Go: A Legal Anthropological Perspective on the Temporalities of Space in Plural Legal Orders," in *The Expanding Spaces of Law: A Timely Legal Geography*, ed. Irus Braverman, Nicholas Blomley, David Delaney, and Alexandre (Sandy) Kedar (Stanford, CA: Stanford University Press, 2014), 30–52.

is reasonable to highlight three major streams that have been shaping this emerging discourse.

The *first* stream of works is about the intersection between time and law, mainly through the lens of physical, objective time. These texts posit that the temporality of law is influenced by how science and technology understand and help legal actors make sense of time. Undeniably, since the Sumerian invention of hour and clock up to the unfolding of reversible Newtonian time, science and technology have been guiding humans' understanding of time, either individually or socially. Rebecca French's article has been fruitful in revealing the distinct models of time from 1880–1920 to 1970–2000+.[44] During the former period, humans understood the linear and stepped model of time, with several dynamics in the form of cyclical and ruptured by the early twentieth century. While the latter is fueled by a massive increase in informational technology advancement, humans are experiencing *messy* and fractal models of time, which contribute to a new kind of subjectification characterized by a *multiphrenic self*.[45]

Another indispensable work, written by Liaquat Ali Khan, uncovers the general principles of temporality that permeate the entire enterprise of law.[46] Khan pioneered the introduction of several symbols significant in extrapolating the law's temporality. For the sake of ingenuity, as appears to be the case, Khan coins several key phrases in construing the principles: temporal proximity, time-series analysis, temporal inertia and temporal triggers, to name a few. Temporalities, he argues, should be broken down into two elements: (1) point in time [t] and (2) duration or timeframe [Δt]. 07.30 p.m., January 3rd or 1984 are some examples of [t], whereas a week, season or semester are to be seen as [Δt]. An important part of Khan's work in understanding the intersection between time and law is the idea of four general principles of temporality that perform a variety of legal functions. The first principle is temporal correlation, which expounds "law uses the correlation between temporality and change to determine legally significant relations."[47] At this point, time correlates rather than causes change, while law "relies on temporal proximity to interweave events, draw inferences, and attach liability."[48] Temporal proximity, Khan argues, is an effective legal tool to determine cause and effect. This principle furthermore captures temporality as an interior part of the human mind, which is capable of understanding both tensed and tense-free temporality. As "temporality is embedded in memorialized facts . . . yet the mind has the ability to misreport the temporal

44 Rebecca French, "Time in the Law," *University of Colorado Review* 72, no. 3 (2001): 663–748.

45 Ibid., pt. D.

46 Liaquat Ali Khan, "Temporality of Law," *McGeorge Law Review* 40, no. 1 (2009): 55–106.

47 Ibid., 69.

48 Ibid., 72.

order of facts stored in memory."[49] The second principle is temporal inertia, which understands that "law maintains temporal inertia by resisting or refusing to acknowledge changes."[50] In brief, inertia implies that law maintains the status-quo. Temporal inertia thus could best be understood as law's core attribute, as it provides "state rules that do not change over a period of time (Δt)."[51] It ensures law's systemic, constant stability and continuity. In practice, inertia could be reflected through the doctrine of precedent and remedy—through remedial injunction. Third is the principle of temporal triggers that illustrates a time trigger as a point in time (t) that initiates or terminates a legal event.[52] Time could allocate law, legal action, power, right and obligation into being and also put them to an end.

Our *second* stream of works is about time as a constitutive part of legal theory. In this context, legal philosophers have highlighted legal temporalities to raise question about what constitutes law and the legal system. Recalling law as a social phenomenon rather than the science of norms that is independent from psychological attitudes, the connection between jurisprudence and time will make sense.[53] In this framework, associating jurisprudence with hermeneutics brings our attention to the idea that by interpreting texts, we are at the same time interpreting all human action and history. To confront the tension between history and jurisprudence, Priel identifies three ways in which time might figure more prominently in jurisprudential inquiry: that is:

> (1) as a *matter of fact* law has a temporal component; (2) law necessarily has a temporal component because law's normative force takes place in time; and (3) law is always a product of a particular culture . . . [which] has a temporal (and geographical) nature.[54]

Under this approach, it would thus make sense to study law properly through such a historical, situated and contingent view in which the only way to apply norms and rules is against "the tacit assumption concerning the translatability of time intervals into normative language."[55] Furthermore, in this field, there have been numerous objections from legal scholars against general treatment of time as objective, measurable and plottable metrics. As

49 Ibid., 77.
50 Ibid., 80.
51 Ibid., 81.
52 Ibid., 87.
53 Dan Priel, "Analytic Jurisprudence in Time," in *Philosophy of Law as an Integral Part of Philosophy: Essays on the Jurisprudence of Gerald J. Postema*, ed. Thomas Bustamante and Thiago Lopes Decat (Oxford: Hart Publishing, 2020), 213–41; Niklas Luhmann, *A Sociological Theory of Law* (Oxon & New York: Routledge, 2014).
54 Priel, "Analytic Jurisprudence in Time," 16.
55 Emmanuel Melissaris, "The Chronology of the Legal," *McGill Law Journal* 50 (2005): 858.

Postema has aptly argued, law operates distinctively from other modes of governance because it orders time. This capacity to order time is, in turn, the key feature of law.[56] While Kelsen's implicit legal validity and Hart's momentary legal system have been mindful of the temporal dimension of law, argued Postema, they rather provide a limited part of the temporal character of law in legal theory. As a response, following Finnis' account of law's essential function to relate the past to the present, Postema's central proposition is that "law provides normative guidance to practically rational human agents by enabling them to integrate its proposed ordering into their cross-temporal practical perspectives."[57] Other than having a public character modeled in generalized directives, laws must also have a "cross-temporally projectable shape."[58]

The *third* body of literature examines law within specific temporalities. These studies argue that diverse forms of historical fact—ranging from post-colonial and racial legacy, past atrocity and violence, criminal evidence or temporal pressures in medical law—have been shaped and reshaped by law. These studies specifically highlight the treatment of legal rules and judgment towards certain *types* of past. Building upon the works of Henri Bergson on the idea of real-time as duration, a number of studies fetch our attention to probe legal temporality as *durée* or duration, that is, acknowledging the multi/plural temporalities of law.[59] In Mawani's words, law "synthesizes past, present, future" and therefore its "internal dynamics influence the conceptions of time it imposes on the world."[60] Recalling law's authority and sovereignty during the colonial experience, she argues, law's presumed timelessness has been capable of shrouding the heterogeneity of temporal experience, thus compels the racial-colonial power relations perpetual.[61]

Some other important works have showcased that legal adjudication is capable of creating a certain reality of the past. Informed by Gadamer's effective historical consciousness and Grosz's untimely futures, Chowdhury coined the term *types of pasts* that are produced by particular forms of adjudicative temporalities.[62] He distinguishes these forms into abstract legal judgment and

56 Gerald J. Postema, "Time in Law's Domain," *Ratio Juris* 31, no. 2 (2018): 160–82.
57 Ibid., 167.
58 Ibid., 175.
59 Mariana Valverde, *Chronotopes of Law: Jurisdiction, Scale and Governance* (Oxon & New York: Routledge, 2015); Kathryn McNeilly, "Are Rights Out of Time? International Human Rights Law, Temporality, and Radical Social Change," *Social & Legal Studies* 28, no. 6 (2019): 817–38, https://doi.org/10.1177/0964663918815729; Kathryn McNeilly, "The Temporal Ontology of the Human Rights Council's Universal Periodic Review," *Human Rights Law Review* 21 (2021): 1–21; Mawani, "Law as Temporality: Colonial Politics and Indian Settlers"; Renisa Mawani, "The Times of Law," *Law & Social Inquiry* 40, no. 1 (2015): 253–63.
60 Mawani, "The Times of Law," 256.
61 Mawani, "Law As Temporality: Colonial Politics and Indian Settlers."
62 Tanzil Chowdhury, *Time, Temporality and Legal Judgment* (Oxon & New York: Routledge, 2020): 100–106.

concrete legal judgment.[63] In the former, "one observes pasts which imbue features of space—divisible, uniform, juxtaposed and simultaneous—that lend themselves to chronologizing."[64] Meanwhile, in the latter, legal adjudication produces *variegated pasts* that are built on enduring and sedimented pasts.[65] In concrete legal judgment, he contends, one might observe a way for radical social change, for such judgment recognizes the legal subject as "one which constitutes and is constituted by its socio-economic ecology."[66] The variegated pasts in concrete legal judgment reveal *contingency and situatedness* that may "reveal facts with potentially exculpatory effect which are worth considering as well as illustrating how and why certain pasts are excluding from judicial-factual analysis."[67] The discussion on legal temporality and fact construction ushers us into Chowdhury's two primary sources, including Kelman's unconscious interpretation and Nousianen's triad of reality construction, text and time.[68] Specifically in criminal law, Chowdhury postulates that legal temporality, either narrow or broad time frames, ties with fact construction: "wherein the broad time-frames have a tendency to causally connect events to a more remote point in the past, and the narrow time frames as singular and disconnected from causally proximate event."[69] Following this argument, he pushes the claim that time frame indeterminacy precedes the central claim of concrete legal judgment on "the tension between rules and standards as different forms of legal directives" in which "a legal norm's degree of *formal realizability* is conditioned on the time frames adopted."[70] Thus, there are some phenomena that describe the time frames adopted by judges as whether to apply legal norms as a rule or *sensed* norm—that is, applicable in 'real-life situations' that subsume "the factual situation into a pre-ordained category as if the legal norm had already anticipated it," or as a standard or *senseless* norm that "can be tailored to a factual situation that it sees as unique, rather than as a particularization of a general rule."[71]

Arguably, while we might be akin to see these bodies of literature as separate compartments in legal discipline, in fact they can provide potential insight from one to another. Building on the existing works, legal temporalities (or

63 Tanzil Chowdhury, *Time, Temporality and Legal Judgment* (Oxon & New York: Routledge, 2020).
64 Ibid., 146.
65 Ibid.
66 Ibid., 152.
67 Ibid., 100.
68 Tanzil Chowdhury, "Temporality and Criminal Law Adjudication's Multiple Pasts," *Liverpool Law Review* 38, no. 2 (2017): 187–206; Mark Kelman, "Interpretive Construction in the Substantive Criminal Law," *Stanford Law Review* 33, no. 4 (1981): 591–673.
69 Tanzil Chowdhury, "Time Frames and Legal Indeterminacy," *Canadian Journal of Law and Jurisprudence* 30, no. 1 (2017): 67.
70 Ibid., 71.
71 Ibid., 72.

temporalities in legal reasoning, to be precise) in this study are construed on the following premises:

(1) by producing and organizing certain types of pasts in the selected court's decisions across contexts, legal judgment creates narratives (e.g., transition, trauma and uncertainty) through examining experiences of historical injustice as interpretive temporal evidence;
(2) such a narrative precipitates and instantiates a critical attunement that juxtaposes law, history and injustice in the forms of, for instance, liability, exculpatory and blameworthiness; and
(3) the juxtaposition (of law, history and injustice) through legal decision-makers' reasoning process could potentially transform society's memory and expectations, emanating from the perplexities of continuing, persistent forms of injustice into the novel and unexpected.

Crafting the style of thinking

Before continuing, we need to unfold some methodological aspects of this study. Although described in a rather general sense, this section hopefully will not attenuate one's joy of methodological craftsmanship.[72] That is, this work primarily employs an interdisciplinary doctrinal method in legal study. It is a doctrinal legal research enriched by legal philosophy that enables us to conceptualize, as Davies correctly suggests, legal theory as performative and prefigurative. In that sense, our theorization is performative insofar as theory of law is seen as a process, and prefigurative insofar as it directs our view to "more practical, localised, and often tentative efforts to model new forms of practical–theoretical legality."[73] Within this framework, this study employs three methods of legal philosophy that share some basic features found in doctrinal legal research. Informed by Taekema and van der Burg, the methods involved are: author analysis, argumentation analysis and construction and reflective equilibrium.[74]

First of all, one would easily discover that the chapters of this book will contain an analysis of some texts in philosophy and phenomenology discussing time and temporality. Specifically, this study's philosophical orientation

72 Paolo Amorosa and Claire Vergerio, "The Canon as Method, or, the Strange Joy of Footnotes," *Critical Legal Thinking*, 2023, https://criticallegalthinking.com/2023/01/31/the-canon-as-method-or-the-strange-joy-of-footnotes/.

73 Davies, *Law Unlimited: Materialism, Pluralism, and Legal Theory*, 19.

74 Sanne Taekema and Wibren van der Burg, "Legal Philosophy as an Enrichment of Doctrinal Research Part I: Introducing Three Philosophical Methods," *Law and Method* 1, no. 01 (2020): 1–19; Sanne Taekema and Wibren van der Burg, "Legal Philosophy as an Enrichment of Doctrinal Research–Part II: The Purposes of Including Legal Philosophy," *Law and Method* 1, no. 01 (2022): 1–19.

works around Bergson's (1859–1941) and Deleuze's (1925–1995)—two prominent French philosopher-phenomenologists—publications related to time as duration. Instead of independently analyzing the works of these authors, this study bases some of its claims on these philosophical views. This strategy could save the doctrinal character of this study. That said, we are not attempting here to extract or situate Bergson-Deleuze's views of time as duration upon a certain legal construct; instead, we are working *with* their views in framing an alternative approach to examine legal constructs.

In relation to this strategy, it is also important to note the significance of Deleuzian jurisprudence to this study. Deleuzian jurisprudence is widely understood as a jurisprudential view that brings attention to law's process, creativity, possibilities and potentials.[75] The reference to Deleuze among critical legal scholars is not relatively new, although we cannot say it is a common exercise.[76] Deleuze's jurisprudence basically appreciates a system of cases, which is inferred by many writers as a kind of philosophy of legal singularity.[77] Relatedly, this kind of jurisprudential framework also becomes, to quote Marneros:

> a practical and creative philosophy of law—not a law that is reduced to the institutionally or systemically dogmatic sense of the word, but one which acquires a new impetus as to how to organize, how to respond to singular situations and how to live.[78]

Of particular importance is the power of differentiation, which according to Deleuze can be found in the system of (legal) cases. That is to say, differentiation through Deleuze's eyes is difference between (legal) singularities. If law, as in life, is flows of desire, the image of it cannot be seen as deriving from a static, pre-given identity. The image of law and legal practice does not

75 See generally Christos Marneros, *Human Rights after Deleuze: Towards an An-Archic Jurisprudence* (Bloomsbury Publishing, 2022); Christos Marneros, "'It Is a Nomos Very Different from the Law': On Anarchy and the Law," *Acta Universitatis Lodziensis. Folia Iuridica*, no. 96 (2021): 125–39; Harison Citrawan, "A Deleuzian Reading on Hart's Internal Point of View," *Padjajaran Jurnal Ilmu Hukum (Journal of Law)* 9, no. 1 (2022): 135–51.

76 Pierre Legrand, *Comparative Law and the Task of Negative Critique* (Oxford & New York: Routledge, 2023).

77 Alexandre Lefebvre, "A New Image of Law: Deleuze and Jurisprudence," *Telos* 130 (2005): 103–26; Kyle McGee, "Creation, Duration, Adjudication: A Review of Alexandre Lefebvre's The Image of Law: Deleuze, Bergson, Spinoza," *Law & Literature* 21, no. 3 (2009): 480–91; Nathan Moore, "Icons of Control: Deleuze, Signs, Law," *International Journal for the Semiotics of Law-Revue Internationale de Sémiotique Juridique* 20, no. 1 (2007): 33–54; Laurent de Sutter, *Deleuze's Philosophy of Law*, trans. Nils F. Schott (Edinburgh: Edinburgh University Press, 2022).

78 Marneros, *Human Rights after Deleuze: Towards an An-Archic Jurisprudence*, 167.

suppress life but rather is part of or immanent to it. We can point out at least four important characteristics in this jurisprudential framework, namely that (1) jurisprudence exists in the future, (2) jurisprudence is immanent, (3) jurisprudence is indifferent to truth and falsity and (4) jurisprudence is the redistribution of the law and laws.[79] As we will notice later, these jurisprudential characteristics are basically the grounds for us to engage with some other related fields, such as legal epistemology and cognitive science.

Furthermore, this study's theoretical orientation is constructed through analysis of arguments and argument construction. Each chapter, as one can later observe, particularly in Part II, is situated within some contending views or debates about certain concepts or approaches. Say, for instance, the judicial dilemma of whether or not today's generation should legally repair injuries for victims of historical discrimination. One side may see that such a reparation is well-justified on the basis of so-called 'intergenerational debt.' Meanwhile, the other side maintains that injuries of past discrimination should be situated within a linear timeline while some change and rectification during this timeline might have superseded the injuries that happened in the past. Between these contending views, our previous method (i.e., author analysis) is then employed to provide an alternative view. This method is critical in providing a 'sound and convincing' argument. Soundness here refers to a logically defensible argument, while convincingness belongs to subjective perception toward a certain judgment.[80]

To achieve that end, three steps are involved: the first is an argument inventory.[81] The following chapters are initiated with a discussion of competing discourse and views from scholars of various backgrounds. The next step is a separate argument analysis.[82] In this analysis, each contending view will be highlighted separately, and from there, a normative reflection will be undertaken based on a specific normative theory (e.g., continuing with our previous example, the question of collective legal responsibility for past wrongdoings should be responded to through a time-mindful framework that conflates the past, present and future, hence discarding the dichotomy generated from the previous inventory step). The last step is an analysis of the argument as whole.[83] This analysis would unmask the whole philosophical assumption toward the elements of legal temporalities (again following our example, because law's time is understood as duration, therefore judicial practices should frame the time of responsibility *in* duration as well).

79 Moore, "Icons of Control: Deleuze, Signs, Law," 44–45.
80 Taekema and van der Burg, "Legal Philosophy as an Enrichment of Doctrinal Research Part I: Introducing Three Philosophical Methods," 7.
81 Ibid., 8.
82 Ibid.
83 Ibid., 9.

Another procedure employed is the reflective equilibrium process. The main idea of this process is that, quoting from Taekema and van der Burg, "we collect all relevant and initially plausible beliefs and confront them with each other to test, partly reject and refine them until we have constructed a coherent theory."[84] This Rawlsian belief insists on affirming certain theoretical underpinnings and building upon them to construct a further coherent argument. In this process, one may find in this book some ethical perspectives that radiate the theoretical construction of: legal inquiry (e.g., Grosz's theory of the untimely), responsibility practice (e.g., Postema's legal time-mindfulness) and intuitive reasoning (e.g., Bergson-Deleuze's intuition). It is also fair to say that these ethical perspectives are *considered judgments* being applied in this study.

One should note, however, that these methods are not necessarily sequential or separated. Rather, these methods are blended or mixed into a certain kind of hermeneutic tendency. In that sense, this study is filled with interpretive and reflective dialogues that attempt to understand the way judges conceptualize their reasoning process which guides them in shaping legal inquiry and justifying collective responsibility in historical injustice adjudication. The working paradigm follows the legal hermeneutic tradition that emphasizes law's value and meaning based on the selection of cases, which can be found in Chapters 1 through 3 on intuitive judicial reasoning. It grapples not with the ways judges ought to understand the law, but rather with their act of understanding itself.[85] Yet, the legal hermeneutical aspect of this study does not necessarily generate a method for *how* this study is conducted, but it is useful in providing the *structures* of the study, including: the selection of cases, theory evaluation and construction and analysis of doctrine and legal principles.

This study's hermeneutical disposition is practically implemented through a comparative lens used in the case-studies (Chapter 1–3). The case-studies posit the arguments within the field of comparative jurisprudence to the extent that such a comparison employs legal philosophy as its underlying methodological reflection.[86] Suggested by the work of William Ewald on comparative jurisprudence and Pierre Legrand's negative comparative law, this study offers an alternative to the traditional comparative law presuppositions that

84 Ibid., 11.

85 Carel Smith, "The Vicissitudes of the Hermeneutic Paradigm in the Study of Law: Tradition, Forms of Life and Metaphor," *Erasmus Law Review* 4 (2011): 21–38; Joy Twemlow, "Critical Phenomenology as a Good Friend," *Critical Legal Thinking*, 2023, https://criticallegalthinking.com/2023/02/02/critical-phenomenology-as-a-good-friend/.

86 Taekema and van der Burg, "Legal Philosophy as an Enrichment of Doctrinal Research Part I: Introducing Three Philosophical Methods"; Taekema and van der Burg, "Legal Philosophy as an Enrichment of Doctrinal Research–Part II: The Purposes of Including Legal Philosophy."

predicate the study object as external to the observer. It is indeed the case that Ewald's comparative jurisprudence is an *intermediate theory* between the contextualist and the textualist approaches in comparative law studies.[87] Comparative jurisprudence somehow links the *yield* of comparative studies with the philosophical reflections generated by jurisprudence.[88] That is to say in understanding a foreign legal system, " 'the law' is best understood as a style of conscious thought: that what we should be seeking to understand is not law in books nor law in action but law in minds."[89] Accordingly, the key to understanding this methodological underpinning is through the two-way interaction between rules and the working of rules through a jurist's mind. Such a view requires comparativists to be attentive to legal epistemology, which is interested in not only what but also how foreign lawyers know the law. In other words, being critical in this kind of methodological underpinning is the exercise of mode of *difference*. Suggested by Legrand's negative critique, one could understand such a mode of differentiation as:

> re-articulation of the comparison of laws in terms of the laws' difference and of differential analysis of the laws' difference, a meaning-making strategy with considerable liberatory epistemic promise, a new kind of arrangement leaving the laws enisled, that is, 'outside one another', an interpretive stance 'respecting and preserving this exteriority and this distance' so that, instead of any enforced subsumption under a prescribed and artificial overarching harmony, dispersion ultimately holds, thereby bringing to bear upon the comparison of laws 'an extraordinary force of justice'.[90]

Following Ewald's and Legrand's assertions, the comparative method in the case study seeks to examine the court's conscious ideas at work in dealing with the judge's cognitive dilemmas (i.e., issues of collectivity-anonymity, temporal objectification and the image of linearity). Rather than seeking and explaining differences between legal traditions, this study is more interested in sketching differences in terms of cognitive structures of legal practice

87 William Ewald, "The Jurisprudential Approach to Comparative Law: A Field Guide to 'Rats,'" in *Legal Theory and the Legal Academy*, ed. Maksymilian Del Mar, William Twining, and Michael Guidice (London: Routledge, 2017), 333–39, https://doi.org/10.4324/9781315091907.

88 William Ewald, "Comparative Jurisprudence (II): The Logic of Legal Transplants," *The American Journal of Comparative Law* 43, no. 4 (1995): 489–510; Ewald, "The Jurisprudential Approach to Comparative Law: A Field Guide to 'Rats'."

89 William Ewald, "Comparative Jurisprudence (I): What Was It Like to Try a Rat," *University of Pennsylvania Law Review* 143 (1994): 704; William E. Butler, "Periodization and International Law," in *Research Handbook on the Theory and History of International Law*, 2nd ed. (Edward Elgar Publishing, 2020), 281–95.

90 Legrand, *Comparative Law and the Task of Negative Critique*, 4.

through textual analysis.[91] This attitude can plausibly lead us to observe a certain virtue-ethical dimension of legal reasoning through a philosophical reflection. That being the case, reading comparative jurisprudence through the Deleuzian lens demonstrates this study's differentiation as an attempt to understand law-as-process that requires immersion.[92] In this process of understanding, one must also concede that there is a sort of imaginative process by comparativists-at-law in a sense that, quoting from Curran, it is an act that occurs "in the penetration by the legal comparatist of foreign legal cultures, as the comparatist begins to understand new categories, new patterns of interpretation."[93] Such a level of differentiation comes with the urgency of delineating the cognitive structure of legal reasoning in the inquiries undertaken by the courts in cases being compared.

Structuring the argument

To help navigate the overarching idea of the study, a brief summary of the argument structure is provided as follows.

Part I will mainly address the question of how judges could enter into the multiplicity of past injustice experiences. It primarily showcases the ethics of intuitive judicial reasoning in historical injustice cases. This part claims that intuition is part of a judicial mode of thinking performed by legal decision-makers to express justifying reasons within their distinctive epistemic frame. It is a method to access normative arguments stemming from virtue. That said, intuitive judicial reasoning in this sense is a kind of judicial practice, a judge's mode of thinking that enables them to create and craft forms of lawful relations considering their epistemic justification toward the temporal experience of injustice. As part of the creative process, intuition is a basic form of legal knowledge through which legal institutions (i.e., the courts) shape the forms of lawful relations. Accordingly, we can claim that intuitive judicial reasoning is a method that generates access to (1) a kind of inquiry that does not follow progressively from the past or present and (2) coherence that governs temporal patterns based on which a certain lawful

91 Geoffrey Samuel, "Epistemology and Comparative Law: Contributions from Sciences and Social Sciences," in *Epistemology and Methodology of Comparative Law*, ed. Mark Van Hoecke (Oxford & Portland, OR: Hart Publishing, 2004), 35–78.

92 Sutter, *Deleuze's Philosophy of Law*. Correspondingly, according to de Sutter, in a Deleuzian framework, "[j]urisprudence experiments with the invention of principles that present the three traits Nietzsche calls for. The first trait is a demand concerning size: a principle must not be larger than what it conditions. The second trait is a demand concerning becoming: a principle must metamorphose along with what it conditions. The third trait is a demand concerning signification: a principle in each case is determined only along with what it determines." 71.

93 Mathias Siems, *Comparative Law* (Cambridge University Press, 2022), 118.

relation may attain social purposes over time. Moreover, such intuitive judicial reasoning is part of the virtue approach to legal reasoning which can be found in empathy. To this extent, empathy needs to be seen as part of judicial intuitive methodology, as it provides a way to access creative minds. Part I is divided into three chapters. The case study provided in Chapter 1-3 should be read as our attempt to exemplify historical injustice adjudication. Employing comparative law as a style of thinking, the case-studies depict how intuitive judicial reasoning is applied by the courts in selecting justifying reasons for collective responsibility through three narratives of historical injustice adjudication, namely: transitory racial discrimination, traumatic colonial extractivism and uncertain climate crisis.

The ethics of intuitive judicial reasoning formulated in Part I would inescapably implicate an epistemological dimension of historical injustice adjudication. In Part II, we seek to draw an alternative framework for *what* and *how* judges understand about historical injustice adjudication through the lens of legal temporalities. This alternative epistemology builds upon two main features, namely: untimely legal inquiry and time-mindful legal responsibility. Part II consists of four chapters. Chapter 4 argues that legal reasoning is understood as a *process* of justification based on schemes of intelligibility that represent the virtuality of norms and facts in the actuality of a case. Such a representation of the virtual into the actual essentially signifies the inherent temporal dimension of law and legal reasoning, while such temporality in legal reasoning is fundamental in recognizing the role of narrative that mediates judges' creative and experimental capacity to capture the multiplicity of experiences of injustice. Chapter 5 argues for intuitive judicial reasoning as an aretaic model of judicial decision-making. Based on the case-studies, judicial intuition is seen as a mode of thinking performed by legal decision-makers in expressing justifying reasons for collective responsibility in historical injustice adjudication. Intuition, in this sense, is a method that enables judges to create forms of lawful relations, considering their epistemic justification toward experiences of injustice. Through a kind of empathic intuition, we may later appreciate a new image of judicial reasoning in a sense that judicial adjudications would no longer be seen in terms of homogeneity and generality, as they are now reframed as "a composite, layered experience in a multifaceted and hybrid reality."[94] Chapter 6 discusses the idea of untimely legal inquiry, that is, a framework of historical injustice as temporal legal inquiry. This chapter suggests that historical injustice should be framed as a kind of legal inquiry that is seen through an untimely approach. The untimely itself is essentially an approach for legal decision-makers to detach themselves from historical

94 Andreia Oliveira and Felix Rebolledo, "The Image as a Process of Invention within Artistic Research," in *The Dark Precursor: Deleuze and Artistic Research*, ed. Paulo de Assis and Paolo Giudici (Leuven University Press, 2017), 396.

inquiry and present-time injustice, that is, seeing the present as an extension of the past instead of treating the past and present as separate modalities of time or even othering the past from the present. Finally, Chapter 7 concerns collective legal responsibility as a form of lawful relation in historical injustice adjudication. As will be argued later, this form of lawful relation should be framed under the concept of legal time-mindfulness from which we can engender a view that collective responsibility practice must be fundamentally tied to the principle of coherence in a temporally extended social life. This kind of temporal coherence in construing collective responsibility practice accounts for a reflective engagement between individual, agential and societal temporalities.

Bibliography

Amorosa, Paolo, and Claire Vergerio. "The Canon as Method, or, the Strange Joy of Footnotes." *Critical Legal Thinking*, 2023. https://criticallegalthinking.com/2023/01/31/the-canon-as-method-or-the-strange-joy-of-footnotes/.

Amsterdam, Anthony G., and Jerome S. Bruner. *Minding the Law*. Cambridge, MA: Harvard University Press, 2009.

Arendt, Hannah. *Responsibility and Judgment*. New York: Schocken, 2003.

Barkan, Elazar. *The Guilt of Nations: Restitution and Negotiating Historical Injustices*. New York & London: W.W. Norton & Company, 2000.

Barkan, Elazar. "Historical Reconciliation: Redress, Rights and Politics." *Journal of International Affairs* (2006): 1–15.

Benda-Beckmann, Franz von, and Keebet von Benda-Beckmann. "Places That Come and Go: A Legal Anthropological Perspective on the Temporalities of Space in Plural Legal Orders." In *The Expanding Spaces of Law: A Timely Legal Geography*, edited by Irus Braverman, Nicholas Blomley, David Delaney, and Alexandre (Sandy) Kedar, 30–52. Stanford, CA: Stanford University Press, 2014.

Beynon-Jones, Siân Maeve, and Emily Grabham. "Introduction." In *Law and Time*, edited by Siân Maeve Beynon-Jones and Emily Grabham, 1–28. Oxon & New York: Routledge London, 2019.

Brożek, Bartosz. "Legal Interpretation: Towards a New Paradigm?" *Teoria Polityki*, no. 4 (2020): 79–92.

Brożek, Bartosz. *The Legal Mind: A New Introduction to Legal Epistemology*. Cambridge: Cambridge University Press, 2020.

Brożek, Bartosz, Michał Furman, Marek Jakubiec, and Bartłomiej Kucharzyk. "The Black Box Problem Revisited. Real and Imaginary Challenges for Automated Legal Decision Making." *Artificial Intelligence and Law* (2023): 1–14.

Butler, William E. "Periodization and International Law." In *Research Handbook on the Theory and History of International Law*, 2nd ed., 281–95. Edward Elgar Publishing, 2020.

Chowdhury, Tanzil. "Temporality and Criminal Law Adjudication's Multiple Pasts." *Liverpool Law Review* 38, no. 2 (2017): 187–206.

Chowdhury, Tanzil. "Time Frames and Legal Indeterminacy." *Canadian Journal of Law and Jurisprudence* 30, no. 1 (2017): 57–76.

Chowdhury, Tanzil. *Time, Temporality and Legal Judgment*. Oxon & New York: Routledge, 2020.

Citrawan, Harison. "A Deleuzian Reading on Hart's Internal Point of View." *Padjadjaran Jurnal Ilmu Hukum (Journal of Law)* 9, no. 1 (2022): 135–51. https://doi.org/10.22304/pjih.v9n1.a7.

Cox, Courtney M. "The Uncertain Judge." *University of Chicago Law Review* 90, no. 3 (2023): 739–811.
Cusato, Eliana, Rebecca Mignot-Mahdavi, Sofia Stolk, and Renske Vos. "In Praise of Multiplicity: Suspending the Desire to Change the World." *Leiden Journal of International Law* (2023): 1–5.
Davies, Margaret. *Law Unlimited: Materialism, Pluralism, and Legal Theory*. New York: Routledge, 2017. https://doi.org/10.4324/9781315775913.
Dixon, Peter J. "Reparations and the Politics of Recognition." *Contested Justice* (2015): 326–51. https://doi.org/10.1017/cbo9781139924528.016.
Ewald, William. "Comparative Jurisprudence (I): What Was It Like to Try a Rat." *University of Pennsylvania Law Review* 143 (1994): 1889–2149.
Ewald, William. "Comparative Jurisprudence (II): The Logic of Legal Transplants." *The American Journal of Comparative Law* 43, no. 4 (1995): 489–510.
Ewald, William. "The Jurisprudential Approach to Comparative Law: A Field Guide to 'Rats'." In *Legal Theory and the Legal Academy*, edited by Maksymilian Del Mar, William Twining, and Michael Guidice, 333–39. London: Routledge, 2017. https://doi.org/10.4324/9781315091907.
Fisher, Elizabeth, Eloise Scotford, and Emily Barritt. "The Legally Disruptive Nature of Climate Change." *The Modern Law Review* 80, no. 2 (2017): 173–201.
French, Rebecca. "Time in the Law." *University of Colorado Review* 72, no. 3 (2001): 663–748.
Fricker, Miranda. *Epistemic Injustice: Power and the Ethics of Knowing*. Oxford: Oxford University Press, 2007.
Goldberg, John C P. "Rethinking Injury and Proximate Cause." *San Diego Law Review* 40, no. 4 (2003): 1315.
Greenhouse, Carol J. "Time's Up, Timed Out: Reflections on Social Time and Legal Pluralism." *The Journal of Legal Pluralism and Unofficial Law* 46, no. 1 (2014): 141–53.
Gross, Ariela. "When Is the Time of Slavery-The History of Slavery in Contemporary Legal and Political Argument." *California Law Review* 96 (2008): 283.
Hayner, Priscilla B. *Unspeakable Truths: Transitional Justice and the Challenge of Truth Commissions*. 2nd ed. New York & London: Routledge, 2011.
Herik, Larissa Van den. "Addressing 'Colonial Crimes' through Reparations? Adjudicating Dutch Atrocities Committed in Indonesia." *Journal of International Criminal Justice* 10, no. 3 (2012): 693–705. https://doi.org/10.1093/jicj/mqs033.
Jakubiec, Marek. "Between Legal Philosophy and Cognitive Science: The Tension Problem." *Ratio Juris* 35, no. 2 (2022): 223–39.
Joshi, Yuvraj. "Racial Transition." *Washington University Law Review* 98 (2020): 1181.
Kelman, Mark. "Interpretive Construction in the Substantive Criminal Law." *Stanford Law Review* 33, no. 4 (1981): 591–673.
Khan, Liaquat Ali. "Temporality of Law." *McGeorge Law Review* 40, no. 1 (2009): 55–106.
Klinsky, Sonja, and Jasmina Brankovic. *The Global Climate Regime and Transitional Justice*. New York: Routledge, 2018.
Lefebvre, Alexandre. "A New Image of Law: Deleuze and Jurisprudence." *Telos* 130 (2005): 103–26.
Legrand, Pierre. *Comparative Law and the Task of Negative Critique*. Oxford & New York: Routledge, 2023.
Luhmann, Niklas. *A Sociological Theory of Law*. Oxon & New York: Routledge, 2014.
MacCormick, Neil. *Rhetoric and the Rule of Law: A Theory of Legal Reasoning*. Oxford: Oxford University Press, 2005.
MacLean, James. *Rethinking Law as Process: Creativity, Novelty, Change*. Oxon & New York: Routledge, 2012.

Maksymilian, Del Mar. "The Spatio-Temporality of Objectification in Legal Theory: Concepts of Legality between Theory and Practice." *Problema: Anuario de Filosofía y Teoría Del Derecho*, no. 2 (2008): 127–55.
Mar, Maksymilian Del. *Artefacts of Legal Inquiry: The Value of Imagination in Adjudication*. Bloomsbury Publishing, 2020.
Marneros, Christos. " 'It Is a Nomos Very Different from the Law': On Anarchy and the Law." *Acta Universitatis Lodziensis. Folia Iuridica*, no. 96 (2021): 125–39.
Marneros, Christos. *Human Rights after Deleuze: Towards an An-Archic Jurisprudence*. Bloomsbury Publishing, 2022.
Mawani, Renisa. "Law as Temporality: Colonial Politics and Indian Settlers." *UC Irvine Law Review* 4, no. 1 (2014): 65–95.
Mawani, Renisa. "The Times of Law." *Law & Social Inquiry* 40, no. 1 (2015): 253–63.
McGee, Kyle. "Creation, Duration, Adjudication: A Review of Alexandre Lefebvre's The Image of Law: Deleuze, Bergson, Spinoza." *Law & Literature* 21, no. 3 (2009): 480–91.
McKinnon, Rachel. "Epistemic Injustice." *Philosophy Compass* 11, no. 8 (2016): 437–46.
McNeilly, Kathryn. "Are Rights Out of Time? International Human Rights Law, Temporality, and Radical Social Change." *Social & Legal Studies* 28, no. 6 (2019): 817–38. https://doi.org/10.1177/0964663918815729.
McNeilly, Kathryn. "The Temporal Ontology of the Human Rights Council's Universal Periodic Review." *Human Rights Law Review* 21 (2021): 1–21.
Melissaris, Emmanuel. "The Chronology of the Legal." *McGill Law Journal* 50 (2005): 839–62.
Miller, Zinaida. "The Injustices of Time: Rights, Race, Redistribution, and Responsibility." *Columbia Human Rights Law Review* 52 (2020): 647–737.
Minnerop, Petra, and Friederike Otto. "Climate Change and Causation: Joining Law and Climate Science on the Basis of Formal Logic." *Buffalo Environmental Law Journal* 27, no. 1 (2019): 49.
Moore, Nathan. "Icons of Control: Deleuze, Signs, Law." *International Journal for the Semiotics of Law-Revue Internationale de Sémiotique Juridique* 20, no. 1 (2007): 33–54.
Murphy, Liam. "The Artificial Morality of Private Law: The Persistence of an Illusion." *University of Toronto Law Journal* 70, no. 4 (2020): 453–88. https://doi.org/10.3138/utlj.2019-0103.
Mussawir, Edward. *Jurisdiction in Deleuze: The Expression and Representation of Law*. London: Routledge, 2011.
Nerhot, Patrick. "The Law and Its Reality." In *Law, Interpretation and Reality: Essays in Epistemology, Hermeneutics and Jurisprudence*, edited by Patrick Nerhot, 50–69. Dordrecht: Springer, 1990.
Neuwirth, Rostam Josef. "Future Law, the Power of Prediction, and the Disappearance of Time." *Law, Technology and Humans* 4, no. 2 (2022): 38–59.
Oliveira, Andreia, and Felix Rebolledo. "The Image as a Process of Invention within Artistic Research." In *The Dark Precursor: Deleuze and Artistic Research*, edited by Paulo de Assis and Paolo Giudici, 395–400. Leuven University Press, 2017.
Osiel, Mark J. *Mass Atrocity, Collective Memory and the Law*. Routledge, 2017.
Posner, Eric A., and Adrian Vermeule. "Reparations for Slavery and Other Historical Injustices." *Columbia Law Review* 103 (2003): 689.
Postema, Gerald J. "Time in Law's Domain." *Ratio Juris* 31, no. 2 (2018): 160–82.
Priel, Dan. "Analytic Jurisprudence in Time." In *Philosophy of Law as an Integral Part of Philosophy: Essays on the Jurisprudence of Gerald J. Postema*, edited by Thomas Bustamante and Thiago Lopes Decat, 213–41. Oxford: Hart Publishing, 2020.
Raz, Joseph. "On the Autonomy of Legal Reasoning." *Ratio Juris* 6, no. 1 (1993): 1–15.

Renault, Emmanuel. *The Experience of Injustice: A Theory of Recognition*. New York: Columbia University Press, 2019.
Ring, Sinéad. "On Delay and Duration: Law's Temporal Orders in Historical Child Sexual Abuse Cases." In *Law and Time*, edited by Siân M. Beynon-Jones and Emily Grabham, 93–107. London: Routledge, 2019.
Roht-Arriaza, Naomi. "Reparations Decisions and Dilemmas." *Hastings International and Comparative Law Review* 27 (2003): 157.
Samuel, Geoffrey. "Epistemology and Comparative Law: Contributions from Sciences and Social Sciences." In *Epistemology and Methodology of Comparative Law*, edited by Mark Van Hoecke, 35–78. Oxford & Portland, OR: Hart Publishing, 2004.
Samuel, Geoffrey. *Epistemology and Method in Law*. London & New York: Routledge, 2016.
Schauer, Frederick. "The Jurisprudence of Reasons." *Michigan Law Review* 85, no. 5/6 (1987): 847–70.
Schaus, Steven. "A Simple Model of Torts and Moral Wrongs." *Notre Dame Law Review* 97 (2021): 1029.
Sebok, Anthony J. "Two Concepts of Injustice in Restitution for Slavery." *Boston University Law Review* 84 (2004): 1405.
Sharma, Sarah. *In the Meantime: Temporality and Cultural Politics*. Durham & London: Duke University Press, 2014.
Shore, Marci. "Germany Has Confronted Its Past. Now It Must Confront the Present." *Foreign Policy*, August 2022.
Siems, Mathias. *Comparative Law*. Cambridge University Press, 2022.
Smith, Carel. "The Vicissitudes of the Hermeneutic Paradigm in the Study of Law: Tradition, Forms of Life and Metaphor." *Erasmus Law Review* 4 (2011): 21–38.
Solum, Lawrence B. "Outcome Reasons and Process Reasons in Normative Constitutional Theory." *University of Pennsylvania Law Review* 172, no. 4 (2024): 913–88.
Sunstein, Cass R. *Legal Reasoning and Political Conflict*. Oxford University Press, 2018.
Sutter, Laurent de. *Deleuze's Philosophy of Law*. Translated by Nils F. Schott. Edinburgh: Edinburgh University Press, 2022.
Taekema, Sanne, and Wibren van der Burg. "Legal Philosophy as an Enrichment of Doctrinal Research Part I: Introducing Three Philosophical Methods." *Law and Method* 1, no. 01 (2020): 1–19.
Taekema, Sanne. "Legal Philosophy as an Enrichment of Doctrinal Research–Part II: The Purposes of Including Legal Philosophy." *Law and Method* 1, no. 01 (2022): 1–19.
Thorne, Benjamin. "An Atrocity Archive: Sensory Expression of Past-Present-Future." *Law and Humanities* 15, no. 2 (2021): 272–78.
Tromp, Nevenka. "In Search for Truth at Mass Atrocities Trials: Will Judges and Lawyers Have the Last Word." *Journal of Comparative Law* 13, no. 1 (2018): 61–82.
Twemlow, Joy. "Critical Phenomenology as a Good Friend." *Critical Legal Thinking*, 2023. https://criticallegalthinking.com/2023/02/02/critical-phenomenology-as-a-good-friend/.
Valverde, Mariana. *Chronotopes of Law: Jurisdiction, Scale and Governance*. Oxon & New York: Routledge, 2015.
Waller, James. *Confronting Evil: Engaging Our Responsibility to Prevent Genocide*. New York: Oxford University Press, 2016.
Wright, Richard W. "The Grounds and Extent of Legal Responsibility." *San Diego Law Review* 40 (2003): 1425–531.

Part I

Transition, trauma and uncertainty

Part I examines the narratives of transition, trauma and uncertainty in legal cases. Building on Ricoeur's narrativity, these narratives of judicial reasoning have a close relationship with temporalities in two senses.[1] On the one hand, as already described in the Introduction, examining these narrative accounts will enable us to understand how judges find and select justifying reasons in a legal case. On the other hand, via Bergsonian time, we can later understand that any inquiries into lawful relations (i.e., legal responsibility) are *intuited* by judges within duration—these inquiries are therefore "the location and the environment of differences in kind; it is even their totality and multiplicity."[2]

That being the case, this section attempts to situate judicial reasoning in the empirical context of multiplicity of experiences of injustice. Case-studies exposed in the next three chapters (Chapters 1 through 3) need to be seen as narrative accounts through which we can better view how and the extent to which judges' modes of reasoning can capture the multiplicity of unjust experiences. These narrative accounts (i.e., transition, trauma and uncertainty) are comprised of contextual temporal realities and the ways these realities are reflected in judicial decision. These accounts are therefore about how specific temporalities are intuited by judges in selecting some relevant legal qualifications. In this multiplicity of narratives, we will highlight some Encounters—or *plot* as Ricoeur suggested; that is: "the intelligible whole that governs a succession of events in any story"—[3]faced by the courts, which include the judges' recognition of: the well-beings of long-discriminated racial minorities, the exploitative resource governance in a post-colonial setting and the localization of severe impacts of climate change.

1 Paul Ricoeur, "Narrative Time," *Critical Inquiry* 7, no. 1 (1980): 169–90.
2 Gilles Deleuze, *Bergsonism*, trans. H. Tomlinson and B. Habberjam (New York: Zone Books, 1991), 32.
3 Ricoeur, "Narrative Time," 171.

DOI: 10.4324/9781003518693-2

Table I.1 Case-studies of intuitive legal reasoning

Case	*Temporalities of injustice*	*Encounter*	*Legal principles*	*Grounds for responsibility*
Injury reparation in *African-American slave descendant reparation, United States*	Transitory character of racial discrimination	Experience of persistence of racial discrimination	Statutory limitation extension	Liminality of clock time and experience of discrimination
Injury from extractivism in *Water privatization citizen lawsuit, Indonesia*	Traumatic unequal relationship in resource governance	Experience of exploitative colonial and authoritarian regimes	Water as human rights and *res commune*	Governance as a spatiotemporal relationship
Climate crisis injury in *Corporate climate responsibility lawsuit, the Netherlands*	Uncertainty of causation in climate responsibility	Experience of the living environments of local residents due to climate crisis	Unwritten standard of due care	Non-causal relationship of climate harms

In the first case study about the narratives of the continuing injury of racial injustice (Chapter 1), we can find the question about reparation entitlement due to the legacy of slavery centuries ago in *Re African American Slave Descendants Litigation*. The District Court of Illinois in this case intuits the question by extending the temporal limitation insofar as such intuition allows the court to capture the multiple narratives of unjust experiences. In our second case study (Chapter 2), the Indonesian Court applies human rights language to express the collective trauma of exploitative policy inherited from past colonial and authoritarian regimes. The right to water in the narratives of this case comes up as a form of judicial intuition that encounters the trauma of colonial extractivism. In the third case study (Chapter 3), the Dutch Civil Court encounters the unease and tension between localization of climate injustice and individualization of collective responsibility in the struggle against the climate crisis. While this court acknowledges the harm experienced by the claimants through sensitizing the gravity of climate crisis, the judges simultaneously intuit such encounters by enacting the principle of unwritten standard of due care in society. Table I.1 helps us situate the overall description of this section's case studies.

Reading Table I.1, one should not be persuaded to grasp the case studies as a comparative attempt that traditionally looks for similarities or differences between legal traditions as represented by the diversity of cases. Nor should one see this as an attempt to homogenize and generalize the adjudicative institutions between countries and methods of reasoning applied in their corresponding traditions. In fact, our comparison is between *intuitive judgments* within their own contexts, based on which such a comparison aims to canvass the methodological underpinning of intuition based on empirical settings. Seeing through the lens of judicial reasoning, the narratives of legal principles as described in Table I.1 (e.g., the statutory limitation tolling in the slavery descendant reparation case, the unwritten standard of due care related to the company's climate commitment and the transcendental nature of water resource governance) are all essentially judicial techniques through which the judges intuit the multiplicity of experiences of injustice. Intuition, in this framework, is what brings these legal principles into the judge's mind, or we can say that intuition becomes "the deflection, the divergence, the deviation, the digression"[4] which *generates* some selected experiences as "the durational in temporality, as differentiated moments, as difference in kind and not a difference in degree."[5] These legal principles indicate that the judges no longer reason the cases in terms of objectified linearity but instead try to attend to the multiple experiences of the case. Ultimately, this process of attending to the multiplicity allows the judges to *actualize* collective legal responsibility which is emanating from the *virtual* temporalities of injustices (i.e., memory of past injustices). And this is basically the main reason why in each narrative we will be employing corresponding theoretical frameworks that can help us to better understand the wider societal context of injustice narrated by the court.

4 Felix Rebolledo Palazuelos, Tania Galli Fonseca, and Andreia Machado Oliveira, "A Philosophical Perspective on Intuition as a Method within Artistic Process," *Studies in Visual Arts and Communication: An International Journal* 5, no. 1 (2018): 10.

5 Ibid.

Chapter 1

Transitory racial discrimination

In this chapter, our inquiry into racial discrimination narratives is divided into three sections. First, it draws the context of the multiplicity of discrimination upon several thematic legal cases. The multiplicity can be grasped here in the context of the ever-changing faces of discrimination, or, as Justice Powell in the affirmative action case in *Bakke* claims, the 'transitory consideration' of discrimination.[1] Within this multiplicity we can identify the structure of experiential temporalities of discrimination upon reading several legal cases at the United States courts. Some thematic legal issues covered in this analysis, which notably have long been framed under the umbrella term of historical injustice, include racial discrimination and exclusion, same-sex marriage and rape shield rules-related cases. Following this structure of experiential temporalities, the second section attempts to situate the transitory character of discrimination in the country by specifically examining the courts' intuitive reasoning in *Re African American Slave Descendants Litigation*.[2] From *Slave Descendants*, we can assert that the court's expression of the timeliness principle upon the reparation claim is actually judicial technique that intuits racial injustice. In *Slave Descendants*, the court's intuitive reasoning process furthermore suggests that the timeliness principle is perceived by the judges within a kind of tension between the chronological and experiential view of time. Finally, the third section will deal with collective legal responsibility actualization. Framing time as duration in a Bergsonian sense implies that legal temporalities are undisputedly perspectival in this inquiry. By specifically emphasizing the judge's extension of statutory limitation of the claim, our inquiry later finds that the transitory character of racial injustice has been primarily contested due to the *givenness* of time. Such a givenness of time is

1 University of California Regents v. Bakke BT—US (1978); Yuvraj Joshi, "Racial Transition," *Washington University Law Review* 98 (2020): 1181; Yuvraj Joshi, "Racial Time," *University of Chicago Law Review* 90 (2023).

2 In re African-Am. Slave Descendants Litig., 375 F. Supp 2d. 721, 726 (N.D. Ill. 2005) (n.d.); In re African-American Slave Descendants Litig., 471 F.3d 754, 762 (7th Cir. 2006) (n.d.).

DOI: 10.4324/9781003518693-3

reflected by the court's interpretation of legal principles (i.e., tolling doctrine, equity theories, etc.) in their travail to actualize collective legal responsibility for reparation. Despite the court's rejection of almost all of the plaintiffs' claims, the judges have ostensibly intuited the Encounter[3]—i.e., the persistent or continuing injustice against a certain group of people—based on which they have attempted to decide empathically by using the details of rules and principles relevant to the case.

The multiplicity of discrimination

As a rule of thumb, the experiential view approach to time advocated in this study understands time as a continuity which is found in duration.[4] As already noted in the Introductory chapter, borrowing from Bergson's theory of time, duration is the continuity of the materialization of memory. Through Bergson, we may learn that "[o]ur [i.e., legal decision maker's] perceptions, sensations, emotions, and ideas occur under two aspects: the one clear and precise, but impersonal; the other confused, ever-changing, and inexpressible."[5] That is, the former is divisible and susceptible to measurement mathematically, while the latter is qualitative and ever-changing.

Applying the two aspects of duration to some legal cases related to the historical experiences of discrimination in the United States courts may generate three forms of temporalities. *First*, the temporalities of injustice flow through perception-memory that are essentially transitory, while at the same time they also hinge upon certain moments as an impetus toward legal change. We may glean from this experiential reality that memory is a normative object within a judge's consciousness. Through Bergson's duration, we can find the significance of perception-memory in experiential temporality. Take, for instance, several 'moments' reflected in the United States courts' references to the years 1868 and 1896, *Brown v. Board of Education*,[6] ratification of the Fourteenth Amendment, *Lucas v. Michigan*,[7] *Korematsu v. United States*[8] and so on. These moments of reference, or in Bergsonian terms "circuits or layers of memory," are memories to which judges' perception leaps and recollects, as a kind of back-and-forth movement into the actual that they encounter. Those references are not something manifestly *given*, but rather, we could say, an impetus toward change. In fact, the further the judges'

3 On temporal Encounter, see details in Chapter 5.

4 Jenann Ismael, "Temporal Experience," in *The Oxford Handbook of Philosophy of Time* (Oxford University Press, 2011).

5 Henri Bergson, *Time and Free Will: An Essay on the Immediate Data of Consciousness* (Routledge, 2014), 129. (emphasis added)

6 Brown v. Board of Education BT-US (1954).

7 Michigan v. Lucas BT-US (1991).

8 Korematsu v. United States BT-US (1944).

memory leaps, the larger their perception may be. This process expands the time experienced and makes time more contingent. Understood that way, the judges' 'turn back the clock' metaphor, which we can easily find in some court decisions in the country, can be grasped in terms of an 'expanding actual'—i.e., since memory leaps further and comes back from the virtual. As a result, the actual present becomes more contingent, and the way law treats legal subjects is no longer an abstract but rather as a concrete, singular subject with variegated experiences. The rather open-texture clauses under the United States Constitution, e.g., the "Equal protection clause" or "Establishment clause," are naturally discursive (instead of bluntly executive), so that some judges' equivocal views of social discrimination or racial division are best seen as a process of becoming. Through the memory recollection process, law's cross-temporally projectable shape is manifested—as opposed or complementary to the 'cross-sectional' shape[9]—with the view to repair and restructure the damage done and to avoid repetition of failure. Based on this explanation, it would be fair to say that a judge's perception-memory leap construes the transitory nature of events and the changing selves of legal subjects in historical cases. Duration involves transition being prioritized to the multiplicity (succession of gapless discrete experiences) as continuity in a spatial array.[10]

The *second* reality is that the temporalities of injustice are experienced in the intensity of anticipating the law. As in almost all events, anticipating the unknown compels us to expect both the expectable and the unexpected. Take, for example, experiential time of a long-discriminated same-sex couple's right to marriage defended by the judges in *Obergefell v. Hodges* (2015).[11] The court highlights expectancy as duration amidst the existing sedimented perceptions and memories against same-sex couples in the country. Intensity of expectancy could be reflected, in this case, by the claimants' narratives of "hurtful for the rest of time,"[12] "continuing uncertainty their unmarried status creates in their lives"[13] and "endur[ing] a substantial burden."[14] The court in *Obergefell* recollected these experiences from the virtual past into the actual present. Historical facts in the court's decisions about prolonged, enduring injustices were not understood as a mere timeline—a chronology to

9 David A. Super, "Temporal Equal Protection," *North Carolina Law Review* 98 (2019): 59–122.

10 Duncan Kennedy, *Legal Reasoning: Collected Essays* (Aurora, CO: Davies Group Publishers, 2008); Fernando Atria, *On Law and Legal Reasoning* (Oxford & Portland, OR: Bloomsbury Publishing, 2002); Carol J. Greenhouse, "Just in Time: Temporality and the Cultural Legitimation of Law," *Yale Law Journal* 98 (1988): 1631.

11 Obergefell v. Hodges BT—S. Ct. (2015).

12 Ibid., 135:2594–95.

13 Ibid., 135:2595.

14 Ibid.

assist them in categorizing and subsuming fact patterns. Rather, these should be grasped as layers of memory which guide the judges to construe and designate the Plaintiff's waiting or expecting in the actual present, such can be found in *Obergefell*.[15] Additionally, in another setting, anticipating as duration can also be reflected as the urge to accelerate the court's proceeding, for instance, in rape shield rules-related cases. The duration of the victim's trauma in this kind of legal plot is contingent upon the call for witnesses to be made by the authority who, through the eye of an 'intellect' outsider, then decides and contains the slices of the victim's experiences. We could propound expectancy as a normative object within the device experienced through waiting for the law. Expectancy could be vividly reduced or increased by legal rules, and importantly, the foregrounding of intensity within duration may exhibit both the interval and simultaneity of necessity, tradition and suffering.

The *third* reality that stands out is that the temporalities of injustice inhabit the character/personality alteration. This proposition suggests that personality is another normative object within the temporalities that is experienced through alteration.[16] Back to Bergson's conceptualization of duration, where character or personality is considered a trajectory of self-creation that emanates from the past.[17] That said, personality is seen as a continuity of change that is indivisible. It is therefore seen as part of human self-creation within the duration.[18] In this sense, there are two types of character/personality, namely *personal* and *impersonal*. Any attempts to be mindful of the former

15 Waiting as law's device at some point borrows from Kafkaesque narrative about guardian before the law in his *The Trial*. Franz Kafka, "Devant La Loi," *Le Portique. Revue de Philosophie et de Sciences Humaines*, no. 15 (2005); Henk Van Houtum, "Waiting before the Law: Kafka on the Border," *Social & Legal Studies* 19, no. 3 (2010): 285–97.

16 Achille Mbembe, *Critique of Black Reason*, trans. Laurent Dubois (Durham & London: Duke University Press, 2017). In relation to racial discrimination, for instance, according to Mbembe, there is currently a sort of 'vertiginous assemblage' of blackness and race, particularly in globalization of markets and neoliberalism era. In this era, Mbembe argues, "time passes quickly and is converted into the production of the money-form. Capital, having reached its maximal capability for flight, sets off a process of escalation. The vision that defines the neoliberal moment is one according to which "all events and situations in the world of life can be assigned a market value." The process is also characterized by the production of indifference; the frenzied codification of social life according to norms, categories and numbers; and various operations of abstraction that claim to rationalize the world on the basis of corporate logic. Capital, notably finance capital, is haunted by a baneful double and defines itself as unlimited in terms of both ends and means. It does more than just dictate its own temporal regime. Having taken as its responsibility the "fabrication of all relations of filiation," it seeks to reproduce itself "on its own" in an infinite series of structurally insolvent debts." 3 (citation omitted)

17 Donald Landes, "From a Privileged Image of Durée to the Core of a New Metaphysics," in *The Bergsonian Mind*, ed. Mark Sinclair and Yaron Wolf (Oxon & New York: Routledge, 2021), 99–112.

18 Ibid.

would require something personal upon which, quoting Landes, "the movement of a durational reality requires an immediate and absolute knowledge that is lost with the generalizing tendency of language and concepts."[19] In this personal type, intuition in adjudicative decisions could be understood in terms of "sympathizing with the object to be known involves entering into it . . . thereby gaining a 'personal' and immediate knowledge of it,"[20] whereas the latter impersonal type gains knowledge from an 'outside' intellect, conceptualizing the object in terms of space and movement into a static being.[21] Simply put, the former emanates from *intuition* and the latter from *intellect*. Take, for instance, the application of the Rape Shield Clause in the country.[22] The heterogeneity of the court's approaches in applying the clause is sourced from the judge's proclivity to rule subsumption; that is, a case to appear before the judge only in light of applying the rule. Meanwhile, if we believe that duration must be understood as continuity, character qualifications should also be understood as successive interpenetrative wholes rather than juxtaposed parts. That being the case, judges are being attentive to experiential time if they can interpret that the past (prior accusation) and the present (actual accusation) are continuous and indivisible.[23] Without necessarily going deeper into the matter, suffice it to say now that there is a clear tension between judges who, on the one hand, are assertive toward intellect and, on the other hand, ones who attentive toward intuition.

Thus far, the basic structure of experiential temporalities in historical injustice adjudication has been glossed over. There are three important things we may conclude at this point. First, the reality of time is translated into three modalities of temporal inquiry (past-, future- and present-ness). Second, temporal inquiry is made of a temporal device, understood as a series of interrelated normative objects (memory, expectancy and personality) built upon judges' intuition on realities and their attitude toward time. Third, from these normative objects, we may extract three salient features of experiential temporality in legal reasoning, including: reflective remembrance, intense expectancy and character alteration. In the following section, we proceed to situate these features in the context of *African American Slave Descendants Litigation* in order to better explain how intuition plays a role in attending to the transitory character of racial discrimination.

19 Ibid., 101.
20 Ibid.
21 Henri Bergson, "Creative Evolution," in *Henri Bergson: Key Writings* (Bloomsbury Publishing, 2002).
22 Michigan v. Lucas BT—US, 500; Barbe v. McBride BT—F. 3d (2008).
23 R. Michael Cassidy, "Character, Credibility, and Rape Shield Rules," *Georgetown Journal of Law & Public Policy* 19 (2021): 145; Jules Epstein, "True Lies: The Constitutional and Evidentiary Bases for Admitting Prior False Accusation Evidence in Sexual Assault Prosecutions," *QLR* 24 (2005): 609.

Intuiting the transition of racial discrimination

To understand judicial intuition towards transitory racial discrimination, we will reflect on the reparative legal claim against enduring injuries encapsulated in *Re African American Slave Descendants Litigation*.[24] Specifically, it is critical to highlight how judicial intuition toward the transitory character of racial discrimination provides access for judges to capture the multiplicity of experiences of injustice.

In this 2004 case law, the District Court of Illinois dealt with a reparation civil suit for slaves' descendants resulting from chattel slavery centuries ago. Having been rejected in the first instance, the case went to appellate court at the Seventh Circuit of the United States Federal Court of Appeals in 2005. The claim for reparation in *Slave Descendants* was filed by a class of Plaintiffs who acted on their behalf (claiming to have been enslaved during the post-slavery period in the country) and on their slave-ancestors' behalf. The Plaintiffs formally requested reparation for injuries against some companies deemed to have profited from and been involved in slavery.[25] The Plaintiffs' allegations are that these companies have violated numerous rules, including

> conspiracy, conversion, unjust enrichment, replevin, violation of Title 42, § 1982 (guaranteeing property rights of all citizens), intentional infliction of emotional distress, negligent infliction of emotional distress, and several counts alleging violation of state-based Unfair Deceptive Acts and Practices (UDAP) in the jurisdictions where the cases were initially filed (New York, Texas, California, Illinois, Louisiana, and New Jersey.[26]

24 Bob Carlson, "Why Slavery Reparations Are Good for Civil Procedure Class," *Saint Louis University Law Journal* 47 (2003): 139; Martha Biondi, "The Rise of the Reparations Movement," *Radical History Review* 87, no. 1 (2003): 5–18; Richard A. Epstein, "The Case against Black Reparations," *Boston University Law Review* 84 (2004): 1177; Lolita Buckner Inniss, "A Critical Legal Rhetoric Approach to in Re African-American Slave Descendants Litigation," *St. John's Journal of Legal Commentary* 24 (2009): 649; Robert Westley, "The Accursed Share: Genealogy, Temporality, and the Problem of Value in Black Reparations Discourse," *Representations* 92, no. 1 (2005): 81–116.

25 The companies are including FleetBoston Financial Corporation, CSX Corporation, Aetna Inc., Brown Brothers Harriman & Company, New York Life Insurance Company, Norfolk Southern Corporation, Lehman Brothers Corporation, Lloyd's of London, Union Pacific Railroad, JP Morgan Chase, R.J. Reynolds Tobacco Company, Brown and Williamson, Liggett Group Inc., Canadian National Railway, Southern Mutual Insurance Company, American International Group ("AIG") and Loews Corporation. According to the Plaintiffs, "The defendants are companies or the successors to companies that provided services, such as transportation, finance, and insurance, to slaveowners. At least two of the defendants were slaveowners; the predecessor of one of the bank defendants once accepted 13,000 slaves as collateral on loans and ended up owning 1,250 of them when the borrowers defaulted, and the predecessor of another defendant ended up owning 346 slaves, also as a consequence of a borrower's default."

26 Inniss, "A Critical Legal Rhetoric Approach to in Re African-American Slave Descendants Litigation," 652–53.

Without going through all the details of this lawsuit, our specific object of investigation in this section is the idea of *timeliness*, proffered by the courts as the critical (temporal) feature of the reparation claim. Arguably, the meaning-making process of the timeliness principle by the court is fundamentally an assertion of judicial intuition toward the transitory character of racial discrimination in the country. By rendering the court's explication of the statute of limitations, intuitive legal reasoning is claimed to be the judges' mode of reasoning, attempting to fully capture the multiplicity of historical injustice experiences.

In this historical injustice reparation claim, the court enshrines four underlying principles to answer the feasibility of Plaintiff's claims, including that (1) there should be a specific connection between the Plaintiffs and the Defendants, in which the former lack constitutional standing to bring the claim; (2) the court is restricted by prudential limitations that prohibit it from giving an answer to such a broad inquiry of social importance; (3) the issue of slavery reparation falls within the ambit of authorities outside the court—i.e., the political question doctrine; and (4) the reparation claim should be timely, meaning that it should be within the applicable statutes of limitations.[27] Arguably, the temporal aspect of the claim, enshrined under Principle (4), underpins all other aspects of procedures, political questions, authority and social importance of this reparation inquiry.[28] This principle thus insists that the Plaintiffs should have demonstrated that their claims are timely or fall within the applicable temporal limitations.

At the moment, we may want to ask as to *when*, or rather, *how*, a complaint is timely? In response to this, the District Court sheds light on the timeliness principle by scrutinizing the concept of statutory limitations. In its general proposition about statutory limitation, the court approaches the case under a strict chronological frame. Two important concepts frequently addressed by litigants when dealing with statutes of limitations, so the court argues, are the concepts of accrual and tolling. The District Court declares that,

> A cause of action 'accrues' when a suit may be maintained thereon, and the law in this regard differs from state-to-state and by nature of action." *The proverbial clock starts to run when the action accrues. It is not the date on which the wrong that injures the plaintiff occurs, but the date—often the same, but sometimes later—on which the plaintiff discovers*

27 In re African-American Slave Descendants Litig., 375 F. Supp 2d. 721, 726 (N.D. Ill. 2005) paragraphs 780–81.

28 Raff Donelson, "Reparations, Responsibility, and Formalism: A Reply to Carnes," *Philosophia* 49, no. 2 (2021): 643–49. Our claim here can be viewed as a sort of temporalization of Donelson's argument about historical responsibility, which rather focuses on justificatory claim on the political questions, authority, and social importance of reparation inquiry. See also Janna Thompson, *Should Current Generations Make Reparation for Slavery?* (Cambridge, UK: Polity Press, 2018).

> *that he has been injured.* While discovery of the injury in some cases may be complex, in others it would be immediately obvious, as in the case of the brutal application of the lash, the turning of the screw, or the tightening of the leg chains nightly to a post. As a complement to accrual, *tolling is a concept which suspends the running of a limitations period to an accrued action. The proverbial clock is stopped when the action is tolled.*[29]

As a general observation, it is suggestive that the court exclusively views the claim for reparation based on chronologizing series of historical events.[30] It is primarily represented by the work of the proverbial clock, which is seen as the judge's technique to contain and fragment time that bars claims for reparation. In relation to the merit of the case, the court states that

> [g]iven that the institution of chattel slavery in the United States ended in 1865, Plaintiffs' century-old claims would have accrued by 1865 at the latest. The longest limitations period for any of Plaintiffs' century-old claims is five years, which would have run well over a century prior to the filing of the instant Complaint. If cognizable claims ever existed, those claims were owned by former slaves themselves, and became time-barred when the statutes of limitations expired in the nineteenth century. As such, Plaintiffs' century-old claims are barred by the statutes of limitations in every jurisdiction.[31]

Furthermore, the court insists that the Plaintiffs who claim that slavery persists because of the defendants' misrepresentation about their involvement in slavery, "reveal no more than that Defendants have made generalized denials of the merits of Plaintiffs' lawsuit."[32]

Nevertheless, such an inquiry into the statute of limitation reflects, to use a Bergsonian term, a suspension of the spontaneous link between perception and recollection (of memories) in adjudication. From a chronological frame of time, it is undeniably reasonable should the court have decided not to reason any further from a strict approach to the statute of limitations, insisting that the law's time bars any reparative claim. A broader canvas, however, is broached by the court by probing into the possibility of extending the temporal limitation in three theories of (1) discovery rule, (2) continuing violation

29 In re African-American Slave Descendants Litig., 375 F. Supp 2d. 721, 726 (N.D. Ill. 2005) paragraphs 771–72. (emphasis added)

30 Janna Thompson, *Taking Responsibility for the Past: Reparation and Historical Injustice* (Cambridge, UK: Polity Press, 2002), 81–83.

31 In re African-American Slave Descendants Litig., 375 F. Supp 2d. 721, 726 (N.D. Ill. 2005) at 773.

32 Ibid., 774.

doctrine and (3) equity theories (i.e., estoppel and tolling). Referring to our previous concept of law's transition as *duration*, we could suggest that such a theoretical observation showcases an intuitive legal reasoning through which they discover the Encounter; that is, the suspension of the spontaneous link between law's time and the experiences of injustice. To elaborate this argument further, let us pay closer attention to the three theories.

First, the court claims that the discovery rule is primarily a rule that "postpones the beginning of a limitations period until such time as the plaintiff discovers the injury or, through reasonable diligence, should have discovered the injury."[33] In this case, the court argues that the mere fact that the plaintiffs' ancestors did not know exactly how much profit was made from their slave labor is not enough to establish that the discovery rule should apply in this case. In that sense, argued the court, "[t]he federal common law discovery rule does not permit the plaintiff to delay filing its lawsuit until all foreseeable harms arising from the injury are actually experienced, but only until the plaintiff discovers the predicate injury."[34] The court furthermore maintains that

> [t]he predicate injury in this instance was the institution of slavery itself. Plaintiffs make a veiled attempt to tie the beginning of the statutes of limitations periods to the discovery of the damages that flowed from slavery rather than the predicate injury itself. Again, the discovery doctrine only extends the statutes of limitations until the predicate act is discovered, not until all discovery of its consequences is completed.[35]

The law's time in this line of reasoning structure distinguishes foreseeable harms arising from (1) actual experienced injury and (2) predicate injury. Suffice it to say here that the important element of this particular theory is not necessarily the duration of experience itself, but rather the timeliness of filing the suit based on the discovery of the predicate act. It underlines a separation within the judge's mind between the *actuality* of discovering injury from claiming such an injury.

Second, the continuing violence, as the court stipulates,

> allows the plaintiff to file an action when there is a continuous series of injuries stemming from the same injury. Under this doctrine, the statutes of limitations are not tolled per se but rather left open *until a final injury has accrued*.[36]

33 Ibid., 775.
34 Ibid., para. 775.
35 Ibid., 775–76. (emphasis added, citation omitted)
36 Ibid., para. 776. (emphasis added)

In intuiting injury as a continuation, the court essentially creates a distinction between the 'finality' of injury and the mere 'alleged effects' of injury. The court furthermore argues that

> [a]ll of the other ills and consequences that flowed from this injury, no matter how dreadful, do not constitute new or continuing claims. *They are merely the alleged effects of an injury that occurred over a century ago, and not a continuing series of acts.*[37]

Continuing violence, as an angle to intuit the transitory character of discrimination, was grasped by the court in a rather processual sense; that is, they chiefly contain the effects of historical slavery into either the final injury or consequences of injury.

Third, the equity theories register two branches, namely estoppel and equity tolling theories. Equity in this sense enables an individuated scrutiny of fairness, and if it succeeds, may provide discretionary relief. The estoppel theory, according to the court, "allows a plaintiff to bring a cause of action after a statute of limitations has expired when the defendant takes active steps to prevent the plaintiff from suing on time."[38] Arguably, timeliness touches on the experiential character of time in this theoretical elaboration that attempts to sensitize temporal claims beyond the chronology bar.[39] Nevertheless, the court exhibits that the plaintiffs

> have not asserted any facts alleging that any Defendant concealed information in a way that would have prevented Plaintiffs' ancestors from asserting their claims within the proscribed statutes of limitations periods. Plaintiffs do not allege that Defendants concealed the injury.[40]

Subsequently, and we might spot intuitive reasoning at this point, the court claims that "the injury was not concealed, but rather obvious when inflicted. *Plaintiffs merely make vague generalizations about Defendants and their perceived practices. Plaintiffs' vague assertions are not enough to satisfy the requirements for equitable estoppel.*"[41] Furthermore, the equitable tolling is applicable when "a plaintiff, despite due diligence, is unable to obtain enough information to conclude that there is a basis for a claim."[42]

37 Ibid. (emphasis added)
38 Ibid., para. 777.
39 T. Leigh Anensom, "From Theory to Practice: Analyzing Equitable Estoppel under a Pluralistic Model of Law," *Lewis & Clark Law Review* 11 (2007): 633.
40 In re African-American Slave Descendants Litig., 375 F. Supp 2d. 721, 726 (N.D. Ill. 2005) paragraph 778.
41 Ibid. (emphasis added)
42 Ibid.

Theoretically distinct from the previously equitable estoppel, equitable tolling

> permits a plaintiff to sue after the statute of limitations has expired if through no fault or lack of diligence on his part he was unable to sue before, even though the defendant took no active steps to prevent him from suing.[43]

The court, however, argues that the doctrine of equitable tolling does not apply in this instance because the basis for the claim cannot be concluded by a mere *chronicle* of social inequities and injustices. The court intuitively maintains that

> Plaintiffs' ancestors knew of their injury at the time that it occurred. *They knew, or should have known, that they were wrongfully being forced to work without compensation, and that somebody was making a profit from their labor. Yet, neither Plaintiffs nor their ancestors ever asserted these claims in a court of law until now.* Plaintiffs have not shown that they acted with all due diligence in attempting to obtain vital information about their claims, and assert them timely . . . . Plaintiffs merely make vague assertions and generalizations as to their claimsand the state of the legal system. Plaintiffs' vague assertions and generalizations are not enough to toll the statutes of limitations on their claims. Plaintiffs' Complaint is nothing more than an attempt to by-pass the various statutes of limitations by chronicling the social inequities and injustices that have befallen African-Americans as a result of slavery. *The statutes of limitations, however, are not to be disregarded by courts out of a vague sympathy for particular litigants.*[44]

Other than extending the temporal limitation, the temporal frame of the *Slave Descendants* ostensibly resonates with the court's broader argument in determining the standing or personal stake doctrine. The doctrine of standing ensures that a litigant is the proper party to bring a matter before a federal court for adjudication, primarily by asking if that specific litigant has a sufficient stake in that matter to invoke the federal judicial process.[45] This injury, therefore, should be particularized only to the claimant.[46] The court, however, found that the Plaintiffs do not satisfy the doctrine's conditions, thus failing to support their standing to maintain the suit as required by Article

43 Ibid.
44 Ibid., para. 771. (emphasis added)
45 Ibid., para. 744.
46 Ibid., para. 745.

III of the United States Constitution. They fail, according to the court, for five reasons: (1) Plaintiffs cannot satisfy the first and most basic requirement of constitutional standing—a concrete and particularized personal injury; (2) Plaintiffs cannot establish a personal injury sufficient to confer standing by merely alleging some genealogical relationship to African-Americans held in slavery over 100, 200 or 300 years ago; (3) In attempting to litigate the unopposed issue of slavery rather than their personal injuries, Plaintiffs also cannot satisfy the second requirement of constitutional standing—injury that is fairly traceable to the conduct of the defendants; (4) Plaintiffs do not allege that they had any present property interest that was injured as a result of these specific Defendants' actions, nor that any action of the Defendants wronged them in any way that would be cognizable under tort theory; and (5) Plaintiffs fail to allege any conduct by the 17 specifically named Defendants that individually affected any of the Plaintiffs.[47]

Relatedly, we can furthermore discover corresponding instances at the case's appellate level at the United States Court of Appeals Seventh Circuit (CoA). The CoA explains the absence of the Plaintiffs' legal standing by employing a scenario that carries temporal imagination in it:

> if there were a legal wrong, it would not be a wrong to any living persons unless they were somehow the authorized representatives to bring suits on behalf of their enslaved ancestors. With some exceptions to be noted, the plaintiffs are suing to redress harms to third parties (their ancestors), without being authorized to sue on behalf of those parties. *It is like a suit by a descendant of a Union soldier, killed in battle, against a Civil War era gun manufacturer still in business that sold guns to the Confederacy in violation of federal law.*[48]

In its conclusion, the CoA argues that

> although most of the plaintiffs and class members are suing as descendants rather than as representatives of their ancestors' estates authorized to sue on those ancestors' behalf, a few do claim to be suing in such a representative capacity. *It is highly unlikely that the estate of anyone who died a century or more ago, or indeed more than half a century ago (for although many former slaves survived into the twentieth century, very few would still have been alive 50 years ago, which is to say in 1956, 91 years after the end of the Civil War), has not yet been closed.* But the district judge accepted that the purported representatives had a right to sue on behalf

47 Ibid., para. 752.
48 In re African-American Slave Descendants Litig., 471 F.3d 754, 762 (7th Cir. 2006) paragraph 760.

> of their ancestors, and the defendants offer only a perfunctory rebuttal. We shall assume without deciding that some of the plaintiffs are legal representatives of their slave ancestors. These plaintiffs not only escape the objection to standing that the suits seek damages for injuries actually suffered by third parties (the ancestors—no longer third parties, but the real parties in interest, merely represented by the plaintiffs), but have less to prove. They just have to prove the injury to the ancestors; the trickle-down question is elided.
>
> *In all likelihood it would still be impossible for them to prove injury, requiring as that would connecting the particular slavery transactions in which the defendants were involved to harm to particular slaves.* But in any event, suits complaining about injuries that occurred more than a century and a half ago have been barred for a long time by the applicable state statutes of limitations. *It is true that tolling doctrines can extend the time to sue well beyond the period of limitations—but not to a century and more beyond.*[49]

The intuitive reasoning in *Slave Descendants* entails a categorial inquiry that enables judges to engage in the meaning-making process of procedures, political questions, authority and the social importance of reparation inquiry. It is manifest that the concept of timeliness of a claim, as these courts exhibit, is intuitively rendered upon chronologizing the accruing and tolling harm, in which time seemingly plays as a natural force that affects the judge's reasoning. Such an approach to accrual and tolling theories indicates some presuppositions in the judge's mode of reasoning, including that (1) the chronological temporal limitation is always in the background of all legal doctrines and theories; (2) the chronology of history implies the state of likelihood over time either in terms of the individual's well-being or of the diminishing properties, and it somehow shrinks the possibility to see anew; and (3) the individual or group's self-identification may be seen as an extended character to represent harm.[50] Conceiving of these implications, timeliness itself entails several premises in the courts' attempt to actualize collective legal responsibility for reparations.

Actualizing collective responsibility

In most discussions about reparation of past injustices in America, the idea of collective responsibility revolves around the issue of compensating the

49 Ibid., 762. (emphasis added)

50 This kind of subjectivity can be seen from the court's recognition to some of the plaintiffs' status as the legal representative of their slave ancestors.

nation's guilt—e.g., eligibility, compensation and calculation of 'the debt.'[51] To enable judges' reasoning to capture the multiplicity of experiences, the transitory character of discrimination should be understood in a *pure* temporal sense. That said, the transitory frame of reparation claim is to be grasped accordingly in the sense of duration; that is, Justice Powell's 'transitory consideration' in *Bakke* should be regarded as both singularity and multiplicity. In the first sense, the transitory discrimination is better grasped as continuity—a single and indivisible whole of memory and perception, while in the latter sense, this transition compounds multiple and variegated simultaneous lived experiences.

The transitory character of racial discrimination investigated in *Slave Descendants* reflects the way judges intuit through the three experiential features mentioned in Section 1 (i.e., reflective remembrance, intense expectancy and character alteration). At the same time, this engagement entails a kind of novel direction in understanding historical collective legal responsibility in the United States. For that reason, rather than restricting ourselves to the

51 David Lyons, "Unfinished Business: Racial Junctures in US History and Their Legacy," in *Justice in Time: Responding to Historical Injustice*, ed. Lukas H. Meyer (Baden-Baden: Nomos Verlagsgesellschaft, 2004), 271–98; Ariela Gross, "When Is the Time of Slavery-The History of Slavery in Contemporary Legal and Political Argument," *California Law Review* 96 (2008): 283; Colleen Murphy, "The Movement for Black Lives and Transitional Justice," in *The Movement for Black Lives: Philosophical Perspectives*, ed. Brandon Hogan, Michael Cholbi, Alex Madva, and Benjamin S. Yost (New York: Oxford University Press, 2021), 116; Elena Maculan and Alicia Gil Gil, "The Rationale and Purposes of Criminal Law and Punishment in Transitional Contexts," *Oxford Journal of Legal Studies* 40, no. 1 (2020): 132–57; Noha Aboueldahab, "The Politics of Time, Transition, and Justice in Transitional Justice," *International Criminal Law Review* (2021): 809–16, https://doi.org/10.1163/15718123-bja10079; Natascha Mueller-Hirth and Sandra Rios Oyola, "Defusing Time Bombs: Towards an Understanding of Time and Temporality in Peacebuilding," in *Time and Temporality in Transitional and Post-Conflict Societies*, ed. Natascha Mueller-Hirth and Sandra Rios Oyola (Oxon & New York: Routledge, 2018), 180–87. In contemporary practices of historical injustice litigation, the term 'transitional justice' has been broadly applied to dealing with both post-authoritarian regimes and established democratic countries. In a way, there has been an inclination in transitional justice practice towards treating distinctively past, present and future, whereas the theory has been moving towards a fluid process that engaging various actors to repress injustice; thus builds, quoting Aboueldahab, "a complex set of interactions, ebbs, and flows that take place across space and time." 810. Seen as a fluid process, the current transitional justice framework designs criminal law for the purpose of reparation of victims rather than typically as a means of state control. In this framework, Maculan and Gil assert additional aspirations of criminal law strictly related to the specific transition circumstance; that is, for truth-seeking, reconciliation, peacebuilding, and foundational mechanism. These legal aspirations could plausibly yield three critical problems of time in the current normative shifts that assign judges or courts to a politics and history juridification tasks. These are, according to Mueller-Hirth and Oyola, "conflicts and negotiations of local and institutional temporalities, the relationships of power that underlie constructions and experiences of different temporalities, and the relationships between time and memory." 181.

bounded domain of clock-time responsibility, an engagement with an experiential view will flourish judicial capacity to be attentive to the richness of transition seen as a collective (temporal) imagination among legal actors.[52] The past, read in this way, is "always already contained in the present, not as its cause or its pattern but as the present's latency, virtuality, and potential for being otherwise."[53] That said, radical social transformation in the country requires the court to 'dislocate' the present, bringing the past as a resourceful modality to challenge and granting the Encounter to the present injustices.

In actualizing collective legal responsibility in *Slave Descendants*, there are two leaps taking place at this point; that is: attitudes toward the present and the future—or we can say a liminality of clock time and experience. In that regard, we can think of transitory considerations of discrimination as any struggles that are materialized within these leaps.

First, the court asserts that collective legal responsibility is grounded in a chronicle of events or a natural temporal artifact while simultaneously trying to capture the link between the past and present in the transition. This kind of reflective remembrance involves the judges' perception and memory that interact and leap to the virtuality of norms, rules and historical facts about the injuries of slave ancestors. They are then going on to the actual allegations of harm made by the Defendants. Memories therefore contain past virtual injuries, while the actual perception is shaped by the claimed harmful experiences. References to the chronological historical moments and precedents are essentially attempts by the court to process what we call 'memory recollection,' which shapes the judge's perception in the actual case. In a way, as Lefebvre has correctly suggested, "[m]emory rush back not as they were, that is, as former presents, but instead as they inhabit the perception that solicited them. Actualized in the perception, they entertain new and unprecedented relations."[54] As we have seen in the court's rulings, the past is not diminished; rather, it coexists with the present—a court decision is somewhat a creation of the past. There is a kind of perpetual exchange between the past and the present from which the court finds them indiscernible, yielding the convolutions between the question of *when* and *how* harms and injuries occurred.

Second, the court endeavors to search for narratives of harmful material representation that wield the futurity of transition. The court sensitizes the claimants' intense expectancy of reparation by experimenting with the

52 Maksymilian Del Mar, *Artefacts of Legal Inquiry: The Value of Imagination in Adjudication* (Bloomsbury Publishing, 2020).

53 Elizabeth Grosz, *The Nick of Time: Politics, Evolution, and the Untimely* (Durham & London: Duke University Press, 2004), 254.

54 Alexandre Lefebvre, "A New Image of Law: Deleuze and Jurisprudence," *Telos* 130 (2005): 189.

statutory limitation. Arguably, the four theories (of the discovery rule, the continuing violation doctrine, equitable estoppel or equitable tolling) are forms of judicial intuition to anticipate the future of reparation claims. They do so by invoking various scenarios, for instance, encapsulating that

> [should] they [the ancestors] knew, or should have known, that they were wrongfully being forced to work without compensation, and that somebody was making a profit from their labor. Yet, neither Plaintiffs nor their ancestors ever asserted these claims in a court of law until now.

Or another scenario conveyed by the CoA, which reads,

> Suppose a class member could prove that he was descended from one of the slaves insured by Aetna or transported by the Union Pacific Railroad (another defendant) or bought with money lent to the buyer by the predecessor of the JPMorgan Chase Bank (still another defendant), and that these transactions were illegal and that the descendants of slaves are among the people whom the laws were intended to protect. Had he not been insured or transported or bought with a bank loan, how would the financial welfare of his remote descendant be affected? Would the ancestor have been freed, or perhaps never enslaved in the first place? As the plaintiffs stress, slavery was profitable; is it conceivable that slaveholders would have been unable to insure, transport, and finance the purchase of slaves if northern companies had been excluded from the provision of these services or had refused to violate their states' laws that sought to keep them from providing the services?[55]

That said, the scenarios in *Slave Descendants* are a significant feature for future projections within the transition.[56] They open a conversation that persuades legal actors to enter into a certain epistemic justification in which any future judges might provide new responses to the scenarios.[57]

Third, the personal stake doctrine provides a way to understand the transitory character of discrimination beyond the binaries of innocence/guilt, wrongdoer/victim (and their agencies), good/bad victimhood and so on. This claim somehow confirms that race is historically artificial and always in the process of becoming.[58] The queries of agents and agencies in *Slave Descend-*

55 In re African-American Slave Descendants Litig., 471 F.3d 754, 762 (7th Cir. 2006) para. 760.

56 For a deeper elaboration on the temporal capacity of scenario, *See* Del Mar, *Artefacts of Legal Inquiry: The Value of Imagination in Adjudication.*

57 Ibid.

58 Ariela Gross, *What Blood Won't Tell: A History of Race on Trial in America* (Cambridge, MA: Harvard University Press, 2008). Examining race on trial throughout the American history, Gross asserts that "Over the course of two centuries, 'race' has been a moving target.

ants are reflected through a kind of legal subjectivity addressed by the court. As a claimant, the court suggested, a subject should have experienced injury or any foreseeable harm that is final and accrued. That said, it is not that the voice of the litigant directly determines the outcome of a decision, but rather, as the court contends, the temporal dimensions in the form of the statute of limitations are not to be disregarded out of a vague sympathy for particular litigants. Victimhood, so to speak, is thus not built upon any vague assertions and generalizations.[59] To recall, experiential temporality insists on a simulated judicial experience that goes beyond individual or group interests. As a part of the normative dimensions of transition, we can think of the question of identity-character (and their personal stakes) as being the core idea of 'present-ness' in transitioning America. In this sense, our reference to legal time-mindfulness (later discussed in Part II) that maintains the value of integrity and fidelity enables the normative environment for the law's cross-temporally projectable shape, from which we can understand that intuition could become an evaluative dimension of expression of justice and coherence.

Ultimately, two arguments are important to note here. First, an intuition toward injustice is found within the link between integrity and fidelity—such as friendship or loyalty. In that sense, according to Postema, "[s]triving for law's systemic and temporally extended integrity is an expression of that fidelity. Time-oriented, time-ordering law gives focus, direction, and content to this fundamental obligation of fidelity of each member to each other."[60] Second, reading Bergson guides us to posit 'moral aspiration' as an appeal to justice based on the enactment of a myth. Reading the two perspectives together, in this ethical dimension, we can argue that justice is an intuited extended value. Justice could be grasped as both moral and physical personalities that emerge from social institutions and habits. Social 'moral obligation' is then understood as an external process that presses an individual from outside. Justice is then intuited so that personal morality could break from static morality to a more open one.

From the earliest days of colonial history throughout the early republic, the antebellum era, the days of Jim Crow, and the civil rights movement, individuals, groups, and nationalities have moved in and out of racial identities, and the word 'race' itself has meant different things at different times. Even in the heyday of scientific racism, in the mid-nineteenth century, courts never relied on racial science alone to determine an individual's racial identity, but always invoked some combination of reputation, performance, and association as well." 296.

59 Cheryl Lawther, "'Let Me Tell You': Transitional Justice, Victimhood and Dealing with a Contested Past," *Social & Legal Studies* 30, no. 6 (2021): 890–912; Gross, *What Blood Won't Tell: A History of Race on Trial in America.*

60 Gerald J. Postema, "Time in Law's Domain," *Ratio Juris* 31, no. 2 (2018): 177.

Conclusion

All things considered, the main assertion of this case study is that construing intuitive legal reasoning is not necessarily based on the outcome of the judgment, but rather, about putting emphasis on the necessity to appreciate the shift from the regularity and expediency of adjudication to a kind of creative and experimental judgment.[61] We may also contend that the temporal encounter in *Slave Descendants* has made the case a singularity through judicial intuition. Despite the court's rejection of the claims, the judges intuitively empathize with the encounter—the persistent or continuing injustice against a certain group of people—from which they have attempted to decide by using the details of rules and principles relevant to the case.[62]

Reference list

Aboueldahab, Noha. "The Politics of Time, Transition, and Justice in Transitional Justice." *International Criminal Law Review* (2021): 809–16. https://doi.org/10.1163/15718123-bja10079.

Anensom, T. Leigh. "From Theory to Practice: Analyzing Equitable Estoppel under a Pluralistic Model of Law." *Lewis & Clark Law Review* 11 (2007): 633.

Atria, Fernando. *On Law and Legal Reasoning*. Oxford & Portland, OR: Bloomsbury Publishing, 2002.

Barbe v. McBride BT—F. 3d (2008).

Bergson, Henri. "Creative Evolution." In *Henri Bergson: Key Writings*. Bloomsbury Publishing, 2002.

Bergson, Henri. *Time and Free Will: An Essay on the Immediate Data of Consciousness*. Routledge, 2014.

Biondi, Martha. "The Rise of the Reparations Movement." *Radical History Review* 87, no. 1 (2003): 5–18.

Brown v. Board of Education BT—US (1954).

Carlson, Bob. "Why Slavery Reparations Are Good for Civil Procedure Class." *Saint Louis University Law Journal* 47 (2003): 139.

Cassidy, R. Michael. "Character, Credibility, and Rape Shield Rules." *Georgetown Journal of Law & Public Policy* 19 (2021): 145.

Donelson, Raff. "Reparations, Responsibility, and Formalism: A Reply to Carnes." *Philosophia* 49, no. 2 (2021): 643–49.

Epstein, Jules. "True Lies: The Constitutional and Evidentiary Bases for Admitting Prior False Accusation Evidence in Sexual Assault Prosecutions." *QLR* 24 (2005): 609.

Epstein, Richard A. "The Case against Black Reparations." *Boston University Law Review* 84 (2004): 1177.

61 Alexandre Lefebvre, *The Image of Law: Deleuze, Bergson, Spinoza* (Stanford: Stanford University Press, 2008), 173–95. Or, borrowing from McNeilly, we may see this as the way legal actors embrace the untimeliness from the timeliness. Kathryn McNeilly, "Are Rights Out of Time? International Human Rights Law, Temporality, and Radical Social Change," *Social & Legal Studies* 28, no. 6 (2019): 817–38, https://doi.org/10.1177/0964663918815729.

62 See also Lefebvre, *The Image of Law: Deleuze, Bergson, Spinoza*, 193–95.

Greenhouse, Carol J. "Just in Time: Temporality and the Cultural Legitimation of Law." *Yale Law Journal* 98 (1988): 1631.
Gross, Ariela. *What Blood Won't Tell: A History of Race on Trial in America.* Cambridge, MA: Harvard University Press, 2008.
Gross, Ariela. "When Is the Time of Slavery-The History of Slavery in Contemporary Legal and Political Argument." *California Law Review* 96 (2008): 283.
Grosz, Elizabeth. *The Nick of Time: Politics, Evolution, and the Untimely.* Durham & London: Duke University Press, 2004.
Houtum, Henk Van. "Waiting before the Law: Kafka on the Border." *Social & Legal Studies* 19, no. 3 (2010): 285–97.
In re African-American Slave Descendants Litig., 375 F. Supp 2d. 721, 726 (N.D. Ill. 2005) (n.d.).
In re African-American Slave Descendants Litig., 471 F.3d 754, 762 (7th Cir. 2006) (n.d.).
Inniss, Lolita Buckner. "A Critical Legal Rhetoric Approach to in Re African-American Slave Descendants Litigation." *St. John's Journal of Legal Commentary* 24 (2009): 649.
Ismael, Jenann. "Temporal Experience." In *The Oxford Handbook of Philosophy of Time.* Oxford University Press, 2011.
Joshi, Yuvraj. "Racial Transition." *Washington University Law Review* 98 (2020): 1181.
Joshi, Yuvraj. "Racial Time." *University of Chicago Law Review* 90 (2023).
Kafka, Franz. "Devant La Loi." *Le Portique. Revue de Philosophie et de Sciences Humaines*, no. 15 (2005).
Kennedy, Duncan. *Legal Reasoning: Collected Essays.* Aurora, CO: Davies Group Publishers, 2008.
Korematsu v. United States BT—US (1944).
Landes, Donald. "From a Privileged Image of Durée to the Core of a New Metaphysics." In *The Bergsonian Mind*, edited by Mark Sinclair and Yaron Wolf, 99–112. Oxon & New York: Routledge, 2021.
Lawther, Cheryl. "'Let Me Tell You': Transitional Justice, Victimhood and Dealing with a Contested Past." *Social & Legal Studies* 30, no. 6 (2021): 890–912.
Lefebvre, Alexandre. "A New Image of Law: Deleuze and Jurisprudence." *Telos* 130 (2005): 103–26.
Lefebvre, Alexandre. *The Image of Law: Deleuze, Bergson, Spinoza.* Stanford: Stanford University Press, 2008.
Lyons, David. "Unfinished Business: Racial Junctures in US History and Their Legacy." In *Justice in Time: Responding to Historical Injustice*, edited by Lukas H. Meyer, 271–98. Baden-Baden: Nomos Verlagsgesellschaft, 2004.
Maculan, Elena, and Alicia Gil Gil. "The Rationale and Purposes of Criminal Law and Punishment in Transitional Contexts." *Oxford Journal of Legal Studies* 40, no. 1 (2020): 132–57.
Mar, Maksymilian Del. *Artefacts of Legal Inquiry: The Value of Imagination in Adjudication.* Bloomsbury Publishing, 2020.
Mbembe, Achille. *Critique of Black Reason.* Translated by Laurent Dubois. Durham & London: Duke University Press, 2017.
McNeilly, Kathryn. "Are Rights Out of Time? International Human Rights Law, Temporality, and Radical Social Change." *Social & Legal Studies* 28, no. 6 (2019): 817–38. https://doi.org/10.1177/0964663918815729.
Michigan v. Lucas BT—US (1991).
Mueller-Hirth, Natascha, and Sandra Rios Oyola. "Defusing Time Bombs: Towards an Understanding of Time and Temporality in Peacebuilding." In *Time and Temporality*

in Transitional and Post-Conflict Societies, edited by Natascha Mueller-Hirth and Sandra Rios Oyola, 180–87. Oxon & New York: Routledge, 2018.
Murphy, Colleen. "The Movement for Black Lives and Transitional Justice." In *The Movement for Black Lives: Philosophical Perspectives*, edited by Brandon Hogan, Michael Cholbi, Alex Madva, and Benjamin S. Yost, 116. New York: Oxford University Press, 2021.
Obergefell v. Hodges BT—S. Ct. (2015).
Postema, Gerald J. "Time in Law's Domain." *Ratio Juris* 31, no. 2 (2018): 160–82.
Super, David A. "Temporal Equal Protection." *North Carolina Law Review* 98, no. 1 (2019): 59–122.
Thompson, Janna. *Taking Responsibility for the Past: Reparation and Historical Injustice*. Cambridge, UK: Polity Press, 2002.
Thompson, Janna. *Should Current Generations Make Reparation for Slavery?* Cambridge, UK: Polity Press, 2018.
University of California Regents v. Bakke BT—US (1978).
Westley, Robert. "The Accursed Share: Genealogy, Temporality, and the Problem of Value in Black Reparations Discourse." *Representations* 92, no. 1 (2005): 81–116.

Chapter 2

Traumatic post-colonial extractivism

This chapter focuses on the role of judicial intuition in capturing the collective trauma of past injustices. Sketching the arguments through a narrative approach, our focus is on how judges' intuition shapes collective legal responsibility related to water (mis)management in the *Jakarta Water Remunicipalization* citizen lawsuit (CLS) in 2015-2018. Reading the case in this manner allows us to understand the judges' intuition toward experiences of injustice, which guides them to select legal qualifications emanating from the collective trauma of unequal relationships in resource governance. That said, distinct from the previous narrative of transition of discrimination, we will here examine the narrative of trauma of extractivist governance.

The case-study aims (1) to explain the concept of judicial intuition in the context of spatial jurisdiction disputes, (2) to identify some aesthetic elements of law informed by linguistic aspects used by legal decision-makers in the CLS and (3) to investigate the creation of lawful relations related to resource governance. Informed by our methodological underpinnings, it is suggested that the collective legal responsibility practice in Jakarta water (mis)management CLS is essentially built upon images of the spatiotemporal configuration of lived experience shaped by what we may call legal property 'hybridization.' This hybridization includes the court's interpretation of constitutional segregation of public and private authorities, universality of rights (to water) and the concept of effectiveness within the liberal-political economy. The CLS decision fundamentally demonstrates overlapping affective dialogues between qualitative risks and resource management projections grounded in the trauma of past colonial and authoritarian regimes.

The case study is organized into three sections. First, it delineates the context of legal temporalities in resource governance, based on which we problematize the pervasive logic of spatiality in understanding water resource management. A brief description of *chronotope* as a supporting analytical theory will be provided, as well as how it can be useful in understanding the embeddedness of time in the legal inquiry into resource governance. Second, a chronotopic analysis of the *Jakarta Water Remunicipalization* CLS (2015–2018) will be unfolded. Through this analysis, we can see the courts'

DOI: 10.4324/9781003518693-4

'hybridization' of legal properties over water resource governance through their narratives of water as human rights and *res commune*. This hybridization can be framed as a form of intuition—it is an image of the spatiotemporal configuration of citizens' lived experiences. It at the same time implies a stretching-narrowing process of space and time related to water governance through the means of legal techniques. Third, we will investigate the actualization of collective legal responsibility in the CLS, in which we can later argue that such a form of lawful relation interacts with the game of spatial and temporal scales and affect. As a result, while the global question of water governance has been revolving around the *who* and *what* of governance, our investigation suggests that the inquiry into *how* governance is exercised would be no less important.

The multiplicity of governance

Let us first situate the context of the case study. *Jakarta Water Remunicipalization* lawsuit is largely seen as part of the global water remunicipalization movement. Conceptually, it exemplifies an intricate relationship between space, time and law. This sort of relationship entails a spatiotemporal dimension of resource governance, in which water (spatial) governance essentially hinges upon some legal properties that represent the temporalities of citizens' lived experience.

One of the ways to describe the law's spatiotemporal interaction is through the concept of governance.[1] Informed by governmentality studies, this concept is broadly considered as a set of governmental practices and technologies exercised by various kinds of actors.[2] By applying governmentality framework, nonetheless, we are not necessarily attempting to understand the government's action in spatiotemporal relations sensemaking, but rather, it seeks to highlight the sort of Foucauldian problematics of the government.[3] To wit, it addresses a network of governance, or, to be precise, borrowing from Rose and Miller, it emphasizes governance as "a whole range of apparatuses pertaining to government and a complex body of knowledge and

1 David Delaney, *The Spatial, the Legal and the Pragmatics of World-Making: Nomospheric Investigation* (New York: Routledge, 2010).

2 Nikolas Rose and Peter Miller, "Political Power beyond the State: Problematics of Government," *The British Journal of Sociology* 61 (January 2010): 271–303, https://doi.org/10.1111/j.1468-4446.2009.01247.x; Nikolas Rose, Pat O'Malley, and Mariana Valverde, "Governmentality," *Annual Review of Law and Social Science* 2 (2006): 83–104.

3 Michel Foucault, "Governmentality," in *The Foucault Effect: Studies in Governmentality*, ed. Graham Burchell, Colin Gordon, and Peter Miller (Chicago: The University of Chicago Press, 1991), 87–104; Margo Huxley, "Geographies of Governmentality," in *Space, Knowledge, and Power*, ed. Jeremy Crampton and Stuart Elden (Hampshire: Ashgate, 2007); Kevin Walby, "Contributions to a Post-Sovereigntist Understanding of Law: Foucault, Law as Governance, and Legal Pluralism," *Social & Legal Studies* 16, no. 4 (2007): 551–71.

'know-how' about government, the means of its exercise and the nature of those over whom it was to be exercised."[4]

Situating the concept of governance in the discourse of law and the city draws our attention to a form of experience of injustice emanating from the water governance dispute. In this context, there is currently an emerging discourse and social activism about water remunicipalization in the Global North as well as in the South.[5] Taking into account the nature of network-governance, water remunicipalization can be defined as "the passage of water services from privatization in any of its various forms—including private ownership of assets, outsourcing of services, and public-private partnerships (PPPs)—to full public ownership, management, and democratic control."[6] Notably, as Lobina furthermore suggests, "concessions, lease contracts, other PPPs, and water privatization are one and the same thing: all these terms refer to the transfer of management control to the private sector, at various degrees."[7] In practice, at least in the last 20 to 30 years, several municipal-level movements have come up with the idea of public demand for reclaiming water resources, challenging the long-lasting private control over water in their respective cities.[8]

It is suggested that water privatization movements reflect a contestation over historical injustice claims caused by so-called extractivist governance. While the term *extractivisim* encompasses a wide range of social, political and economic dimensions, we may identify some key strands from the literature. For the sake of brevity, some findings are borrowed from Chagnon et al., in that they have sketched four common threads about extractivism, including:

(1) extractivism involves *appropriation* of natural and human resource wealth, producing a drain that damages or depletes its source in a potentially irreversible way;

4 Rose and Miller, "Political Power beyond the State: Problematics of Government," 272.

5 Emanuele Lobina, "Water Remunicipalisation: Between Pendulum Swings and Paradigm Advocacy," in *Urban Water Trajectories* (Springer, 2017), 149–61; Thomas M. Hanna and David A. McDonald, "From Pragmatic to Politicized? The Future of Water Remunicipalization in the United States," *Utilities Policy* 72 (2021): 101276.

6 Emanuele Lobina, "Calling for Progressive Water Policies," in *Our Public Experience: The Global Experience with Remunicipalisation* (Amsterdam, London, Paris, Cape Town & Brussels: Transnational Institute (TNI), Public Services International Research Unit (PSIRU), Multinationals Observatory, Municipal Services Project (MSP) and the European Federation of Public Service Unions (EPSU), 2015), 7.

7 Ibid.

8 David A. McDonald and Erik Swyngedouw, "The New Water Wars: Struggles for Remunicipalisation," *Water Alternatives* 12, no. 2 (2019): 322–33.

(2) extractivism is premised on *capital accumulation and centralization of power*. It can occur because of relational power disparities (inequalities/imbalances) and alienation;
(3) *drain*, associated with extractivisms, can be analyzed as resource and wealth flows in time and space (at and through different nested levels, including local, state, regional, and global);
(4) extractivism is a modality of capital accumulation in current global capitalist development that *conditions, constrains and pressures lives* of virtually all humans and other-than-humans. However, it is not dependent on or synonymous with global capitalism and has been embedded in other systems.[9]

Of our particular interest is the idea of flowing wealth in time and space that conditions constrains and pressures the lives of virtually all humans and other-than-humans. Considering this particular element of extractivism, it follows that the term *governance* in the context of extractivist governance can be read as an ongoing exploitative, unequal relationship—it is therefore, as our theoretical orientation indicates, a duration.[10] When extractivist governance is interpreted in this way, we may begin to see water remunicipalization as an expression of reclaim the water governance. In this framework, governmentality studies have also suggested that the claim to governance should be interpreted as a network that includes a greater variety of actors, both state and nonstate, rather than exclusively in terms of juridico-normative discourse. Understandably, an examination of the game of networks of actors is required in order to determine the who, what and how of governance.[11]

But one may ask, how can we find a way to indicate judges' experimental and creative inquiry into the extractivist governance framework? We

9 Christopher W. Chagnon, Francesco Durante, Barry K. Gills, Sophia E. Hagolani-Albov, Saana Hokkanen, Sohvi M. J. Kangasluoma, Heidi Konttinen, Markus Kröger, William LaFleur, and Ossi Ollinaho, "From Extractivism to Global Extractivism: The Evolution of an Organizing Concept," *The Journal of Peasant Studies* 49, no. 4 (2022): 763. (emphasis added)

10 Aníbal Quijano, "Coloniality and Modernity/Rationality," *Cultural Studies* 21, no. 2–3 (2007): 168–78; Nelson Maldonado-Torres, *Outline of Ten Theses on Coloniality and Decoloniality* (Paris, 2016), https://fondation-frantzfanon.com/wp-content/uploads/2018/10/maldonado-torres_outline_of_ten_theses-10.23.16.pdf.

11 McDonald and Swyngedouw, "The New Water Wars: Struggles for Remunicipalisation." It is important to highlight McDonald and Swyngedouw's hypothesis on the inquiry of the *how* to govern. They argued that "remunicipalisation will continue to grow in the medium term due to widespread dissatisfaction with privatisation on the part of elected officials, civil servants and citizens, but that differences within the remunicipalisation movement, combined with ongoing fiscal restraints and growing resistance from powerful multilateral actors, may make it difficult to sustain this growth without significant changes to strategy, engagement and resources," 323.

can argue that by analyzing the legal problem of governance in terms of duration, judges can enter into various dimensions of *temporal* realities beyond their inclination toward parochialism that views governance as a merely physical control over *space*. That said, to be prompted by *experimental* and *creative* inquiry, the inquiry into governance should also touch upon an inquiry into time and temporalities. Consequently, we can deduce at the moment that by navigating the plenitude of citizens' experiences, temporalities are virtually shaping the spatial governance of resources.[12] Furthermore, underpinned by our understanding regarding the inherent temporalities in legal reasoning (later discussed thoroughly in Chapter 4), we can expound on judges' creativity in hybridizing different linguistic aspects of consciousness, so that they can assign meaning and value to a certain object of inquiry.

In the context of extractivist governance, the multiplicity of experiences of injustice asserts a conflation of citizens' lived experiences in the past and present.[13] Within such an understanding, our next challenge would be how to identify the narratives that reflect or symbolize the multiplicity of citizens' lived experiences that congeal into the spatialization of water governance responsibility. Supplanted by Bakhtin's literary concept of *chronotope*[14]—read in this context as the ways legal actors use legal techniques to synthesize the spatial and temporal frame of an inquiry—we can proceed from the basic premise that legal responsibility practice is an aesthetic representation of governance over resources construed upon a spatiotemporal configuration of lived experience.[15] As a form of literary concept, our reference to Bakhtin's *Chronotope* insists on a narrative relationship between, on the one hand, people and events, and on the other hand, time and space.[16] The concept itself claims the fundamental unity of the narrative of time and space.[17] Bakhtin,

12 Kirsten Campbell, "The City of Law," *International Journal of Law in Context* 9, no. 2 (2013): 192–212, https://doi.org/10.1017/S1744552313000086; Mark Purcell, "Possible Worlds: Henri Lefebvre and the Right to the City," *Journal of Urban Affairs* 36, no. 1 (2014): 141–54, https://doi.org/10.1111/juaf.12034.

13 Stef Craps, *Postcolonial Witnessing: Trauma Out of Bounds*, vol. 2 (Springer, 2013).

14 Mikhail Mikhaĭlovich Bakhtin, *The Dialogic Imagination: Four Essays* (University of Texas Press, 2010).

15 Irus Braverman, Nicholas Blomley, David Delaney, and Alexandre Kedar, "Expanding the Spaces of Law," in *The Expanding Spaces of Law: A Timely Legal Geography*, ed. Irus Braverman, Nicholas Blomley, David Delaney, and Alexandre (Sandy) Kedar (Stanford, CA: Stanford University Press, 2014), 1–29; Nicholas Blomley, "Performing Property: Making the World," *Canadian Journal of Law and Jurisprudence* 26 (2013): 23–48.

16 Bakhtin, *The Dialogic Imagination: Four Essays*.

17 Michael Holquist, "The Fugue of Chronotope," in *Bakhtin's Theory of the Literary Chronotope: Reflections, Applications, Perspectives*, ed. Nele Bemong, Pieter Borghart, Michel De Dobbeleer, Kristoffel Demoen, Koen De Temmerman, and Bart Keunen (Gent: Academia Press, 2010), 19–34.

however, did not get the chance to clearly state one definition of *chronotope*. The closest thing to a definition Bakhtin ever wrote was that

> [I]n the literary artistic scholarship, spatial and temporal indicators are fused into carefully thought-out, concrete whole. Time, as it was, thickens, takes a flesh becomes artistically visible, likewise, space becomes charges and repulsive to the movements of time, plot and history. The intersection of axes and fusion of indicators characterizes the artistic *chronotope*.[18]

Arguably, we can demonstrate the role of legal temporalities in understanding the governance of a city (and its resources) based on this assertion. In that context, Bakhtin's *chronotope* is to be understood as the ways legal techniques are employed by legal decision-makers to synthesize the spatial and temporal frames of an inquiry. This synthesis will in turn shape judges' intuition in assigning meaning to extractivist governance.[19]

One might ask, how could the concept of *chronotope* be relevant to law's comprehension of governance? Borrowing from existing literatures, particularly in critical legal scholarship, we can say that law, especially reflected by the court's reasoning, is full of narrative where time "takes a flesh" and "space becomes charges and repulsive to the movement of time."[20] In a way, legal cases record, appropriate and fix narrative into legal concept, operating in what Delaney coins as *nomoscape*, "[an] enormously complex and dynamic components of social- and life-worlds . . . condition[ing] the workings of nomic fields of power within which we are always positioned, through which we navigate."[21] Therefore, navigating powers and technologies through governance operates under certain *scalar* effects upon which legal decision-makers rely.[22] According to critical legal scholar Mariana Valverde, scalar effects essentially deal with both the amount of spatial and temporal effects of a particular mode of governance (or jurisdiction in Valverde's term) under observation.[23] In this context, in discussing spatial scales, lawyers commonly grasp governance as territorial capacity in a sense that law works in the traditional distinctive layers of legal orders (e.g., between

18 Bakhtin, *The Dialogic Imagination: Four Essays*, 84.

19 See generally Mariana Valverde, *Chronotopes of Law: Jurisdiction, Scale and Governance* (Oxon & New York: Routledge, 2015).

20 Irene Van Oorschot, "Doing Times, Doing Truths: The Legal Case File as a Folded Object," in *Law and Time*, ed. Siân M. Beynon-Jones and Emily Grabham (Oxon & New York: Routledge, 2019), 229–46.

21 Delaney, *The Spatial, the Legal and the Pragmatics of World-Making: Nomospheric Investigation*, 121–22. (emphasis added)

22 Mariana Valverde, "Jurisdiction and Scale: Legaltechnicalities as Resources for Theory," *Social & Legal Studies* 18, no. 2 (2009): 139–57.

23 Mariana Valverde, "Studying the Governance of Crime and Security: Space, Time and Jurisdiction," *Criminology & Criminal Justice* 14, no. 4 (2014): 379–91.

local (sub-national), national, and international (world) jurisdictions). While in terms of temporal scale, which seemingly gets less attention amongst lawyers, governance plays a role in determining the shape and meaning-making process of lawfulness according to the passage of time. The two scales, like the use of a map for geographers, articulate the shape of legal power and knowledge. This results in the idea of governance that "sorts the where, the who, the what, and the how of governance through a kind of chain reaction, whereby if one question (where, who) is decided, then the answers to the other questions [what, how] seem to follow automatically."[24] Such a chain reaction is a kind of *game*, according to Valverde, who then outlines the following configuring elements:

1. where: territories;
2. who: authorities (whether sovereign, delegated or private);
3. what: the objects of governance (e.g., potholes are municipal; aboriginal reserves are federal);
4. how—which in turn has two dimensions:

    (a) governing capacities, and
    (b) rationalities of governance.[25]

At the moment, we can find a conflation of space, time and affect that can guide us in identifying narratives that reflect the temporalities of citizens' lived experience. The idea of resource governance has now been temporalized in the sense that a legal case is now better framed as an essence—that is, it becomes a singularity. Through this framework, an inquiry into extractivist governance is guided by the questions of *first*, where and who governs a particular issue (i.e., water governance) and *second*, the capacity of this resource governance in practice. Admittedly, however, it is a kind of common sense, particularly through our lawyerly vision, that the answer to 'where and who' justifies 'what and how' of governance, in which power is being "exercised, spatialized, and contested."[26]

Intuiting the trauma of extractivism

Our focus is examining the *Jakarta Water Remunicipalization* citizen lawsuit. To recall, seen as part of the global remunicipalization movement, the contestation over water resources in the city has been revolving exclusively around

24 Valverde, "Jurisdiction and Scale: Legaltechnicalities as Resources for Theory," 144.
25 Ibid.
26 Shiri Pasternak, "Jurisdiction," in *Routledge Handbook of Law and Society*, ed. Mariana Valverde et al. (Oxon & New York: Routledge, 2021), 178.

the spatial aspect of governance. In this sense, water is seen as part of the spatial resources of a city—thus, it is considered a property, an object that is subject to control and possession. The spatial element of water governance is also reflected in this 2015 lawsuit, in which the Indonesian courts dealt with the claim about mismanagement in Jakarta's water governance. The Plaintiffs (Nurhidayah et al.) initially filed a lawsuit to the Central Jakarta District Court (*Pengadilan Negeri Jakarta*) against a group of public and private Defendants, including the Central and Jakarta local administrations, PDAM Provinsi DKI Jakarta (a local public-owned company), and PT. Aetra Air Jakarta and PT. PAM Lyonnaise Jaya (two multinational private companies). Similar to other water remunicipalization movement claims around the world, the Plaintiffs ask the court to revoke the water privatization agreement that is between PDAM Provinsi DKI Jakarta and the two multinational private companies, which was concluded back in 1997.

Let us sketch a brief summary of the case proceedings. The first-level civil trial was held at the Jakarta District Court in 2015. Although the case is basically processed under civil procedure, the Plaintiffs submitted the claim in the form of a citizen lawsuit (CLS). One should note, however, that CLS is yet to be recognized under the country's legal system. In this context, the closest procedure to CLS is environmental and consumer protection lawsuits.[27] Interestingly, the trial court accepted the case and decided that by entering into the water privatization agreement in 1997, the Defendants had conducted unlawful wrongdoing that "resulted losses to the Jakarta local administration and its citizens."[28] Later at the appellate level in 2016, the Jakarta High Court overturned this decision, claiming that on a procedural basis the lawsuit failed to fit into the characteristics of CLS.[29] In 2017, the case underwent the proceedings at the Supreme Court, who then decided to overturn the High Court decision, arguing that the first-level trial has evidently been correct in applying the laws.[30] A year later, the case was brought up to the case review (*peninjauan kembali*) level when the Supreme Court declared that the lawsuit was invalid because the Plaintiffs failed to fulfill their legal standing for claiming a CLS.[31]

27 Cholidin Nasir, "Pengawasan Terhadap Kebijakan Pemerintah Melalui Mekanisme Citizen Lawsuit," *Jurnal Konstitusi* 14, no. 4 (2017): 906–26; Rizkita Alamanda, "Gugatan Warga Negara (Studi Kasus: Gerakan Samarinda Menggugat," *Jurnal Hukum Lingkungan Indonesia* 1, no. 2 (2014): 101–10; Abdul Fatah, "Citizen Lawsuit in Environmental Cases," *Lentera Hukum* 6 (2019): 289.

28 PN Jakarta Pusat, Nurhidayah et al. v. PT. Aetra Air Jakarta et al. (527/Pdt.G/2012/PN JKT. PST) (2012).

29 PT DKI Jakarta, Nurhidayah et al. v. PT. Aetra Air Jakarta et al. (588/PDT/2015/PT DKI) (2015).

30 Mahkamah Agung Rep. Indonesia, Nurhidayah et al. v. PT. Aetra Air Jakarta et al. (31K/Pdt/2017) (2017).

31 Mahkamah Agung Rep. Indonesia, Nurhidayah et al. v. PT. Aetra Air Jakarta et al. (841 PK/Pdt/2018) (2018).

This section considers the way judges select justifying reasons in the CLS through intuition. Table 2.1 shows our overarching description of how the judge's mode of reasoning is capable of encountering the multiplicity of experiences of water injustice in Jakarta. In particular, we are interested in examining the judge's intuitive reasoning when encountering the trauma with extractivist governance in the past. By using *chronotopic* analysis, we can argue that the court's intuitive reasoning helps them assign the meaning and value of qualitative elements of water resources injustice in the city, from which we can draw a nexus between the judges' attention to experiences of injustice and their justifying reasons. Understood in this way, water (spatial)

Table 2.1 List of judicial decisions on *Jakarta Water Remunicipalization* citizen lawsuit

Court decision	*Outcome*	*Justifying reasons*				*Mode of reasoning*
		Nature of claim	*Freedom of contract*	*Causality*	*Water as human right*	
Trial at Jakarta District Court (527/Pdt.G/ 2012/PN JKT.PST., 24 March 2015)	Invalidating the Agreement; Defendants have conducted unlawful acts	V	V	V	V	Intuitive reasoning
Appellate at Jakarta High Court (588/PDT/ 2015/PT DKI., 12 January 2016)	Overturning District Court; Invalidating the citizen lawsuit	V	X	X	X	Intellect reasoning
Cassation at Supreme Court (31 K/Pdt/ 2017, 10 April 2017)	Overturning appellate decision; Invalidating the Agreement	V	V	V	V	Intuitive reasoning
Case review at Supreme Court (841 PK/Pdt/ 2018, 30 November 2018)	Overturning cassation decision; Invalidating the citizen lawsuit	V	X	X	X	Intellect reasoning

governance is virtually canvassed under the multiplicity of societal trauma of colonialism and authoritarianism, asserting a conflation of the citizens' past, present and future lived experiences. As a result, we can later claim that the multiplicity of trauma with extractivist governance is essentially an image of the spatiotemporal configurations of water governance in the country.

Reading *Jakarta Water Remunicipalization* entails a depiction of how intuitive legal reasoning hybridizes four justifying reasons. This hybridization ultimately implies a stretching-narrowing process of space and time. These include (1) the nature of the claim (i.e., public and private separation), (2) freedom of contract (i.e., the invalidity of the privatization agreement), (3) causality of harm (i.e., private company financial loss causes burdens to the citizens) and (4) access to water as a human right (i.e., the state's obligation to guarantee the quality, quantity and continuity of water service). Our *chronotopic* analysis can help us understand how the courts assigned the meaning and value of qualitative elements of water resources jurisdiction in Jakarta. To reiterate, assigning *chronotope* to this case would enable us to understand that the issue of water governance is not only about *who* and *what* governance is but also *how* it is being exercised.

Let us examine the first justifying reason related to the nature of the CLS. In examining the case, the court at each level makes an inquiry into the nature of public-private affairs in managing water as part of the city's resources. Relevant to this inquiry is the contested public nature of CLS. The fundamental question is whether a CLS can formally involve non-public actors as defendant (e.g., suing private water provider companies). Since there is not yet a clear and established legal basis related to CLS proceedings in the Indonesian court, references were made to other resources outside of the positive laws of the country. Such a legal vacuum also creates further legal complications in such a way that the nature of CLS becomes a major disagreement between courts at every level of this case, from the trial court up to the case-review level at the Supreme Court. While the Plaintiffs did not claim legal responsibility exclusively against the two private foreign companies, they still included these companies as Co-defendants.

Specific attention needs to be given to the debate between both parties at the appellate level (*tingkat banding*) in which they contested whether the water privatization is an act of civil contract (i.e., between the Jakarta administration and the private companies) or a local administrative action (i.e., a Jakarta Governor's decision). In their appeal argument, the Plaintiffs claimed that the water privatization agreement, which was signed on June 6, 1997, was the primary *cause* of years of material and immaterial losses suffered by the government and its citizens. They indicate that the agreement was an arrangement to exclusively benefit the multinational private companies, and it is considered a violation of people's right to have access to clean water. Meanwhile, the private Defendants held the claim that the dispute actually deals with administrative decisions and thus has no grounds for a compensatory civil claim. Seeing from the administrative law framework, the Defendants assert that there were two support letters made by the Jakarta Governor and the Minister of Finance to justify the conclusion of the agreement. These administrative documents become the the Defendants' evidence to address the subtle public-private character of the lawsuit.[32] Accordingly, the appellate and case review courts then conclude that "the civil suit is formally invalid due to the incorporation of other parties outside of the government, which are PT. Aetra Air Jakarta and PT. PAM Lyonnaise Jaya."[33] The nature of a citizen lawsuit, as these courts argue, is that it should only involve public or governmental institutions.

The *second* legal principle under examination is freedom of contract. It deals with the judges' assessment regarding the validity of the water privatization agreement. According to the Plaintiffs, the agreement violates the freedom of contract principle stipulated under the Indonesian Civil Code. This argument, claimed by the Plaintiffs, comes from the fact that the late President Soeharto, persuaded by the World Bank's privatization plan, issued a 'directive' to the Ministry of Public Works in 1995. This directive stipulated two critical points:

1) The need for proper handling of clean water supply for DKI Jakarta and its surroundings for the benefit of the wider community;
2) The handling is to involve two private companies by setting the handling limit, namely Ciliwung River in the west and east, where each company is assigned the task of providing clean water of ± 20 m3/s each. (p. 19)

The presidential directive was then followed by two other supporting letters from the Jakarta Governor and the Minister of Finance. These executive interventions are seen as an external pressure that forces the Jakarta's public-owned company, PDAM Jaya, to enter into the agreement with other two multinational private companies to control access to water in Jakarta. In their arguments, the Plaintiffs pointed out that the authoritarian atmosphere during the late President Soeharto's regime was behind this unlawful action, because at that time such an executive directive was commonly regarded as a sort of quasi-legislation, "whose normative force was somehow beyond the constitution."[34] The trial and the cassation courts, which can be seen as the

32 See generally David A. McDonald, "Public Ambiguity and the Multiple Meanings of Corporatization," in *Rethinking Corporatization and Public Services in the Global South* (London: Zed Books, 2014), 1–30; Jane Mans Bridge, "On the Contested Nature of the Public Good," in *Private Action and the Public Good* (Yale University Press, 1998), 3.

33 Mahkamah Agung Rep. Indonesia, Nurhidayah et al. v. PT. Aetra Air Jakarta et al. (841 PK/Pdt/2018) at 14.

34 PN Jakarta Pusat, Nurhidayah et al. v. PT. Aetra Air Jakarta et al. (527/Pdt.G/2012/PN JKT. PST) at 142.

ones applying intuitive reasoning, affirm the Plaintiff's argument. Quoting from the Supreme Court's opinion in 2017, the court considered that

> [t]he Judges [of the Jakarta District Court] have been correct in applying the law related to the existence of unlawful acts in the establishment of the Jakarta Water Privatization Cooperation Agreement which violates Article 1320 of the Civil Code. This is because Defendant VII [PDAM Jaya], in entering into a cooperation agreement with Co-Defendants I [PT. Aetra Air Jakarta] and II [PT. PAM Lyonnaise Jaya], *was not free as they were under the influence and intervention of the President.* Whereas it should be a Regional Owned Enterprise in accordance with the provisions of Article 15 in conjunction with Article 45 of the Local Regulation Number 13 of 1992, the cooperation agreement is decided by the Management (Directors) after obtaining the approval of the Governor and consideration from the Supreme Audit Agency without the intervention of the President.[35]

It is interesting to point out at the moment how the Supreme Court attempts to brush their argument on a broader canvas of the historical background of the agreement. The court's reference to the 'freedom of contract' principle is critical at this point because the Plaintiffs, confirmed by the judges at the Supreme and the District Courts, display not only a signal of violation of the basic contract law principle but also a symbol of a certain quasi-normative force that causes such a violation.

The *third* justifying reason is about the causality of harm. The Jakarta District Court and the Supreme Court encompass the likely causal relationship between the agreement and the company's shortfall compensation. This shortfall compensation is in turn claimed to be burdening citizen consumers in the form of regular tariff increases. The Supreme Court maintains that

> [t]he opinion of the Judges [of Jakarta District Court] . . . citing the Supreme Audit Agency's report correctly shows how a shortfall can occur due to the high charge of water, which is not followed by an increase in tariffs, and it causes the tariff for drinking water in DKI Jakarta Province to be the highest compared to other regions in Indonesia. The calculation and determination of the water charge by Co-Defendants I and II were not transparent and unbalanced. As a result of the shortfall in 2007, PDAM Jaya's debts amounted to Rp. 116,976,729,331.00 and as of September 30, 2008 amounted to Rp.131,989,359,912.00 and accumulated losses for 2007 amounted to Rp. 1,776,158,302,289.00 and as of September 30, Rp. 1.659,828,124,603.00;

35 Mahkamah Agung Rep. Indonesia, Nurhidayah et al. v. PT. Aetra Air Jakarta et al. (31K/Pdt/2017) paragraph 86. (citations omitted, author's emphasis)

> In addition, the response of Defendant V [Governor of Jakarta] on July 9, 2013 stated that based on the Financial Statements of PDAM Jaya for the years ended December 31, 2012 and 2011, prepared by the Public Accounting Firm of Abubakar Usman & Partners, . . . it is stated that since the implementation of the agreement from 1998 to 2012 PAM Jaya recorded an accumulated loss of Rp. 1,179,747,577,095.00 (2011: Rp. 1,264,001,493,352.00) . . . ;
>
> These matters are caused by: (1). Inequality in making the cooperation agreement and its attachments (addendum rebasing), thus only securing the position of PT Palyja and harming PDAM Jaya; (2). PDAM Jaya's Board of Directors did not perform adequate planning, monitoring, and evaluation so as to make commitments that were detrimental to the community and regional finances;[36]

Through linking the series of company shortfalls, government losses and escalation of tariffs, the Plaintiffs have attempted to construe the nature of harm; that is, whether it resulted from the disputed privatization agreement. At this point, we can also point out that the past is 'recreated' by the courts' intuition by conflating the temporal dynamics between, on the one hand, the periodization of financial losses and, on the other hand, the regularity and continuity of tariff burdens (i.e., per semester). The following Supreme Court's assessment provides such instances:

> it is evident that the shortfall is a definite result of the PKS clause, which is designed in such a way as to benefit the private sector, which must be accepted and agreed upon by PDAM Jaya at the time of making the PKS. The exact formula shortfall is due to the water charge clause that adheres to the full cost recovery system in the Cooperation Agreement which is not supported by the increase in the rate of the Supreme Court of the Republic of Indonesia;
>
> Since 2007 the Jakarta water tariff was decided by Defendant V not to increase, but the large shortfall burden borne by PDAM Jaya was not only caused by the tariff (water price) which had not increased since 2007 but because of the water charge set by Defendant VII with the Co-Defendants [PT Palyja and PT Aetra] very high and even unreasonable which caused the high shortfall expense approved by Defendant VII;
>
> This can be seen from the Cooperation Agreement which promises that every six months (every semester), the water charge will increase. Article 28.4. of the Cooperation Agreement regarding the Adjustment of Benefits states that the Basic Benefits will be adjusted at the beginning of each semester over the entire period in accordance with the benefits indexation

36 Ibid., 90–92.

> formula. This means that at the beginning of each semester, throughout the validity period of the cooperation, the water charge will continue to increase (adjusted). If the tariff does not increase so that a difference is formed, there will be a shortfall, which is the burden of PDAM Jaya. Article 28.4. of the Cooperation Agreement regarding the Adjustment of Rewards mentions: "The parties agree that the first basic benefit or the new basic benefit whichever applies will be adjusted at the beginning of each semester over the entire term.[37]

The *fourth* justifying reason pertains to water as a human right. The right to water discourse came into the discussion given that, at the same time, the Indonesian Constitutional Court concluded that the entire 2004 Water Resources Law was in violation of the constitution. In that judicial review, the Constitutional Court sets out two fundamentals regarding water governance in the country, namely that (1) water has a distinctive characteristic in the country (particularly different from the Western view of resources) and (2) the ways the Indonesians 'make use' (*memanfaatkan*)—not 'exploit'—of water ought to escape from the exploitative nature of colonial practices in the past reflected in the water resources management system. In the case, the Constitutional Court declares that

> History bears witness that since a long time ago, before society bound itself as a nation and state, until now, water is a basic human need that was gifted by *Allah Subhanahuwata'ala*, God Almighty, so that water becomes a public right (*res commune*), namely a right shared by the community. The fighters, from the independence movement to the struggle to defend and fill Indonesia's independence, named the place where this nation lived and defended its life as 'water-land' [*tanah air*] not 'the fatherland' (English) nor '*das Vaterland*' (Germany) which means 'land of father.' The use of the term water-land shows that in the view of the Indonesian people, land and water are two important resources in their lives that cannot be separated from one another. Indonesian citizens know and understand that Wage Rudolf Supratman, the composer of the National Anthem *Indonesia Raya*, which was sung and played on October 28, 1928, known as Youth Pledge Day, wrote in the first sentence, "Indonesia, my water-land.[38]

In this opinion, the Constitutional Court has depicted the peculiar position of water being part of natural resources for the Indonesian people, which is historically justified during the process of the nation-building resulting from colonialization. The judicial review itself mainly dealt with the possibility

37 Ibid., 93–95.
38 Mahkamah Konstitusi [Constitutional Court] February 18, 2013, 85/PUU-XI/2013 (Indon.)

of water privatization and it somehow informs the Jakarta water privatization CLS. Notably, the Supreme Court in the CLS in 2017 declares that the privatization agreement was in violation of Jakarta Bylaws 13/1992 simply because "after the conclusion of this agreement, the services of clean and drinking for Jakarta citizens have not been improving in terms of quality, quantity and continuity."[39]

The critical aspect of our *chronotopic* analysis is how water governance is shaped not only by spatial but also temporal scales.[40] Specifically, the narrative of temporalities that we can grasp from the intuitive judicial reasoning presented in the trial and the cassation courts concerns with traumatic experiences of the exploitative colonial and authoritarian regimes. Through such Encounters, intuitive judges can find the multiplicity of experiences stemming from the social trauma of unequal relationships related to resource governance. These Encounters are evidently subtle as they are judiciously concealed behind the numbers, prices, graphs, maps and statistics related to water resource governance. Nevertheless, they reflect the best scenario that introduces the claim's difference *in kind*, which then guides the intuitive judges to find the essence of the lawsuit and to draw on the traumatic past of authoritarianism and the nation's imaginary relationship with water. Suffice it to say at the moment that these experiences of injustice are therefore 'created' by the intuitive judges through the immediacy of trauma.[41]

Actualizing collective legal responsibility

As previously observed in the prior section, water governance could be seen as a mode of governance that comprises interactions, engagements and strategies from various actors, technologies and so on.[42] In this case study, water governance is interpreted loosely to include any arrangement of affairs pertaining to (access to) water resource management. As part of the water remunicipalization movement, there is an element of durability in the existing institutions that "rests on the mutually reinforcing interdependence between their regulative, normative and cultural-cognitive elements."[43]

39 Mahkamah Agung Rep. Indonesia, Nurhidayah et al. v. PT. Aetra Air Jakarta et al. (31K/Pdt/2017) at 158–59.
40 Okke Braadbaart, "Privatizing Water: The Jakarta Concession and the Limits of Contract," in *A World of Water: Rain, Rivers and Seas in Southeast Asian Histories*, ed. Peter Boomgaard (Leiden: KITLV Press, 2007), 297–320.
41 Cathy Caruth, *Unclaimed Experience: Trauma, Narrative, and History* (Baltimore & London: JHU Press, 1996); Abigail Ward, "Understanding Postcolonial Traumas," *Journal of Theoretical and Philosophical Psychology* 33, no. 3 (2013): 170.
42 McDonald and Swyngedouw, "The New Water Wars: Struggles for Remunicipalisation."
43 Emanuele Lobina, Vera Weghmann, and Marwa Marwa, "Water Justice Will Not Be Televised: Moral Advocacy and the Struggle for Transformative Remunicipalisation in Jakarta," *Water Alternatives* 12, no. 2 (2019): 728.

In discerning collective legal responsibility in *Jakarta Water Remunicipalization*, two elements of water governance are of particular importance, namely *who* governs and *what* is to govern. The *first* element of collective legal responsibility is about who governs the water. Unfortunately, the case did not virtually answer this question in a lucid manner. Instead, the courts' narratives appear to exhibit an internal battle of various actors; for instance, between central government agencies, central government against local government, local government against its own company or local government company against foreign private companies. There are two issues relevant to this: who is the 'public administrator' and who are the managing companies? The 2017 Supreme Court decision, for instance, submits that

> the object of the lawsuit is the state's negligence in terms of water management in Jakarta where the state, which in the *a quo* case is being sued, is an element of the State administrator [*penyelenggara negara*], the President up to PDAM Jaya, making and implementing the cooperation agreement policy by handing over water management to the private sector, namely *Lyonnaise des Aux and Thames Overseas* Ltd.[44]

Related to the plaintiffs' legal standing, the 12 plaintiffs in this case claimed that they are

> Indonesian citizens with the status of observers, activists, and consumers of drinking water as well as 8,520,554 (eight million five hundred twenty thousand five hundred fifty-four) Indonesian citizens residing in the DKI Jakarta Province, who are entitled to the fulfillment of human rights guaranteed under the Constitution of the Republic of Indonesia without discrimination in any form.

However, in 2018, the government filed a case review (*peninjauan kembali*) to the Supreme Court, where the judges decided to overturn their 2017 decision. The Supreme Court decided that there was a mistake in their previous decision, claiming that "this lawsuit is formally flawed because it has included other parties outside the government, namely PT. Aetra Air Jakarta and PT. PAM Lyonnaise Jaya as Defendants, hence it no longer fulfils the requirements of a citizen lawsuit."[45] Consequently, the Court declares that the petition of the plaintiffs could not be formally accepted to be processed in court.

44 Mahkamah Agung Rep. Indonesia, Nurhidayah et al. v. PT. Aetra Air Jakarta et al. (31K/Pdt/2017) at 124.

45 Mahkamah Agung Rep. Indonesia, Nurhidayah et al. v. PT. Aetra Air Jakarta et al. (841 PK/Pdt/2018).

One can hardly find a coherent narrative that implies an answer to the *who* question. At the cassation level at the Supreme Court in 2017, according to the Plaintiffs, PDAM Jaya (Jakarta's public-owned water company) admitted that

> [t]he transfer as the administrator and provider of clean water in DKI Jakarta from PDAM Jaya to the private sector actually eliminates the main duties and functions of PDAM Jaya as regulated in the DKI Jakarta Regional Regulation (*Peraturan Daerah*) No. 13 of 1992 concerning Regional Drinking Water Companies for the Special Capital Region of Jakarta which stipulates in detail the objectives, namely the fulfilment of drinking water for the needs of the community in order to improving people's welfare, increasing regional original income, and participating in carrying out regional economic development by carrying out all efforts directly related to the supply and distribution of drinking water that meets the health requirements and good service for the community based on the company's principles; With the loss of the *a quo* main tasks and functions, the goal to increase regional gross income (*pendapatan asli daerah*) has not been achieved; even now, there has been no significant revision to the Agreement, and the potential contract loss is approximately 18 trillion.[46]

The claimants furthermore argued that the diminishing role of PDAM Jaya at the same time made leeway for private companies to produce and distribute clean and drinking water and to be granted monopoly rights over water. While we might obtain a seemingly implicit answer, it is squarely justified to assert that although PDAM Jaya *ought to* have jurisdiction, this does not mean that it 'automatically spells doom' for other scales of governance, such as foreign private companies. Importantly, it should also be noted that the trauma of foreign appropriation shapes the way in which the jurisdiction game determines 'who' should govern.

The *second* element of collective legal responsibility is what to govern, or, to be precise, what is water that is governed. The Supreme Court's reference to the Constitutional Court's opinion in the 2004 Water Resources Law judicial review case has shed some light on this matter. As already shown previously, in the Constitutional Court's deliberation, water is seen to be in the middle of tension between the government's power over resources and the citizen's fundamental right to water. The intuitive reasoning made by the Supreme Court, however, seemed to propound the idea of collective legal

46 Mahkamah Agung [Supreme Court] April 10, 2017, Nurhidayah et al. v. PT. Aetra Air Jakarta et al. (31K/Pdt/2017) (Indon.) (citation omitted))

responsibility on the basis of how such tension is navigated. The Supreme Court argues that

> [t]he guarantee that the state still retains its control over water is an indispensable requirement in assessing the constitutionality of the Water Resources Law. This guarantee can be seen in the six basic principles of limiting the management of water resources. The six basic principles, namely, *first*, users of water resources to meet daily basic needs and for small-holder agriculture are not burdened with water resource management services, as long as the fulfillment of daily basic needs and for smallholder agriculture is obtained directly from water sources. The (central) government and local governments are responsible for developing a drinking water supply system and it must be the priority of government programs. *Second*, the concept of rights in water utilization must be distinguished from the concept of rights in a general sense. The concept of right in right to water must be in line with the concept of *res commune* which should not be an object of economic price. *Third*, the concept of the right to utilize water in the Water Resources Law must be interpreted as a derivative of the right to life guaranteed by the 1945 Constitution. *Fourth*, the principle that "beneficiaries of water resources management services must bear the management costs" must be interpreted as a principle that does not place water as an *object* subject to economic prices. *Fifth*, the customary rights of living customary law communities to water resources are recognized, in accordance with Article 18B paragraph (2) of the 1945 Constitution. *Sixth*, in principle, the exploitation of water for other countries is not permitted. The government can only grant water concessions to other countries if the supply of water for its own needs has been met.[47]

One may notice in this judicial argument the public nature of water and its governance and the way legal principles are enacted to circumvent, as the extractivism account tells us, the flowing wealth in time and space that conditions, constrains and pressures the lives of virtually all humans and other-than-humans.[48] To emphasize, quoting from the Supreme Court's opinion, governing water is fundamentally about fulfilling or providing "daily basic needs and so that smallholder agriculture is not burdened with water resource management services," thus "the exploitation of water for other

47 Ibid., 30. (emphasis added)

48 Lena Salaymeh and Ralf Michaels, "Decolonial Comparative Law: A Conceptual Beginning," *Rabel Journal of Comparative and International Private Law (RabelsZ)* 86, no. 1 (2022): 166–88.

countries is not permitted."[49] The legal concept of (the right to) water appears virtually to be fluid in that it conflates space, temporality and affects of the citizens.[50] The intricate relationship between space, time and affect of water resources in *Jakarta Water Remunicipalization* is reflected in judges' intuitive reasoning toward the way water has been governed during the last 30 years.[51]

Our *chronotopic* analysis has showcased an overlapping dialogue or interaction between national trauma and risk-projection. In the context of the former, it appears that the way law governs resources, such as water, is implicated by the nation's collective experience of foreign dispossession and abuse of power during an authoritarian regime.[52] The trauma is made visible through the historicity of water privatization in Jakarta, which underscores the temporalities of colonial extractivism and the executive abuse of power in directing the decision of the local government to privatize. Meanwhile, the latter is signaled by the way in which the intuitive judges frame water as the national's property and only in a rare and specific circumstance may foreign countries' exploitation be granted. The case at hand signals risk-projection as something that is not exclusively quantifiable through numbers (e.g., a company's or government's economic loss), but also qualitatively experienced by the citizens who have been suffering from water mismanagement for the last 30 years. This overlapping dialogue demonstrates the *contingency* and *situatedness* of legal judgment—in which qualitative experiences are not merely a recollection of past events, but also a projection toward the future of rights to water, claiming for the increasing loss of money and anticipating the potential limited access to water in years to come. We can understand at the moment that given such contingency and situatedness, norms governing water jurisdiction are, in fact, made senseless in a way that they are tailored to the multiplicity of resource governances in the community.[53]

49 Ibid.

50 Andreas Philippopoulos-Mihalopoulos, *Spatial Justice: Body, Lawscape, Atmosphere* (New York: Routledge, 2015); Andreas Philippopoulos-Mihalopoulos, "Atmospheres of Law: Senses, Affects, Lawscapes," *Emotion, Space and Society* 7, no. 1 (2013): 35–44, https://doi.org/10.1016/j.emospa.2012.03.001.

51 Mohamad Mova Alafghani, "Strengths and Limitations of The Indonesian Constitutional Court's '6 Basic Principles' in Resolving Water Conflicts," *Constitutional Review* 9, no. 1 (2023): 179–220.

52 Andrew Rosser, "Towards a Political Economy of Human Rights Violations in Post-New Order Indonesia," *Journal of Contemporary Asia* 43, no. 2 (2013): 243–56; Imam Koeswahyono, Syahriza Alkohir Anggoro, and Muhammad Dahlan, "Old Wine in a New Bottle: Neoliberalism and Water Resources Law 2019 in Indonesia," *JSEAHR* 6 (2022): 26.

53 Dik Roth, "Environmental Sustainability and Legal Plurality in Irrigation: The Balinese Subak," *Current Opinion in Environmental Sustainability* 11 (2014): 1–9; Braadbaart, "Privatizing Water: The Jakarta Concession and the Limits of Contract."

Conclusion

The present chapter has showcased a kind of intuitive judicial reasoning that navigates the immediacy of trauma (of colonial extractivism) in such a way that this mode of reasoning could guide judges to attend to some critical features of resource extractivism. *Jakarta Water Remunicipalization* can be seen as a clear example of the intricate relationship between law, space and time in water governance. Governance, therefore, does not only take place in the economic but also in the cultural dimension, because the temporalities of colonial extractivism assert a conflation of the past, present and future of the citizens' lived experience.[54] Furthermore, it showcases overlapping affective dialogues or interactions between qualitative risks and projections over water mismanagement and trauma against past authoritarian and colonial regimes. As a result, while the question of water remunicipalization has been thus far focusing on the question of who and what of governance, our observation of the Indonesian courts' intuitive reasoning suggests that the inquiry into *how* governance is being exercised is no less determinant in understanding collective responsibility practice.

Reference list

Alafghani, Mohamad Mova. "Strengths and Limitations of The Indonesian Constitutional Court's '6 Basic Principles' in Resolving Water Conflicts." *Constitutional Review* 9, no. 1 (2023): 179–220.

Alamanda, Rizkita. "Gugatan Warga Negara (Studi Kasus: Gerakan Samarinda Menggugat." *Jurnal Hukum Lingkungan Indonesia* 1, no. 2 (2014): 101–10.

Bakhtin, Mikhail Mikhaĭlovich. *The Dialogic Imagination: Four Essays*. University of Texas Press, 2010.

Bhabha, Homi K. *The Location of Culture*. London & New York: Routledge Classics, 2004.

Blomley, Nicholas. "Performing Property: Making the World." *Canadian Journal of Law and Jurisprudence* 26 (2013): 23–48.

Braadbaart, Okke. "Privatizing Water: The Jakarta Concession and the Limits of Contract." In *A World of Water: Rain, Rivers and Seas in Southeast Asian Histories*, edited by Peter Boomgaard, 297–320. Leiden: KITLV Press, 2007.

Braverman, Irus, Nicholas Blomley, David Delaney, and Alexandre Kedar. "Expanding the Spaces of Law." In *The Expanding Spaces of Law: A Timely Legal Geography*, edited by Irus Braverman, Nicholas Blomley, David Delaney, and Alexandre (Sandy) Kedar, 1–29. Stanford, CA: Stanford University Press, 2014.

Bridge, Jane Mans. "On the Contested Nature of the Public Good." In *Private Action and the Public Good*, 3. Yale University Press, 1998.

Campbell, Kirsten. "The City of Law." *International Journal of Law in Context* 9, no. 2 (2013): 192–212. https://doi.org/10.1017/S1744552313000086.

54 Clifford Geertz, "Culture and Social Change: The Indonesian Case," *Man* (1984): 511–32; Philippopoulos-Mihalopoulos, "Atmospheres of Law: Senses, Affects, Lawscapes"; Homi K. Bhabha, *The Location of Culture* (London & New York: Routledge Classics, 2004).

Caruth, Cathy. *Unclaimed Experience: Trauma, Narrative, and History*. Baltimore & London: JHU Press, 1996.
Chagnon, Christopher W., Francesco Durante, Barry K. Gills, Sophia E. Hagolani-Albov, Saana Hokkanen, Sohvi M. J. Kangasluoma, Heidi Konttinen, Markus Kröger, William LaFleur, and Ossi Ollinaho. "From Extractivism to Global Extractivism: The Evolution of an Organizing Concept." *The Journal of Peasant Studies* 49, no. 4 (2022): 760–92.
Craps, Stef. *Postcolonial Witnessing: Trauma out of Bounds*. Vol. 2. Springer, 2013.
Delaney, David. *The Spatial, the Legal and the Pragmatics of World-Making: Nomospheric Investigation*. New York: Routledge, 2010.
Fatah, Abdul. "Citizen Lawsuit in Environmental Cases." *Lentera Hukum* 6 (2019): 289.
Foucault, Michel. "Governmentality." In *The Foucault Effect: Studies in Governmentality*, edited by Graham Burchell, Colin Gordon, and Peter Miller, 87–104. Chicago: The University of Chicago Press, 1991.
Geertz, Clifford. "Culture and Social Change: The Indonesian Case." *Man* (1984): 511–32.
Hanna, Thomas M., and David A. McDonald. "From Pragmatic to Politicized? The Future of Water Remunicipalization in the United States." *Utilities Policy* 72 (2021): 101276.
Holquist, Michael. "The Fugue of Chronotope." In *Bakhtin's Theory of the Literary Chronotope: Reflections, Applications, Perspectives*, edited by Nele Bemong, Pieter Borghart, Michel De Dobbeleer, Kristoffel Demoen, Koen De Temmerman, and Bart Keunen, 19–34. Gent: Academia Press, 2010.
Huxley, Margo. "Geographies of Governmentality." In *Space, Knowledge, and Power*, edited by Jeremy Crampton and Stuart Elden. Hampshire: Ashgate, 2007.
Koeswahyono, Imam, Syahriza Alkohir Anggoro, and Muhammad Dahlan. "Old Wine in a New Bottle: Neoliberalism and Water Resources Law 2019 in Indonesia." *JSEAHR* 6 (2022): 26.
Lobina, Emanuele. "Calling for Progressive Water Policies." In *Our Public Experience: The Global Experience with Remunicipalisation*, 6–18. Amsterdam, London, Paris, Cape Town & Brussels: Transnational Institute (TNI), Public Services International Research Unit (PSIRU), Multinationals Observatory, Municipal Services Project (MSP) and the European Federation of Public Service Unions (EPSU), 2015.
Lobina, Emanuele. "Water Remunicipalisation: Between Pendulum Swings and Paradigm Advocacy." In *Urban Water Trajectories*, 149–61. Springer, 2017.
Lobina, Emanuele, Vera Weghmann, and Marwa Marwa. "Water Justice Will Not Be Televised: Moral Advocacy and the Struggle for Transformative Remunicipalisation in Jakarta." *Water Alternatives* 12, no. 2 (2019): 725–48.
Mahkamah Agung Rep. Indonesia. Nurhidayah et al. v. PT. Aetra Air Jakarta et al. (31K/Pdt/2017) (2017).
Mahkamah Agung Rep. Indonesia. Nurhidayah et al. v. PT. Aetra Air Jakarta et al. (841 PK/Pdt/2018) (2018).
Maldonado-Torres, Nelson. *Outline of Ten Theses on Coloniality and Decoloniality*. Paris, 2016. https://fondation-frantzfanon.com/wp-content/uploads/2018/10/maldonado-torres_outline_of_ten_theses-10.23.16.pdf.
McDonald, David A. "Public Ambiguity and the Multiple Meanings of Corporatization." In *Rethinking Corporatization and Public Services in the Global South*, 1–30. London: Zed Books, 2014.
McDonald, David A., and Erik Swyngedouw. "The New Water Wars: Struggles for Remunicipalisation." *Water Alternatives* 12, no. 2 (2019): 322–33.

Nasir, Cholidin. "Pengawasan Terhadap Kebijakan Pemerintah Melalui Mekanisme Citizen Lawsuit." *Jurnal Konstitusi* 14, no. 4 (2017): 906–26.
Oorschot, Irene Van. "Doing Times, Doing Truths: The Legal Case File as a Folded Object." In *Law and Time*, edited by Siân M. Beynon-Jones and Emily Grabham, 229–46. Oxon & New York: Routledge, 2019.
Pasternak, Shiri. "Jurisdiction." In *Routledge Handbook of Law and Society*, edited by Mariana Valverde, Kamari Clarke, Eve Darian-Smith, and Prabha Kotiswaran, 178–81. Oxon & New York: Routledge, 2021.
Philippopoulos-Mihalopoulos, Andreas. "Atmospheres of Law: Senses, Affects, Lawscapes." *Emotion, Space and Society* 7, no. 1 (2013): 35–44. https://doi.org/10.1016/j.emospa.2012.03.001.
Philippopoulos-Mihalopoulos, Andreas. *Spatial Justice: Body, Lawscape, Atmosphere.* New York: Routledge, 2015.
PN Jakarta Pusat. Nurhidayah et al. v. PT. Aetra Air Jakarta et al. (527/Pdt.G/2012/PN JKT.PST) (2012).
PT DKI Jakarta. Nurhidayah et al. v. PT. Aetra Air Jakarta et al. (588/PDT/2015/PT DKI) (2015).
Purcell, Mark. "Possible Worlds: Henri Lefebvre and the Right to the City." *Journal of Urban Affairs* 36, no. 1 (2014): 141–54. https://doi.org/10.1111/juaf.12034.
Quijano, Aníbal. "Coloniality and Modernity/Rationality." *Cultural Studies* 21, no. 2–3 (2007): 168–78.
Rose, Nikolas, and Peter Miller. "Political Power beyond the State: Problematics of Government." *The British Journal of Sociology* 61 (January 2010): 271–303. https://doi.org/10.1111/j.1468-4446.2009.01247.x.
Rose, Nikolas, Pat O'Malley, and Mariana Valverde. "Governmentality." *Annual Review of Law and Social Science* 2 (2006): 83–104.
Rosser, Andrew. "Towards a Political Economy of Human Rights Violations in Post-New Order Indonesia." *Journal of Contemporary Asia* 43, no. 2 (2013): 243–56.
Roth, Dik. "Environmental Sustainability and Legal Plurality in Irrigation: The Balinese Subak." *Current Opinion in Environmental Sustainability* 11 (2014): 1–9.
Salaymeh, Lena, and Ralf Michaels. "Decolonial Comparative Law: A Conceptual Beginning." *Rabel Journal of Comparative and International Private Law (RabelsZ)* 86, no. 1 (2022): 166–88.
Valverde, Mariana. "Jurisdiction and Scale: 'Legaltechnicalities' as Resources for Theory." *Social & Legal Studies* 18, no. 2 (2009): 139–57.
Valverde, Mariana. "Studying the Governance of Crime and Security: Space, Time and Jurisdiction." *Criminology & Criminal Justice* 14, no. 4 (2014): 379–91.
Valverde, Mariana. *Chronotopes of Law: Jurisdiction, Scale and Governance.* Oxon & New York: Routledge, 2015.
Walby, Kevin. "Contributions to a Post-Sovereigntist Understanding of Law: Foucault, Law as Governance, and Legal Pluralism." *Social & Legal Studies* 16, no. 4 (2007): 551–71.
Ward, Abigail. "Understanding Postcolonial Traumas." *Journal of Theoretical and Philosophical Psychology* 33, no. 3 (2013): 170.

Chapter 3

Uncertain climate crisis

This chapter pivots on the narrativity of climate justice. In this mode of thinking, judges are seen to be navigating the "problematic realness" of climate change.[1] It encompasses the peculiar narratives of climate litigation that allow judges to imagine the crisis via certain means and methods of imagination and fiction. Such narratives are compelling because they present an avenue to *evaluate* the judge's mode of reasoning about climate science and human experiences resulting from the Anthropocene.[2] In reading *Milieudefensie et al. v. Royal Dutch Shell PLC*, we see that intuition is valuable for the judges' justification of collective responsibility practices insofar as it allows them to gesture with creative and experimental legal inquiries into the multiplicity of experiences of climate injustice. Such uncertainty of crisis can be viewed as an unanticipated encounter in the judges' minds—insisting they craft a creative and experimental legal inquiry into the multiplicity of experiences of climate injustice.[3]

Our case-study proceeds as follows: the first section will deal with explaining the climate crisis through the lens of time and temporality. Our brief survey on climate justice temporalities submits that the contestation between

1 Amitav Ghosh, *The Great Derangement: Climate Change and the Unthinkable* (London: The University of Chicago Press, 2016); Chiara Armeni, "Narratives as Tools of Legal Re-Imagination in the Climate Crisis," *Journal of Environmental Law* 33, no. 2 (2021): 485–94.

2 For contemporary critique of Western social imaginary on human-nature relationship in terms of legal subjectivity, see Jana Norman, *Posthuman Legal Subjectivity: Reimagining the Human in the Anthropocene* (Oxon & New York: Routledge, 2022); Sam Bookman, "Catalytic Climate Litigation: Rights and Statutes," *Oxford Journal of Legal Studies* 43, no. 3 (2023): 598–628, https://doi.org/10.1093/ojls/gqad011.

3 Mingzhe Zhu, "The 'Bitcoin Judgements' in China: Promoting Climate Awareness by Judicial Reasoning?" *Review of European, Comparative & International Environmental Law* 32 no. 1 (2023): 158–62; Joana Setzer and Catherine Higham, *Global Trends in Climate Change Litigation: 2022 Snapshot* (London: Grantham Research Institute on Climate Change and the Environment and Centre for Climate Change Economics and Policy, London School of Economics and Political Science, 2022).

DOI: 10.4324/9781003518693-5

various kinds of climate crisis framing is shaped by and simultaneously fabricates the crisis temporalities. In the second section, we seek to examine the narrative structure in *Milieudefensie* that reflects the uncertainty of climate injustice as a form of encounter that conflates the climate crisis' past, present and future. Finally, the last section will explain the way the court infers collective legal responsibility (i.e., of Royal Dutch Shell) for climate injustice by selecting the best explanation stemming from people's experiences of climate crisis.

The multiplicity of climate injustice

Our first task would be to contextualize climate injustice through the lens of temporalities. We will try to survey some ways in which climate crisis is seen as part of our lived experience.[4] This survey involves a viewpoint where the crisis is no longer seen as an external reality or simply as scientific data/object, but rather as a framework based on internal human imagination and experience of the crisis. As we will find later, this framework shows a certain kind of relationship between the climate's past, present and future.[5]

Arguably, narrative is a critical instrument in understanding climate crisis.[6] It is also fundamental in legal reasoning since the legal properties of climate crisis rely heavily on how lawmakers and adjudicators frame the ever-changing narratives of climate. That said, it is through narratives that legal actors can perceive climate chaos as a kind of *hyperobject*, to quote Morton's term.[7] Taking into account the defeasibility of climate science information in the current age of Anthropocene, the role of narrative has never been more significant than before, particularly when we encounter the question of justice in the courtroom. Tracing back to Derrida's force of law, as Rogers has aptly suggested, we may furthermore regard that the narrative of climate change in courts carries a gravity distinct from many other forms of climate narrative.[8] Climate narrative in the courtroom, borrowing from

4 Julian Agyeman, David Schlosberg, Luke Craven, and Caitlin Matthews, "Trends and Directions in Environmental Justice: From Inequity to Everyday Life, Community, and Just Sustainabilities," *Annual Review of Environment and Resources* 41 (2016): 321–40.

5 Friederike E. L. Otto, Sjoukje Philip, Sarah Kew, Sihan Li, Andrew King, and Heidi Cullen, "Attributing High-Impact Extreme Events across Timescales—a Case Study of Four Different Types of Events," *Climatic Change* 149 (2018): 399–412.

6 Phillip Paiement, "Urgent Agenda: How Climate Litigation Builds Transnational Narratives," in *Transnational Environmental Law in the Anthropocene: Transnational Environmental Law in the Anthropocene Reflections on the Role of Law in Times of Planetary Change*, ed. Emily Webster and Laura Mai (London: Routledge, 2021), 121–43, https://doi.org/10.4324/9781003152590.

7 Timothy Morton, *Hyperobjects: Philosophy and Ecology after the End of the World* (Minneapolis & London: University of Minnesota Press, 2013).

8 Nicole Rogers, *Law, Fiction and Activism in a Time of Climate Change* (Routledge, 2019).

Rogers, is a catalyst to enhance the judge's understanding of climate change, putting "climate narratives as script, containing speculations and suggestions for navigating what lies ahead."[9]

Scholars have argued that time plays a fundamental role in shaping the narrative of climate change. In making sense of climate change, time is disruptive in such a way that we are struggling to draw the temporal lag between past and present industrial activities and their future catastrophic consequences. Climate crisis temporality is "wild time," said Rogers, expounding "a future in which the world has been radically transfigured by climate change"; that is, "the chaotic future period in which the logic, institutions, modes of interacting and artefacts of civilization are abruptly or gradually undone as a consequence of climatic and other disruptions."[10] The situation we encounter today is a disruption between slow-pacing geological time and rapid-changing Anthropocene time. To wit, it is a contention between the time sketched by geologists and earth scientists in understanding earth's geological period against the time contoured by "the role of humankind as catalyst for large, unstoppable, planetary forces that are shaping geohistory."[11]

Thinking about climate crisis in terms of time brings us to a further analysis of some of its characteristics. Temporalizing climate crisis asserts that it is fundamentally polycentric in the sense that this anthropogenic crisis "is caused by cumulative GHG emissions as a result of human activities across a range of sectors, at varying scales, in different parts of the world."[12] Particularly, this polycentric nature involves a plurality of agents and spatiotemporal positions, political and socioeconomic factors and, importantly, degrees of involvement.[13] Consequently, it is challenging, if not impossible, for any modes of traditional legal reasoning and argumentation to directly address the reality of this crisis.[14] Moreover, in relation to this polycentric nature, temporalizing climate crisis is meant to inquire about historical injustice.[15] Here, we may see that there is a kind of interference between historical process

9 Ibid., 3; David McDermott Hughes, "A Climate Strategy of Last Resort," *Boston Review*, accessed October 5, 2023, www.bostonreview.net/articles/a-climate-strategy-of-last-resort/?utm_source=Boston+Review+Email+Subscribers&utm_campaign=fbf3a68a02-newsletter_5_10_23&utm_medium=email&utm_term=0_2cb428c5ad-fbf3a68a02-41296216&mc_cid=fbf3a68a02&mc_eid=3b5256212e.

10 Rogers, *Law, Fiction and Activism in a Time of Climate Change*, 4.

11 Ibid., 5. The latter however may include various kinds of 'human' time, as we have addressed in earlier chapters about *chronos* and *kairos*.

12 Orla Kelleher, "Incorporating Climate Justice into Legal Reasoning: Shifting towards a Risk-Based Approach to Causation in Climate Litigation," *Journal of Human Rights and the Environment* 13, no. 1 (2022): 291.

13 Setzer and Higham, "Global Trends in Climate Change Litigation: 2022 Snapshot."

14 R. Henry Weaver and Douglas A. Kysar, "Courting Disaster: Climate Change and the Adjudication of Catastrophe," *Notre Dame Law Review* 93 (2017): 295–356.

15 Historical injustice inquiry will be thoroughly discussed later in Chapter 5.

(i.e., the chronology of climate crisis) and legal temporalities (i.e., legal principle applicable in such a historical process), within which we may discover the so-called *normative uncertainties* reflected in the legal decision-making process.[16]

An alternative way of addressing this kind of temporal discrepancy in climate justice can be found in Posner and Sunstein's *Climate Change Justice*, whose idea was later followed by Posner and Weisbach's work on the same issue. In these influential works, the overall temporal orientation suggested by the authors is rather a forward-looking, welfarist approach. According to Posner and Sunstein, the standard reasons for distributive and corrective justice fall short of providing compelling evidence to hold wealthy nations accountable for the climate crisis.[17] They submit that the distributive approach, which requires affluent states to contribute in a special way to poor states, is akin to ignoring "other redistributive strategies might be much better for helping those who are most disadvantaged."[18] Furthermore, they claim,

> if the goal is to act in accordance with corrective justice, it is important to identify both the actors and the victims; *abstract references to nations as wrongdoers, and to nations as victims, often beg or obscure the key questions*.[19]

As a result, a fair allocation of responsibility should consider what they call the intertemporal dimension, that is, considerations toward climate justice that "bear not only on the allocation of benefits and burdens across nations, but also on their allocation across time."[20]

Implicit in Posner, Sunstein and Weisbach's arguments is the causal complexity of climate change as the key to the process of temporalizing climate change. That is, there should be sufficient nexus between gas emissions reduction policy and any alleged rights violation. Nonetheless, contrary to this practical concern-based argument, Kelleher proves that the distributive and corrective justice approaches are in fact critical elements in achieving so-called climate justice. Kelleher claims that

> [t]he incorporation of these distributive or corrective justice principles into the international climate regime is significant because it helps answer

16 Behnam Taebi, Jan H. Kwakkel, and Céline Kermisch, "Governing Climate Risks in the Face of Normative Uncertainties," *Wiley Interdisciplinary Reviews: Climate Change* 11, no. 5 (2020): e666.

17 Eric A. Posner and Cass R. Sunstein, "Climate Change Justice," *Georgetown Law Journal* 96 (2008): 1565.

18 Ibid., 1573.

19 Ibid. (emphasis added)

20 Eric A. Posner and David Weisbach, *Climate Change Justice* (Princeton: Princeton University Press, 2010), 191.

> the normative question of why a climate justice approach (which emphasizes wealthy developed countries not shirking their responsibility to bear the greatest burden) *should* be relevant in systemic right-based climate litigation.[21]

Kelleher's study casts a crucial light on legal discourse about the causal conundrum required in courts' reasoning, particularly on the face of their willingness to accept a risk-based test for causation or proximity.[22] More specifically, Kelleher addresses what is called systemic rights-based climate litigation, which can be grasped as "legal cases that take a whole-of-system approach by challenging the overall ambition of a government's framework climate mitigation policies, often on fundamental rights (and sometimes on statutory) grounds, before domestic and regional human rights courts."[23] In this type of legal case, the claimants ought to be able to draw a causal relationship between regulatory action and climate harms; that is, they have to prove that

> the state in question is interfering with the climate system, that this is causing or is likely to cause adverse impacts (e.g., more frequent extreme weather events), and that these climate harms reach a certain threshold of seriousness to amount to human rights violations.[24]

Kelleher's study on systemic rights-based climate litigation in Europe, both at the domestic courts and the European Court of Human Rights, indicates that the courts have been willing to entertain a *risk-based* test in assessing the causal proximity of climate crisis. The courts' acceptance of the *risk-contribution* matter of climate crisis has made responsible entities—especially wealthy states and corporations—unable to escape legal liability by relying on the causal proximity principle. Moreover, the practice of climate litigation in the Netherlands, among many other places, proves that

> the courts reasoned that causation plays less of a role in circumstances where the remedy sought was not an award of damages, but instead an order to take mitigation measures—in those circumstances, all that has to be proven is a 'real *risk* of danger.'[25]

In line with these assertions, we are also witnessing that the legal concept of causation appears to be softening in climate change litigation, as Minnerop

21 Kelleher, "Incorporating Climate Justice into Legal Reasoning: Shifting towards a Risk-Based Approach to Causation in Climate Litigation," 301. (emphasis original)
22 Ibid.
23 Ibid., 292.
24 Ibid.
25 Ibid., 307. (citation omitted)

and Otto have claimed. The authors build a sort of matrix of causation which shows that, in this type of litigation, courts have tried to distinguish *co-relation* from *cause and effect* relationship, in which they rather applied weaker tests to the legal concept of causation in order to "recognize fairness consideration."[26] According to this study, a new matrix of causation should be built in order for judges to address the conventional test of causation. This matrix is construed upon three pillars, including: logical elaboration of the notions of 'necessary' and 'sufficient' conditions of a causal relationship; the so-called 'distinctive causal field' that captures a strong connection where sufficient event-specific evidence for a plurality of types of events exists; and the notion of sustenance, which includes the idea of concurrence of climate crisis causes.[27]

Relevant to the issue, recent literature also suggests that causation tests in climate litigation could benefit from the growing evidence in climate science, particularly in the field of climate science attribution. For instance, in an analysis of seventy-three cases of climate litigation from fourteen jurisdictions, according to Stuart-Smith et al., it is suggestive that

> [t]o maximize the chances of establishing causation in the courts, plaintiffs should ensure that (1) cases filed concern impacts that are demonstrably attributable to climate change and (2) that evidence submitted to the courts clearly substantiates the alleged relationship between defendants' emissions and plaintiffs' losses.[28]

Thus far, our brief survey on climate justice temporalities seems to suggest that narrative plays an important role, particularly in judicial reasoning. The crafting (or attribution) of legal responsibility by the courts in climate litigation appears to be contingent upon the way they frame the causality principle. It is thus argued that the causality conundrum is an entry point, or an Encounter to be precise, whence judges *intuit* climate injustice. As we shall point out next, by focusing on *Milieudefensie*, we can call such an Encounter the uncertainty of climate injustice, which is grasped as a kind of unanticipated encounter in judges' minds that leads them to a creative and experimental legal inquiry into the multiplicity of experiences of climate injustice.

26 Petra Minnerop and Friederike Otto, "Climate Change and Causation: Joining Law and Climate Science on the Basis of Formal Logic," *Buffalo Environmental Law Journal* 27, no. 1 (2019): 50.

27 Ibid., 72–73.

28 Rupert F. Stuart-Smith, Friederike E. L. Otto, Aisha I. Saad, Gaia Lisi, Petra Minnerop, Kristian Cedervall Lauta, Kristin van Zwieten, and Thom Wetzer, "Filling the Evidentiary Gap in Climate Litigation," *Nature Climate Change* 11, no. 8 (2021): 654.

Intuiting the uncertainty of climate injustice

The limited nature of (ordinary) legal reasoning to capture climate change crisis is because law is imagined to be a closed system, independent of its environment. Arguably, legal decision-makers gesture intuitively with the encounter of a case, insisting them to a creative and experimental legal inquiry into the multiplicity of experiences of climate injustice. In this framework, this section will focus on drawing the uncertainty of climate injustice as a particular form of encounter.

In a broader sense, the uncertainty of climate injustice is fundamentally construed upon two types of climate imagination, namely ecological and sociological imaginations.[29] Following Noorgard, we can identify four key problems in which sociological imagination can reframe ecological imagination. This reframing involves the problems of (1) why climate change is happening, (2) how we are being impacted, (3) why we have failed to successfully respond so far and (4) how we might be able to effectively do so. Such a reframing will then make the nature-culture relationship more visible, thus preventing humans from getting further into the propensity for nature-culture alienation.[30]

An important caveat needs to be posted at this point. Rogers reminds us about the perils of 'emergency'—or in our context, uncertainty—of climate injustice. In practice, such an emergency can be seen as a pretext for an otherwise unjustified action (in Roger's study, this pertains to climate change activism that involves civil obedience and intersection with criminal laws). The idea of emergency in that sense thus asks for a redefinition of legal norms and principles that can invert unlawfulness into lawfulness. According to Rogers,

> Critical to the establishment of the defense in the United States is the exhaustion of all reasonable and legitimate alternatives on the part of the defendant. The contested interpretation of the nature of reasonable alternatives, or indeed what is reasonable in the face of climate change, provides additional paradoxical possibilities in any application of the defense. One possible interpretation offered by climate change activists, but thus far not accepted by the courts, is that the defense should apply where more moderate law-abiding methods traditionally used to respond to other forms of harm no longer suffice or have been demonstrated to be ineffective in addressing the exceptional catastrophic harm of climate change. In other words, where the legal system has failed to prevent a

29 Kari Marie Norgaard, "The Sociological Imagination in a Time of Climate Change," *Global and Planetary Change* 163 (2018): 171–76.

30 Norman, *Posthuman Legal Subjectivity: Reimagining the Human in the Anthropocene.*

> catastrophe, more radical measures which involve law-breaking are permissible.[31]

By referring to the *uncertainty* of climate crisis, however, we are not attempting to suggest that the legal decision-maker ought to break or oppose the existing law in crafting climate justice responsibility, but instead, they need to treat adjudicative judgment as a way to "actualize a temporally mobile basis of interest and desire in conjunction with tradition."[32]

Within this backdrop, let us highlight the narratives in a climate civil lawsuit between *Milieudefensie et al. v. Royal Dutch Shell PLC* at The Hague District Court in the Netherlands. Climate litigation practice in the country has been seen as one of the most progressive in today's movement against climate injustice. The critical moment was initially in 2015, when the District Court of The Hague decided in *Urgenda v. the Netherlands* that the Dutch government had violated the national civil law by causing climate crisis in the country.[33] This so-called strategic litigation case has been the steppingstone for many other courts—in and outside the country—to justifying collective legal responsibility related to climate crisis obligation.[34] While *Urgenda* definitely has its own merits in shaping climate litigation reasoning in the country,[35] *Milieudefensie*, on the other hand, has a distinct character of reasoning in some ways. To begin with, it is important to understand the significant role of the court's narratives in framing and scaling the uncertainty of climate crisis. In the earlier passage of their opinion, the court in *Milieudefensie* stretches out the global scale of climate crisis

31 Nicole Rogers, "Beyond Reason: Activism and Law in a Time of Climate Change," *Journal for the Study of Radicalism* 12, no. 2 (2018): 170.

32 Alexandre Lefebvre, *The Image of Law: Deleuze, Bergson, Spinoza* (Stanford: Stanford University Press, 2008), 101.

33 See Rechtbank Den Haag [The Hague District Court] June 24, 2015, Urgenda v The Netherlands, Case No. C/09/456689 (Neth.) Hoge Raad [Supreme Court] December 20, 2019, Urgenda v The Netherlands, Case No. 19/00135 (Neth.)

34 I think it is contextual in climate change litigation to exert the term 'strategic' case to distinguish it from 'routine case,' as some climate legal scholars mentioned. Kelleher, nonetheless, coins another interesting term of 'systemic rights-based climate litigation,' which is defined as "legal cases that take a whole-of-system approach by challenging the overall ambition of a government's framework climate mitigation policies, often on fundamental rights (and sometimes on statutory) grounds, before domestic and regional human rights courts." Ibid., 292.

35 Kars J. de Graaf and Jan H. Jans, "The Urgenda Decision: Netherlands Liable for Role in Causing Dangerous Global Climate Change," *Journal of Environmental Law* 27, no. 3 (2015): 517–27; C. W. Chris Backes and G. A. Gerrit van der Veen, "Urgenda: The Final Judgment of the Dutch Supreme Court," *Journal for European Environmental & Planning Law* 17, no. 3 (2020): 307–21.

problem that ought to be tackled by today's mankind. The court considers the following facts:

> § Mankind has been using energy, primarily produced by burning fossil fuels (coals, oil and gas), on a massive scale since the beginning of the Industrial Revolution. Carbon dioxide is released in this process. The chemical compound of the elements carbon and oxygen is designated with the chemical formula CO_2. Some of the released CO_2 is emitted into the atmosphere, where it lingers for hundreds of years, or even longer. Some of it is absorbed by the ecosystems of forests and oceans. This absorption option is steadily becoming smaller due to deforestation and the warming of sea water.
>
> § CO_2 is the primary greenhouse gas which, together with other greenhouse gases, traps the heat emitted by the earth in the atmosphere. This is known as the greenhouse effect, which intensifies as more CO_2 ends up in the atmosphere. This in turn increasingly warms the earth. The climate system has a delayed response to the greenhouse gas emissions: the warming effect of greenhouse gases which are emitted today will only become apparent in thirty to forty years' time. Other greenhouse gases are, inter alia, methane, nitrous oxide and fluorinated gases. The unit 'parts per million' (hereinafter: ppm) is used to express the concentration of greenhouse gases in the atmosphere. *There is a direct, linear link between man-made greenhouse gas emissions, in part caused by the burning of fossil fuels, and global warming. The temperate of the earth has now increased by about 1.1°C relative to the average temperature at the beginning of the Industrial Revolution. Over the past decades, global CO_2 emissions have increased by 2% per year.*[36]

From these two paragraphs, we may identify an interaction between climate science data and Noorgard's so-called sociological imagination. The reframing of ecological to sociological imagination is reflected when the court conceives of reasons why the crisis is happening and the incremental impact of it. Of our particular interest is the way the court recounts some counterintuitive scenarios in the following paragraphs:

> § In climate science—the area of science that studies the climate and climate change—and in the international community there has been consensus for quite some time that the average temperature on earth should not increase by more than 2°C relative to the average temperature in the pre-industrial era. *If the concentration of greenhouse gases in the atmosphere has stayed below 450 ppm by the year 2100, climate science believes*

36 Rechtbank Den Haag, Milieudefensie v. Royal Dutch Shell, Plc (2021).

> *there is a good chance that this target (hereinafter: the 2°C target) will be reached.* In the last couple of years, further insight has shown that a safe temperature increase should not exceed 1.5°C with a corresponding greenhouse gas concentration level of no more than 430 ppm by the year 2100.
>
> § The current greenhouse gas concentration level is 401 ppm. The total global remaining capacity for further greenhouse gas emissions is also known as the carbon budget. Global CO_2 emissions currently run at 40 Gt CO_2 per year. Each year the global CO_2 emissions stay at this level reduces the carbon budget by 40 Gt. *If global CO2 emissions are higher, the carbon budget will decrease by more than 40 Gt.* A carbon budget of 580 Gt CO_2 was remained available from 2017—a best estimate—for a 50% chance of a warming of 1.5°C. Now, three years later, 120 Gt CO_2 of the carbon budget has been used, which means that 460 Gt CO_2 remains. *At unchanged emission levels, the carbon budget will have been used up within the foreseeable future.*[37]

From the quoted passages, we understand that the court does not exclusively treat climate crisis as a technical problem with scientific solutions, as it also causes social loss and damage. Particularly, we can see this attitude when the court made reference to reports of the Intergovernmental Panel on Climate Change (IPCC). For instance, the court asserts that

> § All parts of Europe will encounter the adverse effects of climate change. Individual citizens and companies will run a substantial financial risk as a result of these impacts. As a result of climate change Europe is expected to face more frequent heat waves, which will last longer and become more intense and result in more deaths. Human systems and ecosystems in Europe are vulnerable to climate change, but vulnerabilities will differ per region.[38]

Meanwhile, zooming in on the context of the Netherlands, the court furthermore asserts that

> Climate change-related health problems in Dutch residents include heat stress, increasing infectious diseases, deterioration of air quality, increase of UV exposure, and an increase of water-related and foodborne diseases. In the coming decades, the Netherlands will also face many water-related climate impacts, such as flooding along the coast and rivers, excess water, water shortage, deterioration of water quality, salinization, raised water levels and drought. Periods of either drought and water shortage

37 Ibid., paras. 2.3.3–2.3.4. (citation omitted; emphasis added)
38 Ibid., para. 2.3.6. (citations omitted)

> or problems due to excess water may occur on an annual basis. These changes and uncertainties in water availability will have an impact on agriculture and biodiversity, but also on, for example, the energy sector and the manufacturing industry, for instance in the form of cooling water problems and poor accessibility via rivers in case of drought and network problems due to drought, excess water or other weather extremes.[39]

With this background in mind, the object of dispute in *Milieudefensie* is the scope of Royal Dutch Shell's (RDS) greenhouse gas protocol, in which its legal obligation is categorized into three scopes, covering:

Scope 1: direct emissions from sources that are owned or controlled in full or in part by the organization;
Scope 2: indirect emissions from third-party sources from which the organization has purchased or acquired electricity, steam, or heating for its operations;
Scope 3: all other indirect emissions resulting from activities of the organization, but occurring from greenhouse gas sources owned or controlled by third parties, such as other organizations or consumers, including emissions from the use of third-party purchased crude oil and gas.[40]

Here we have three types of emissions, namely direct emissions, indirect emissions from third-party sources, and other indirect emissions from third-party sources connected with the company. Against these scopes of Shell's greenhouse gas protocol, the Plaintiffs position their claims on the following grounds:

> RDS has an obligation, ensuing from the unwritten standard of care pursuant to Book 6 Section 162 Dutch Civil Code to contribute to the prevention of dangerous climate change through the corporate policy it determines for the Shell group. For the interpretation of the unwritten standard of care, use can be made of the so-called *Kelderluik* criteria, human rights, specifically the right to life and the right to respect for private and family life, as well as soft law endorsed by RDS, such as the UN Guiding Principles on Business and Human Rights, the UN Global Compact and the OECD Guidelines for Multinational Enterprises. RDS has the obligation to ensure that the CO2 emissions attributable to the Shell group (Scope 1 through to 3) will have been reduced at end 2030, relative to 2019 levels, principally by 45% in absolute terms, or net 45% (using the IPCC SR15 report and the IEA's Net Zero emissions by 2050 scenario as a

39 Ibid., para. 2.3.9. (citations omitted)
40 Ibid., para. 2.5.4.

> basis), in the alternative by 35% (using the IEA's Below 2 Degree Scenario as a basis), and further in the alternative by 25% (using the IEA's Sustainable Development Scenario as a basis), through the corporate policy of the Shell group. *RDS violates this obligation or is at risk of violating this obligation with a hazardous and disastrous corporate policy for the Shell group, which in no way is consistent with the global climate target to prevent a dangerous climate change for the protection of mankind, the human environment and nature.*[41]

In its assessment, the court initially restates the main legal inquiry of this case. The court's problematization is that

> [t]he claims of Milieudefensie et al. are directed against RDS, established in the Netherlands, as the parent company of the Shell group. This case revolves around the question of whether or not RDS has the obligation to reduce, at end 2030 and relative to 2019 levels across all emission Scopes (1 through to 3), the CO_2 emissions of the Shell group's entire energy portfolio through the corporate policy of the Shell group.[42]

As we have examined in the previous section, the most critical aspect of intuiting uncertainty in climate litigation is related to the question of causation. It is suggested from a range of literature that an inquiry into causation involves, at its core narratives, claims for the presence of harm or risk of harm.[43] In *Milieudefensie*, the presence of harm or risks is bundled into what judges call a form of interest. Related to this, the court's initial argument builds upon the nature of the Plaintiff's claim, asserting that climate change litigation is admissible insofar as the accrued interests of the claim are justifiably similar. The court exhibits that

> The class actions of Milieudefensie et al. are public interest actions. *Such actions seek to protect public interests, which cannot be individualized because they accrue to a much larger group of persons, which is undefined and unspecified.* The common interest of preventing dangerous climate change by reducing CO_2 emissions can be protected in a class action. The dispute on the admissibility of class actions revolves around the question whether or not they comply with the requirement 'similar interest' in the sense of Book 3 Section 305a Dutch Civil Code. This requirement entails

41 Ibid., para. 3.2. (emphasis added)
42 Ibid., para. 4.1.1.
43 Alison Fernandes, *The Temporal Asymmetry of Causation* (Cambridge, UK: Cambridge University Press, 2023).

> that the interests in question *must be suitable for bundling so as to safeguard an efficient and effective legal protection of the stakeholders.*[44]

From the court's passage, we know that climate change is recognized as part of public interests in such a way that it can only be disputed if and only if there are similar interests suitable for bundling. This condition arguably requires the court to put climate change interest on a certain scale. As we can see in the following paragraphs, the court's opinion hinges on the spatiotemporal scale of climate crisis:

> *The court is of the opinion that the interests of current and future generations of the world's population, as served principally with the class actions, is not suitable for bundling.* Although the entire world population is served by curbing dangerous climate change, there are huge differences in the time and manner in which the global population at various locations will be affected by global warming caused by CO_2 emissions. Therefore, this principal interest does not meet the requirement of 'similar interest' under Book 3 Section 305a Dutch Civil Code.
>
> However, the interests of current and future generations of Dutch residents and (with respect to the Waddenvereniging) of the inhabitants of the Wadden Sea area, a part of which is located in the Netherlands, as served in the alternative with the class actions, are suitable for bundling, even though in the Netherlands and in the Wadden region there are differences in time, extent and intensity to which the inhabitants will be affected by climate change caused by CO_2 emissions. However, *these differences are much smaller and of a different nature than the mutual differences when it concerns the entire global population and do not stand in the way of bundling in a class action. The collective claims are therefore declared not allowable insofar as they serve the interest of the world's population, except for the interest of Dutch residents and the inhabitants of the Wadden region.*[45]

Taking a closer look, we can discover that rather than framing climate crisis interest into generalization and abstraction, the court is quite aware that there exists "huge differences in the time and manner in which the global population at various locations will be affected by global warming caused by CO_2 emissions."[46] That being said, the requirement of "similar interests" should be based upon the court's capacity to *differentiate* space and time,

44 Rechtbank Den Haag, Milieudefensie v. Royal Dutch Shell, Plc, C/09/57193 para. 4.2.2. (citation omitted; emphasis added)
45 Ibid., paras. 4.2.3–4.2.4. (emphasis added)
46 Rechtbank Den Haag, Milieudefensie v. Royal Dutch Shell, Plc, C/09/57193.

and, in this context, the court was more interested in justifying harm and the risk of harm *experienced* by Dutch residents, particularly the inhabitants of the Wadden region. Arguably, we can find in this admissibility question a matter of scaling temporal experiences. Pragmatically speaking, it is impossible for the court to accrue the experiences of global population, which makes it more feasible for the court to justify those with lesser differences in time, extent and intensity. Therefore, this narrative suggests that the bundling of similar interests (or experiences) can be seen as the court's attempt to match the risk and the harm of climate change.

Not only about the experiences of the harmed population, the inquiry into proximate causation also builds upon the question of singularity of event. In this case, specific attention is given to the interpretation of the "event giving rise to the environmental damage" clause. Let us first refer to the normative legal basis of this claim, in which the court highlighted the applicability of Article 7 Rome II (Regulation (EC) No. 864/2007. This provision provides any claimant's choice of applicable law in an environmental damage dispute, which reads:

> The law applicable to a non-contractual obligation arising out of environmental damage or damage sustained by persons or property as a result of such damage shall be the law determined pursuant to Article 4(1), unless the person seeking compensation for damage chooses to base his or her claim on the law of the country in which the event giving rise to the damage occurred.

Relatedly, Article 4(1) of Rome II, as a general rule, stipulates that:

> Unless otherwise provided for in this Regulation, the law applicable to a non-contractual obligation arising out of a tort/delict shall be the law of the country in which the damage occurs irrespective of the country in which the event giving rise to the damage occurred and irrespective of the country or countries in which the indirect consequences of that event occur.

Bearing those provisions in mind, we then need to see the court's reasoning as follows:

> Where *events giving rise to environmental damage* occur in several states, it is not possible to invoke the escape clause (Article 4(3)) in order to concentrate the applicable law with regard to a single act. Thus, the plaintiff may opt for different laws as far as acts by multiple tortfeasors acting in various states are concerned. If, however, an act in country A causes an incident in country B which then leads to an environmental damage in country C, it may be submitted that only the final incident should be

> characterized as the decisive 'event' within the meaning of Article 7. One has to concede that extending the victim's right to choose the law, of each place of act would considerably undermine legal predictability. On the other hand, such generous approach would fit the favor naturae underlying Article 7. Since the tortfeasor may be sued in country A under Article 7 no. 2 Brussels Ibis, extending the victim's option will also facilitate proceedings.

The Defendant argues that the enactment of company policies does not itself create a kind of event giving rise to environmental damage. According to RDS, their corporate policy "is a preparatory act that falls outside the scope of this article because . . . the mere adoption of a policy does not cause damage."[47] Interestingly, the court argues to the contrary, claiming that the RDS' argument "is too narrow, not in line with the characteristics of responsibility for environmental damage and imminent environmental damage nor with the concept of protection underlying the choice of law in Article 7 Rome II."[48] The court envisages that

> [a]lthough Article 7 Rome II refers to an 'event giving rise to the damage', i.e., singular, it leaves room for situations in which multiple events giving rise to the damage in multiple countries can be identified, as is characteristic of environmental damage and imminent environmental damage.[49]

Critical to this opinion is the way in which the court intuits the multiplicity of environmental damages, from which we may see the necessity of abandoning the traditional linear image of causality in order for the law to accommodate claims for climate justice. In this regard, the court subsequently submits that

> [w]hen applying Article 7 Rome II, RDS' adoption of the corporate policy of the Shell group therefore constitutes *an independent cause of the damage*, which may contribute to environmental damage and imminent environmental damage with respect to Dutch residents and the inhabitants of the Wadden region.[50]

Having claimed the inapplicability of Article 7 Rome II to this matter and clarified the multiple natures of the statutory event giving rise to the environmental damage clause, the court resorted the matter to the Dutch national law. The court exhibits that the matter of RDS' reduction of obligation

47 Ibid., para. 4.3.6.
48 Ibid.
49 Ibid.
50 Ibid. (emphasis added)

is contrary to the principle of *unwritten standard of care* under Book 6 Section 162 of the Dutch Civil Code. The rule provides a definition of 'tortious act' as follows:

1. A person who commits a tortious act (unlawful act) against another person that can be attributed to him must repair the damage that this other person has suffered as a result thereof.
2. As a tortious act is regarded a violation of someone else's right (entitlement) and an act or omission in violation of a duty imposed by law or of what according to unwritten law has to be regarded as proper social conduct, always as far as there was no justification for this behavior.
3. A tortious act can be attributed to the tortfeasor [the person committing the tortious act] if it results from his fault or from a cause for which he is accountable by virtue of law or generally accepted principles (common opinion).

According to the court, essential in construing tortious acts in this case is the unwritten standard of care principle, which basically stipulates that "acting in conflict with what is generally accepted according to unwritten law is unlawful."[51] In evaluating this principle, the court has included 14 points of assessment. These points include: (1) the policy-setting position of RDS in the Shell group, (2) the Shell group's CO_2 emissions, (3) the consequences of the CO_2 emissions for the Netherlands and the Wadden region, (4) the right to life and the right to respect for private and family life of Dutch residents and the inhabitants of the Wadden region, (5) the UN Guiding Principles on Business and Human Rights, (6) RDS' check and influence of the CO_2 emissions of the Shell group and its business relations, (7) what is needed to prevent dangerous climate change, (8) possible reduction pathways, (9) the twin challenge of curbing dangerous climate change and meeting the growing global population energy demand, (10) the ETS system and other 'cap and trade' emission systems that apply elsewhere in the world, permits and current obligations of the Shell group, (11) the effectiveness of the reduction obligation, (12) the responsibility of states and society, (13) the onerousness for RDS and the Shell group to meet the reduction obligation and (14) the proportionality of RDS' reduction obligation.[52] As we will later examine, the nature of and the degree to which the unwritten standard of care principle is applicable in this case is based on judges' intuition. While the application of this principle is not without criticism,[53] one may also claim that this kind of

51 Ibid., para. 4.4.1.
52 Ibid., para. 4.4.2.
53 Alexander Zahar, "Human Rights Law and the Obligation to Reduce Greenhouse Gas Emissions," *Human Rights Review* 23, no. 3 (2022): 385–411; Alexander Zahar, "The Missing

reasoning is a lucid perspective on legal principles that is useful to tackling climate crisis. By examining *Urgenda* in 2015, for instance, de Graaf and Jans contend that

> Using international agreements to establish the unwritten standard of due care of the State in this particular case is not the only argument for the court's decision, but it is a remarkable one. In reading the judgment of the court, one could seriously consider that specific provisions in the Dutch Constitution had lost their meaning. Agreements of the State with other states and the latest scientific knowledge seem to transform into binding obligations of the State vis-à-vis Urgenda by interpreting the standard of due care of Article 162(2) of book 6 of the Dutch Civil Code in the face of dangerous climate change. This manner of interpretation is not entirely uncommon since Dutch law allows the courts, when applying and interpreting open or vague norms or concepts in national legislation (e.g., 'good faith', 'due care'), to take into account such international law obligations. These obligations can have what is called a 'reflex effect' in national law.[54]

Following de Graaf and Jans' proposition, we can argue that the reflex effect, as a sort of judicial obligation, fundamentally squares with this study's proposition about judicial intuition in time. The reflex effect encapsulated in such a framework is a method towards the immediate data of 'uncertainty' that generates access to (1) the untimely inquiry that does not necessarily follow progressively from the past or present and (2) the coherence that governs temporal patterns based on which climate crisis responsibilities may attain social purposes over time. This method, therefore, should be grasped as a response to *the* Encounter that allows the court to gesture with the uncertainty of climate crisis applicable to Shell's corporate responsibility actualization. In this regard, the fourteen factors addressed by the court in interpreting the standard due of care principle can be read through Deleuze's *rules* of intuition, namely differentiation (i.e., repositioning the 'problem' of climate change responsibility) and temporalization (i.e., the essence of climate change claim for collective responsibility). Through this reading, we can later find coherence that governs temporal patterns of climate crisis, based on which collective responsibility attains social purpose over time.

Relational Element in Tort Cases on Greenhouse Gas Emissions," *Climate Law* 12, no. 3–4 (2022): 216–41.

54 de Graaf and Jans, "The Urgenda Decision: Netherlands Liable for Role in Causing Dangerous Global Climate Change," 525.

To elaborate such a proposition, let us structure the way the court problematizes climate justice inquiry in *Milieudefensie* based on the following narratives:

(1) "There is a direct, linear link between man-made greenhouse gas emissions, in part caused by the burning of fossil fuels, and global warming. The temperate of the earth has now increased by about 1.1°C relative to the average temperature at the beginning of the Industrial Revolution. Over the past decades, global CO_2 emissions have increased by 2% per year."
(2) "If the concentration of greenhouse gases in the atmosphere has stayed below 450 ppm by the year 2100, climate science believes there is a good chance that this target (hereinafter: the 2°C target) will be reached."
(3) "If global CO_2 emissions are higher, the carbon budget will decrease by more than 40 Gt. . . . At unchanged emission levels, the carbon budget will have been used up within the foreseeable future."
(4) Based on the laws (at national and international levels), "RDS violates this obligation or is at risk of violating this obligation with a hazardous and disastrous corporate policy for the Shell group, which in no way is consistent with the global climate target to prevent a dangerous climate change for the protection of mankind, the human environment and nature."
(5) And therefore, "This case revolves around the question whether or not RDS has the obligation to reduce at end 2030 and relative to 2019 levels across all emission Scopes (1 through to 3) the CO_2 emissions of the Shell group's entire energy portfolio through the corporate policy of the Shell group."

From a temporal perspective, what we can notice from this structure of problematization is a conflation between climate justice's past, present and future. That is, the legal inquiry about corporate's violation of its climate obligation is being intuited to the extent that the present legal inquiry is construed upon both the imagined past and future of climate crisis.[55] As indicated in the previous

55 See Chris Hilson, "Framing Time in Climate Change Litigation," *Oñati Socio-Legal Series, Forthcoming* 9, no. 3 (2019): 361–79. I think Hilson also poses a similar position. Hilson claims three senses in explaining the relationship between climate science and temporal aspects of climate litigation, namely: "First, there is the debate about what GHG emissions are required to keep us within the two degrees warming threshold, above which climate change is widely considered to be dangerous. Time here becomes a matter of how long we have left, based on climate modelling, to take action before we reach two degrees. The risks of climate change here lie in the future. Second, there is an attempt by climate science to discuss the here and now—the present. So for example, while not able to attribute causal responsibility for particular cyclonic activity to climate change, climate scientists have

narrative structure, the use of scenarios (e.g., "If the concentration of greenhouse gases," "If global CO_2 emissions are higher") can be considered a preliminary sorting carried out by intuitive judges *through* perception in their search for salient properties of law. This method of problematization should not be seen as a way to delimit or constrain a problem or inquiry, but rather as a way of

> working with it to render the problem productive of a necessary, inevitable truth within and without—the truth is in the productivity of the operational coherence of the problem as a restatement of its premises, conditions, situation, implications, through to its possible outcomes and a decisive adequate solution.[56]

Actualizing collective legal responsibility

In this last section, we will highlight the ways in which the court in *Milieudefensie* inferred RDS' corporate responsibility for climate injustice. In doing so, the judges essentially selected the best explanation stemming from people's experiences in the climate crisis duration. The court's argument is fundamentally a narrative of "playing with existing rules" in order to contain climate change that has disregarded "established rules."[57] In that sense, we may claim the 'playing with existing rules' as a figurative expression of intuitive reasoning that provides the judges access to legal perception, considering that climate change, as Rogers correctly writes, "constitutes more than an external phenomenon: it is, and will increasingly become, embodied and lived experience."[58]

In actualizing RDS's corporate climate responsibility, the narratives in *Milieudefensie* can be parsed into a single principle of unwritten standard of care. In what follows, we can describe this principle as an expression of intuitive judges that generates access to (1) climate justice inquiry that does not necessarily follow progressively from the past or present, and (2) the

nevertheless shown a degree of correlation between warming and the prevalence of extreme weather events. And third, climate science may be used to try to attribute liability to major GHG emitters for their past, historical emissions. When we see such arguments presented in court cases, these represent future, present and past scientific time frames respectively." (375)

56 Felix Rebolledo Palazuelos, Tania Galli Fonseca, and Andreia Machado Oliveira, "A Philosophical Perspective on Intuition as a Method within Artistic Process," *Studies in Visual Arts and Communication: An International Journal* 5, no. 1 (2018): 7.

57 Rogers, *Law, Fiction and Activism in a Time of Climate Change*, Chap. 6. Rogers claims that in order to understand climate crisis, we (in particular lawyers) should go beyond reason and rules, which then leads us to consider the use of narratives employed by activists. The significance of Rogers's claim in this study is that the phrase 'beyond reason and rules' could be regarded as a way for the judges to escape from the logic of subsumption, thus generating anew some plausible alternatives. See discussion in Chapter 5 about the untimely.

58 Ibid., 155.

coherence that governs temporal patterns of climate crisis, based on which collective legal responsibility may attain social purposes over time.[59]

Let us first address the court's repositioning of the 'problem' of climate change responsibility. In this instance, the court crafts legal responsibility by enacting the legal problem as an Encounter—understood as something that is unanticipated or unrecognized from the past that forces the judges to think and react in an atypical manner. The initial step is the repositioning of RDS's policy-setting in the Shell group. According to the court,

> [f]rom the facts . . . it follows that RDS determines the general policy of the Shell group. The companies in the Shell group are responsible for the implementation and execution of the policy and must comply with applicable legislation and their contractual obligations. The implementation responsibility of the Shell companies does not alter the fact that RDS determines the general policy of the Shell group.[60]

In this context, the company's policy-setting should be placed within the larger Shell group's CO_2 emissions policy. The court views that

> the Shell group is a major player on the worldwide market of fossil fuels. If all Scopes (1 through to 3) are included, the Shell group is responsible for significant CO_2 emissions all over the world. The total CO_2 emissions of the Shell group (Scope 1 through to 3) exceeds the CO_2 emissions of many states, including the Netherlands.

That said, according to the Court, "[i]*t is not in dispute that these global* CO_2 *emissions of the Shell group (Scope 1 through to 3) contribute to global warming and climate change in the Netherlands and the Wadden region.*"[61]

Inevitably, the company's policy-setting has certain implications for its business relations, and in this regard, the Court interprets the standard due of care principle in terms of RDS' check and influence on the CO_2 emissions of the Shell group and its business relations. In this case, the Court draws a distinction between "the CO_2 emissions of (1) the Shell group (RDS and the other Shell companies) and (2) the business relations of the Shell group, including the end-users."[62] According to the Court,

> [d]ue to the *policy-setting influence* RDS has over the companies in the Shell group, *it bears the same responsibility for these business relations as for its own activities*. The far-reaching control and influence of RDS over

59 See more details in Chapter 6 on judicial intuition.
60 Rechtbank Den Haag, Milieudefensie v. Royal Dutch Shell, Plc, C/09/57193 para. 4.4.4.
61 Ibid., para. 4.4.5.
62 Ibid., para. 4.4.22.

> the Shell group means that *RDS' reduction obligation must be an obligation of result for emissions connected to own activities of the Shell group.* This concerns RDS' Scope 1 emissions and the part of RDS' Scope 2 emissions which can be ascribed to the Shell companies. From the perspective of the Shell group as a whole, this constitutes the Scope 1 emissions of the Shell group.[63]

Given that the RDS' operation involves an enormous number of separate corporate entities, the Court expresses a rather broad spectrum in understanding the range of the RDS' check and influence on CO_2 emissions, as follows:

> As regards the business relations of the Shell group, including the end-users, RDS may be expected to take the necessary steps to remove or prevent the serious risks ensuing from the CO_2 emissions generated by them, and to use its influence to limit any lasting consequences as much as possible. This is a significant best-efforts obligation, which is not removed or reduced by the individual responsibility of the business relations, including the end-users, for their own CO_2 emissions.
>
> It is not in dispute that through its purchase policy the Shell group exercises control and influence over its suppliers' emissions. These are the Scope 2 emissions of the Shell group as a whole. This means that through the corporate policy of the Shell group RDS is able to exercise control and influence over these emissions. The subject that is most disputed between the parties is the control and influence RDS exerts over the Scope 3 emissions of the Shell group, which are released by the end users. RDS does not contest that it can exert that control and influence through its energy package, and the composition thereof, produced and sold by the Shell group. This is not altered by the circumstance, emphasized by RDS, that the Shell group has contractual obligations as well as obligations ensuing from long-term concessions, which may limit its freedom of choice as regards the Shell group's energy package. This limitation means that RDS is not fully free to determine the Shell group's energy package; in determining the energy package of the Shell group, RDS will have to take the current obligations into account. *This limitation does not alter the fact that ultimately RDS determines the energy package of the Shell group—and consequently, the range of energy products.* With due observance of its current obligations, RDS is free to decide not to make new investments in explorations and fossil fuels, and to change the energy package offered by the Shell group, such as the reduction pathways require.[64]

63 Ibid.
64 Ibid., paras. 4.4.24–4.4.25. (emphasis added)

While RDS' climate responsibility is framed by the Court under the broader Shell Group's policy setting, a further related question is whether such responsibility should also be framed under dangerous climate change prevention. This question is inevitably paramount in order to draw the *limits* of corporate responsibility in the midst of epistemic scientific knowledge on this issue. The Court infers such limits of responsibility by referring to some of the best available findings recognized at the international level:

> The goals of the Paris Agreement are derived from the IPCC reports. The IPCC reports on the relevant scientific insights about the consequences of a temperature increase, the concentrations of greenhouse gases that give rise to that increase, and the reduction pathways that lead to a limitation of global warming to a particular temperature. Therefore, the goals of the Paris Agreement represent the best available scientific findings in climate science, which is supported by widespread international consensus. The non-binding goals of the Paris Agreement represent a universally endorsed and accepted standard that protects the common interest of preventing dangerous climate change. The court follows this reasoning in its interpretation of the unwritten standard of care. The court assumes that it is generally accepted that global warming must be kept well below 2°C in 2100, and that a temperature rise of under 1.5°C should be strived for. The court also assumes that this requires a limitation of the global concentration of greenhouse gases of up to 450 ppm in 2100 and that a maximum greenhouse gas concentration of 430 ppm must be pursued. *The court notes that in doing so it does not formulate a legally binding standard for the prevention of dangerous climate change in the Netherlands and the Wadden region. The court includes this broad consensus about what is needed to prevent dangerous climate change—viz. achieving the goals of the Paris Agreement—in its answer to the question whether or not RDS is obliged to reduce the Shell group's* CO_2 *emissions via its corporate policy.*[65]
>
> The court establishes that tackling dangerous climate change needs immediate attention. Given the current concentration of greenhouse gases in the atmosphere (401 ppm in 2018), the remaining carbon budget is limited. This applies to both 430 ppm as a limit for a global warming of up to 1.5°C and 450 ppm for a global warming of up to 2°C. *The longer it takes to achieve the required emissions reductions, the higher the level of emitted greenhouse gases, and consequently, the sooner the remaining carbon budget runs out. At unchanged emission levels, the carbon budget will have been used up within twelve years.* As has been described by the IEA in its World Energy Outlook 2020, the next ten years will be crucially important for preventing dangerous climate change. This also follows

65 Ibid., para. 4.4.27.

> from the conclusion of the UNEP (of 2019). The sooner reductions are started, the more time is available before the remaining carbon budget runs out. *The imperativeness for the Netherlands to reduce CO_2 emissions is even greater, because so far the temperature rise in the Netherlands has developed about twice as fast as the global average, with serious and irreversible consequences and risks for the human rights of Dutch residents and the inhabitants of the Wadden region.*[66]

Given these broad considerations and the absence of agreed-upon calculated measures as to *when* a company ought to implement a prevention policy, the Court then sketches some possible reduction pathways that should be undertaken by RDS. In that framework, the court asserts that

> So there is no well-defined and concrete specification for the method according to which the timing of the various companies must be applied in working towards the goal of net zero emissions in 2050. The consensus referred to in legal ground, however, provides sufficient starting points for the specification of the unwritten standard of care on this issue. In light of the broad international consensus that each company must independently work towards achieving net zero emissions by 2050, RDS may be expected to do its part.
>
> In answering the question what can be expected of RDS, *the court considers that an important characteristic of the imminent environmental damage in the Netherlands and the Wadden region at issue here is that every emission of CO_2 and other greenhouse gases, anywhere in the world and caused in whatever manner, contributes to this damage and its increase.* It is an established fact that—apart from its own limited CO_2 emissions—RDS does not actually causes the Scope 1 through to 3 emissions of the Shell group by itself. However, this circumstance and the not-disputed circumstance that RDS is not the only party responsible for tackling dangerous climate change in the Netherlands and the Wadden region does not absolve RDS of its individual partial responsibility to contribute to the fight against dangerous climate change according to its ability.[67]

Another far-reaching argument provided by the court is when dealing with the twin challenges of curbing dangerous climate change and meeting the growing global population energy demand. Such a challenge is put plainly on

66 Ibid., paras. 4.4.27–4.4.28. (emphasis added)
67 Ibid., paras. 4.4.36–4.4.37. (citation omitted, emphasis added)

the surface by RDS as a way to justify its reduction policy. Against this claim, the court considers that

> [t]he parties agree that the world faces a twin challenge . . . However, the importance of access to reliable and affordable energy, as pointed out by RDS, and the Shell group's role in it, have no bearing on RDS' reduction obligation. That interest must always be served within the context of climate targets.[68]

Moreover, maintained the court, these climate targets ought to be understood in line with another global goals—those set out under the United Nations Sustainable Development Goals (SDGs). The court discerns that

> there is a connection between the UNSDG and the climate goals of the Paris Agreement and other agreements made for the implementation of the UN Climate Convention. It is not the intention for SDG 7 ("Ensure access to affordable, reliable, sustainable and modern energy for all"), as cited by RDS, to detract from the Paris Agreement or to interfere with these goals. This also follows from SDG 13 ("Take urgent action to combat climate change and its impacts") and the preamble under 8 of the Paris Agreement, which emphasizes the intrinsic connection between the tackling of dangerous climate and fair access to sustainable development and the eradication of poverty. The UNSDG sustainability goals can therefore not be a reason for RDS to not meet its reduction obligation.[69]

Another way to escape from climate change responsibility is that its reduction obligation has been covered by the emission trading system (ETS) and other 'cap and trade' emission systems that apply elsewhere in the world, as well as by the permits and current obligations of the Shell group. The ETS system itself, as noted by the court,

> is a system which, inter alia, regulates the CO_2 emissions of a wide variety of industries based on the "cap and trade" principle. The objective of the ETS system is to reduce the member states' anthropogenic emissions of greenhouse gases, fulfilling the commitments ensuing from the Kyoto Protocol.[70]

In this framework,

> Companies in the EU that fall under the ETS system may only emit greenhouse gases in exchange for surrendering emission allowances. These

68 Ibid., para. 4.4.40.
69 Ibid., para. 4.4.42.
70 Ibid., para. 4.4.45.

> emission allowances regard Scope 1 emissions and may be purchased, sold or kept. The emission allowances are divided over the companies in the member states.[71]

The Court furthers that,

> [i]f a company emits less CO_2 than allocated, it may sell the corresponding emission allowances. Companies that are about to exceed their CO_2 quota may purchase additional emission allowances. By creating CO_2 scarcity through the ETS system, the EU aims to reduce in absolute terms the total emissions in its member states. The EU views the ETS system as the cornerstone of its climate policy and as an important tool to cost-effectively limit CO_2 emissions.[72]

With this regulatory backdrop in mind, the Court then takes into consideration RDS's interests as follows:

> Given the emissions reduction targets of the ETS system, RDS can rest assured that the interests to be taken into account, which are also at issue in these proceedings, were fully and correctly weighed by the issuing body/bodies when the emission allowances were issued. It concerns the reduction target strived for with the ETS system. To that extent, the ETS system has an indemnifying effect. The indemnifying effect of the ETS system means that—insofar as it concerns the reduction target of the ETS system—RDS does not have an additional obligation with respect to Scope 1 and 2 emissions in the EU that fall under the system. Those are Scope 1 emissions of the Shell group in the EU and the Scope 3 emissions in the EU of the end-users of the products produced and sold by the Shell group, which are covered by the ETS system—as Scope 1 emissions of the consumers. However, the ETS system only affects a part of the CO_2 emissions for which RDS is responsible. Furthermore, the ETS system only applies in the EU, while global Scope 3 emissions influence the dangerous climate change in the Netherlands and the Wadden region. *Finally, the reduction target of the ETS system is not identical to RDS' reduction obligation. Insofar as RDS' reduction obligation extends beyond the reduction target of the ETS system, RDS will have to fulfil its individual obligation. RDS cannot rely on the indemnifying effect of the ETS system insofar as this system entails a less far-reaching reduction target than a net reduction of the CO2 emissions (Scope 1 through to 3), relative to 2019, for the Shell group.*[73]

71 Ibid.
72 Ibid.
73 Ibid., para. 4.4.46. (citation omitted, emphasis added)

Lastly, the Court also addresses the responsibility of states and society as a constructive part of the standard due of care principle. Embarking from RDS's account on the nature of public-private engagement in tackling climate change, arguing that "government policy is needed to bring about the required change of the energy market,"[74] the Court nonetheless does not validate such a view. As a sort of movement differentiating collective legal responsibility, the Court maintains that

> From the passage in the Oxford report, cited by RDS, it follows that public-private partnership and the division of responsibility among the various actors are points of attention. There is general consensus on this. *This issue, the not-disputed responsibility of other parties and the uncertainty whether states and society as a whole will manage to achieve the goals of the Paris Agreement, do not absolve RDS of its individual responsibility regarding the significant emissions over which it has control and influence.* There is also broad international consensus that each company must independently work towards the goal of net zero emissions by 2050. *Due to the compelling interests which are served with the reduction obligation, RDS must do its part with respect to the emissions over it has control and influence. It is an individual responsibility that falls on RDS, of which much may be expected.* Therefore, RDS must do more than monitoring developments in society and complying with the regulations in the countries where the Shell group operates. There is broad international consensus that it is imperative for non-state actors to contribute to emissions reduction and for companies to have an individual responsibility to achieve the reduction targets. *RDS' responsibility differs as regards* (a) *the Shell group (obligation of results) and* (b) *the business relations of the Shell group (significant best-efforts obligation). This subdivision shows that RDS is not the only party that is held responsible for curbing dangerous climate change in the Netherlands and the Wadden region; the solution to this problem is not passed on to RDS alone. However, RDS does bear an individual responsibility, which it can and must effectuate through its corporate policy for the Shell group.*[75]

To this end, since RDS bears a distinct responsibility to reduce emissions, there should be a further assessment by the Court regarding the level of consequences of doing so. That is, the Court also put into consideration the onerousness of RDS and the Shell group to meet the reduction obligation, specifically because RDS makes an argument that "imposing a reduction

74 Ibid., para. 4.4.51.
75 Ibid., para. 4.4.52. (emphasis added)

obligation on [RDS] will lead to unfair competition and a disruption of the 'level playing field' on the oil and gas market."[76] The Court confirms that

> the reduction obligation will have far-reaching consequences for RDS and the Shell group. *The reduction obligation requires a change of policy, which will require an adjustment of the Shell group's energy package.* This could curb the potential growth of the Shell group.[77]

However, the Court argues, and this indicates a kind of problem restatement of intuitive reasoning, that

> the interest served with the reduction obligation outweighs the Shell group's commercial interests, which for their part are served with an uncurtailed preservation or even growth of these activities. Due to the serious threats and risks to the human rights of Dutch residents and the inhabitants of the Wadden region, private companies such as RDS may also be required to take drastic measures and make financial sacrifices to limit CO_2 emissions to prevent dangerous climate change. For these reasons, RDS' argument, namely that accepting the reduction obligation, as advocated by Milieudefensie et al., is highly unusual and has no precedent, does not benefit RDS.[78]

Milieudefensie shows how intuitive reasoning extracts the essence of climate responsibility practice. Or, to put it in the Bergson-Deleuzian sense, the Court has stated and resolved the collective legal responsibility "in terms of time instead of space." That said, the inquiry into climate change responsibility practice was being framed under the time-mindful legal relations grounded on (1) historical worsening and (2) perpetual blameworthiness. The two features are embedded in the Court's structure of argument as follows. The justification of climate responsibility practice is mainly shown by the Court's attention to the multiplicity of the worsening lived experiences associated with climate crisis. Upon a closer look into *Milieudefensie*, the Court quite frequently highlights what they call the 'seriousness and irreversibility' of climate change consequences. Specifically in the Netherlands and the Wadden Region, the consequences of CO_2 emissions are depicted as follows:

> The temperature rise in the Netherlands (approximately 1.7 degrees above the pre- industrial temperature) has so far developed about twice as fast as the global average (approximately 0.8 degrees above the pre-industrial

76 Ibid., para. 4.4.53. (emphasis added)
77 Ibid.
78 Ibid. (citation omitted, emphasis added)

> temperature). The climate change caused by CO_2 emissions will have serious and irreversible consequences for the Netherlands and the Wadden region. The risks for Dutch residents and the inhabitants of the Wadden region are apparent from various sources. The IPCC reports are not specifically focused on the Netherlands. *The fact that these reports do not mention certain risks for Dutch residents and the inhabitants of the Wadden region, as put forward by RDS, does not mean that these risks do not exist. The risks associated with climate change for Dutch residents and the inhabitants of the Wadden region concern health risks and deaths due to climate change-induced hot spells as well as health problems and an increased mortality risk due to increasing infectious diseases, deterioration of air quality, increase of UV exposure, and an increase of water-related and foodborne diseases. They also concern water-related health risks, which the Netherlands and the Wadden region will face, including flooding along the coast and rivers, excess water, water shortage, deterioration of water quality, salinization, raised water levels and drought.* Although the consequences of climate change and the associated risks for the inhabitants of the Wadden region may turn out differently from the risks for Dutch and other residents because the effect of accelerated sea level rise will be limited and hardly noticeable in the Wadden region up to 2030, climate change will equally have serious and irreversible consequences for the inhabitants of the Wadden region; in the more extreme scenarios this area will drown completely in the long term.[79]

That being the case, the consequence of CO_2 emissions is not construed as *causality* but rather as *co-relation*. It reflects, as we have addressed, the 'distinctive causal field' of climate justice. It follows that the court emphasizes the right to life and the right to respect for the private and family lives of Dutch residents and the inhabitants of the Wadden region. According to the claimants,

> [t]hese rights enshrined in Articles 2 and 8 of the European Convention for the Protection of Human Rights and Fundamental Freedoms (ECHR) and Articles 6 and 17 of the International Covenant on Civil and Political Rights (ICCPR) apply in relationships between states and citizens.[80]

However, the court suggests that it "cannot directly invoke these human rights with respect to RDS."[81] Interestingly, the court notes that

> [d]ue to the fundamental interest of human rights and the value for society as a whole they embody, the human rights may play a role in the relationship between Milieudefensie et al. and RDS. Therefore, the court will

79 Ibid., para. 4.4.6. (citation omitted, emphasis added)
80 Ibid., para. 4.4.9.
81 Ibid.

> factor in the human rights and the values they embody in its interpretation of the unwritten standard of care.[82]

Additionally, by referring this claim to *Urgenda*, the court deduces that "Articles 2 and 8 ECHR offer protection against the consequences of dangerous climate change due to CO_2 emissions induced global warming."[83]

To support the premises regarding the applicability of human rights norms in the case, in interpreting the standard of due care principle, the court makes reference to the United Nations Guiding Principles on Business and Human Rights (UNGP). In this context, UNGP can be seen as a source of corporate responsibility. However, the court maintains the urge to clarify some caveats of this reference, explicating the different nature of state and corporate responsibility under the UNGP. The court opines that

> [t]he responsibility of business enterprises to respect human rights, as formulated in the UNGP, is a global standard of expected conduct for all business enterprises wherever they operate. It exists independently of States' abilities and/or willingness to fulfil their own human rights obligations, and does not diminish those obligations. And it exists over and above compliance with national laws and regulations protecting human rights. Therefore, it is not enough for companies to monitor developments and follow the measures states take; they have an individual responsibility.[84]

Through this argument, we can see the way the court's narrative of climate crisis encounter (as the *object* of corporate legal responsibility) gives way to an examination of human rights norms (as the *ground* of corporate legal responsibility). More specifically, what we are seeing here is that the court's intuition about responsibility practice is fundamentally tied to coherence in a temporally extended social life. To support this claim, let us follow the court's subsequent preponderance related to corporate human rights responsibility:

> The responsibility of business enterprises to respect human rights applies to all enterprises regardless of their size, sector, operational context, ownership and structure. Nevertheless, the scale and complexity of the means through which enterprises meet that responsibility may vary according to these factors and with the severity of the enterprise's adverse human rights impacts. The means through which a business enterprise meets its responsibility to respect human rights will be proportional to, among other factors, its size. Severity of impacts will be judged by their scale, scope and irremediable character. The means through which a business enterprise meets its responsibility to respect human rights may also vary depending

82 Ibid., para. 4.4.10.
83 Ibid.
84 Ibid., para. 4.4.13. (citation omitted)

> on whether, and the extent to which, it conducts business through a corporate group or individually. *The court is of the opinion that much may be expected of RDS. RDS heads the Shell group, which consists of about 1,100 companies, and operates in 160 countries all over the world. It has a policy-setting position in the Shell group, which is a major player on the worldwide market of fossil fuels and is responsible for significant CO_2 emissions, which exceed the emissions of many states and which contributes towards global warming and a dangerous climate change in the Netherlands and in the Wadden region with serious and irreversible consequences and risks for the human rights of Dutch residents and the inhabitants of the Wadden region.*[85]

This passage critically suggests that corporate legal responsibility for climate change is perceived through an *extension* of the past (memory) to the perception of the present and expectation of the future. In that regard, such an extension requires the court to be attentive to changes not only on the wrongdoer's (i.e., the company's) part, but it also takes into account *how* such changes took place. This can be clearly shown by another stance of temporalities considered by the court in drawing the effectiveness of the reduction obligation arguments. In this context, the court submits that

> RDS argues that the reduction obligation will have no effect, or even be counterproductive, because the place of the Shell group will be taken by competitors. Even if this were true, it will not benefit RDS. *Due to the compelling interests which are served with the reduction obligation, this argument cannot justify assuming beforehand there is no need for RDS to not meet this obligation.* It is also important here that each reduction of greenhouse gas emissions has a positive effect on countering dangerous climate change. After all, each reduction means that there is more room in the carbon budget. The court acknowledges that RDS cannot solve this global problem on its own. However, this does not absolve RDS of its individual partial responsibility to do its part regarding the emissions of the Shell group, which it can control and influence.
>
> The question also is whether this argument of RDS is actually valid. What this argument assumes is perfect substitution, whereby the place of the Shell group will be taken over one-on-one by other parties. However, it remains to be seen whether this circumstance will transpire. This cannot necessarily be deduced from the examples given by RDS or from the Mulder report submitted by RDS. The examples date from before the Paris Agreement. Therefore, it cannot automatically be assumed that it will be the same, now or in the future. The Mulder report also seems to

85 Ibid., para. 4.4.16. (citation omitted, emphasis added)

> be a snapshot. The Mulder report also only seems to start from a 'business as usual' scenario and not from other scenarios, in which other oil and gas companies also limit their investments in oil and gas, voluntarily, under pressure, or due to retreating investors, or as sustainable methods of energy generation become available worldwide, in the aim to meet the targets of the Paris Agreement. Other companies also have to respect human rights. Finally, the Mulder report does not take account of the causal relationship between production limitation and emission reduction.[86]

Therefore, it follows from the irreducibility of corporate climate change responsibility that such responsibility practices cannot be *measured* in terms of comparison between the more and the less. Corporate climate responsibility is made concrete and is treated as a singularity. The Court's following examination on the proportionality of RDS's reduction obligation is a clear description of such singularity:

> The court has included the proportionality of the reduction obligation in its interpretation of the unwritten standard of care. Proportionality has been discussed before, in the context of various sub-topics. The court considers that the CO_2 emissions for which RDS can be held responsible by their nature pose a very serious threat, with a high risk of damage to Dutch residents and the inhabitants of the Wadden region and with serious human rights impacts. This applies to both current and future generations. *A characteristic feature of dangerous climate change is that every emission of CO2 and other greenhouse gases, anywhere in the world and caused in whatever manner, contributes to this development. In turn, each reduction of greenhouse gas emissions positively contributes to countering dangerous climate. After all, each reduction means that there is more room in the carbon budget. RDS is able to effectuate a reduction by changing its energy package. This all justifies a reduction obligation concerning the policy formation by RDS for the entire, globally operating Shell group*. The compelling common interest that is served by complying with the reduction obligation outweighs the negative consequences RDS might face due to the reduction obligation and also the commercial interests of the Shell group, which are served by an uncurtailed preservation or even increase of CO_2-generating activities. Due to the serious threats and risks to the human rights of Dutch residents and the inhabitants of the Wadden region, private companies such as RDS may also be required to take drastic measures and make financial sacrifices to limit CO_2 emissions to prevent dangerous climate change. RDS has total freedom to comply with its reduction obligation as it sees fit, and to shape the corporate policy of

86 Ibid., paras. 4.4.49–4.4.50. (citation omitted)

> the Shell group at its own discretion. The court notes here that a 'global' reduction obligation, which affects the policy of the entire Shell group, gives RDS much more freedom of action than a reduction obligation limited to a particular territory or a business unit or units.[87]

To this end, what does the case tell us about intuitive judicial reasoning? And where does judicial intuition in time lead the conversation about environmental justice—if there is any such trend or direction? To recall, intuition in this study is viewed as part of reasoning method performed by judges in selecting justifying reasons against the problem of judicial cognitive dilemma. This dilemma, reflected in the problem of uncertainty of climate injustice, necessitates a certain mode of thinking for judges when creating and crafting forms of lawful relations, taking into account their epistemic justification of temporal experience of climate injustice.[88] It is undoubtedly the case that some scholars have clearly challenged this relatively broad and flexible judicial environmentalism.[89] However, as the present chapter has suggested, what is essential from this type of reasoning is the court's attention to time as duration. That is, the experience of climate injustice are made conceivable because judges gain knowledge about the unjust climate crisis through their own (internal) sense of empathy rather than objectified reason.[90] Based

87 Ibid., para. 4.4.54. (emphasis added)

88 Lucy Maxwell, Sarah Mead, and Dennis van Berkel, "Standards for Adjudicating the Next Generation of Urgenda-Style Climate Cases," *Journal of Human Rights and the Environment* 13, no. 1 (2022): 35–63; Bookman, "Catalytic Climate Litigation: Rights and Statutes"; Zhu, "The 'Bitcoin Judgements' in China: Promoting Climate Awareness by Judicial Reasoning?"

89 Katalin Sulyok, "Science, Epistemology and Legitimacy in Environmental Disputes—The Epistemically Legitimate Judicial Argumentative Space," *Leiden Journal of International Law* (2023): 1–28, https://doi.org/10.1017/S0922156523000559. According to Sulyok, "Direct engagement with scientific rationality may not be possible in every case, given the time and monetary constraints of legal proceedings. This gives rise to a need for finding epistemic substitutes for scientific authority. Adjudicators in such cases sometimes turn to everyday knowledge and reason using intuitive rationality. Everyday experience may inform the selection of relevant information forming the premises of the judicial decision. With such a reasoning style, courts can bypass the detailed inferential processes necessary to evaluate the merits of scientific arguments." 15. (citation omitted) As a matter of fact, I think the problem of most critiques of intuitive reasoning is on the approximation of intuition and common sense.

90 For further analysis on the intersection between climate change and transitional justice, see Sonja Klinsky and Jasmina Brankovic, *The Global Climate Regime and Transitional Justice* (New York: Routledge, 2018), Chap. 4. Specifically, they argue that the imaginative tension between narratives in climate change is critical for questions of "justice and transformation." 159. Furthermore, they maintain, "[w]e can tell a convergent climate change story that focuses on the potential for climate change to threaten all humanity and on the resulting need for universal collective action. Because greenhouse gas emissions are so intimately embedded in every aspect of our lives, any sufficient response to this story would necessarily

on the structure of the court's previous argumentation, we may confirm that empathic intuition is valuable for judges to generate (1) an untimely inquiry into climate injustice, and (2) coherence that governs temporal patterns of climate crisis—based on which corporate's climate responsibility attains social purposes over time.

Reference list

Agyeman, Julian, David Schlosberg, Luke Craven, and Caitlin Matthews. "Trends and Directions in Environmental Justice: From Inequity to Everyday Life, Community, and Just Sustainabilities." *Annual Review of Environment and Resources* 41 (2016): 321–40.

Armeni, Chiara. "Narratives as Tools of Legal Re-Imagination in the Climate Crisis." *Journal of Environmental Law* 33, no. 2 (2021): 485–94.

Backes, C. W. Chris, and G. A. Gerrit van der Veen. "Urgenda: The Final Judgment of the Dutch Supreme Court." *Journal for European Environmental & Planning Law* 17, no. 3 (2020): 307–21.

Bookman, Sam. "Catalytic Climate Litigation: Rights and Statutes." *Oxford Journal of Legal Studies* 43, no. 3 (2023): 598–628. https://doi.org/10.1093/ojls/gqad011.

Fernandes, Alison. *The Temporal Asymmetry of Causation*. Cambridge, UK: Cambridge University Press, 2023.

Ghosh, Amitav. *The Great Derangement: Climate Change and the Unthinkable*. London: The University of Chicago Press, 2016.

Graaf, Kars J. de, and Jan H. Jans. "The Urgenda Decision: Netherlands Liable for Role in Causing Dangerous Global Climate Change." *Journal of Environmental Law* 27, no. 3 (2015): 517–27.

Hilson, Chris. "Framing Time in Climate Change Litigation." *Oñati Socio-Legal Series, Forthcoming* 9, no. 3 (2019): 361–79.

Hughes, David McDermott. "A Climate Strategy of Last Resort." *Boston Review*. Accessed October 5, 2023. www.bostonreview.net/articles/a-climate-strategy-of-last-resort/?utm_source=Boston+Review+Email+Subscribers&utm_campaign=fbf3a68a02-newsletter_5_10_23&utm_medium=email&utm_term=0_2cb428c5ad-fbf3a68a02-41296216&mc_cid=fbf3a68a02&mc_eid=3b5256212e.

Kelleher, Orla. "Incorporating Climate Justice into Legal Reasoning: Shifting towards a Risk-Based Approach to Causation in Climate Litigation." *Journal of Human Rights and the Environment* 13, no. 1 (2022): 290–317.

Klinsky, Sonja, and Jasmina Brankovic. *The Global Climate Regime and Transitional Justice*. New York: Routledge, 2018.

Lefebvre, Alexandre. *The Image of Law: Deleuze, Bergson, Spinoza*. Stanford: Stanford University Press, 2008.

be transformational to core social, economic, and technological systems. We can also tell a divergent climate change story that takes as its starting point profound inequalities in human well-being and then interrogates where these inequalities came from and how climate change will intersect with them. This story points us in a different direction, but one that is no less transformational. This story suggests a rethinking of the underlying norms and economic arrangements that have resulted in patterned and profound inequalities within and among countries." Ibid.

Maxwell, Lucy, Sarah Mead, and Dennis van Berkel. “Standards for Adjudicating the Next Generation of Urgenda-Style Climate Cases.” *Journal of Human Rights and the Environment* 13, no. 1 (2022): 35–63.

Minnerop, Petra, and Friederike Otto. “Climate Change and Causation: Joining Law and Climate Science on the Basis of Formal Logic.” *Buffalo Environmental Law Journal* 27, no. 1 (2019): 49.

Morton, Timothy. *Hyperobjects: Philosophy and Ecology after the End of the World*. Minneapolis & London: University of Minnesota Press, 2013.

Norgaard, Kari Marie. “The Sociological Imagination in a Time of Climate Change.” *Global and Planetary Change* 163 (2018): 171–76.

Norman, Jana. *Posthuman Legal Subjectivity: Reimagining the Human in the Anthropocene*. Oxon & New York: Routledge, 2022.

Otto, Friederike E. L., Sjoukje Philip, Sarah Kew, Sihan Li, Andrew King, and Heidi Cullen. “Attributing High-Impact Extreme Events across Timescales—a Case Study of Four Different Types of Events.” *Climatic Change* 149 (2018): 399–412.

Paiement, Phillip. “Urgent Agenda: How Climate Litigation Builds Transnational Narratives.” In *Transnational Environmental Law in the Anthropocene: Transnational Environmental Law in the Anthropocene Reflections on the Role of Law in Times of Planetary Change*, edited by Emily Webster and Laura Mai, 121–43. London: Routledge, 2021. https://doi.org/10.4324/9781003152590.

Palazuelos, Felix Rebolledo, Tania Galli Fonseca, and Andreia Machado Oliveira. “A Philosophical Perspective on Intuition as a Method within Artistic Process.” *Studies in Visual Arts and Communication: An International Journal* 5, no. 1 (2018): 1–11.

Posner, Eric A., and Cass R. Sunstein. “Climate Change Justice.” *Georgetown Law Journal* 96 (2008): 1565.

Posner, Eric A., and David Weisbach. *Climate Change Justice*. Princeton: Princeton University Press, 2010.

Rechtbank Den Haag. Milieudefensie v. Royal Dutch Shell, Plc (2021).

Rogers, Nicole. “Beyond Reason: Activism and Law in a Time of Climate Change.” *Journal for the Study of Radicalism* 12, no. 2 (2018): 157–82.

Rogers, Nicole. *Law, Fiction and Activism in a Time of Climate Change*. Routledge, 2019.

Setzer, Joana, and Catherine Higham. *Global Trends in Climate Change Litigation: 2022 Snapshot*. London: Grantham Research Institute on Climate Change and the Environment and Centre for Climate Change Economics and Policy, London School of Economics and Political Science, 2022.

Stuart-Smith, Rupert F., Friederike E. L. Otto, Aisha I. Saad, Gaia Lisi, Petra Minnerop, Kristian Cedervall Lauta, Kristin van Zwieten, and Thom Wetzer. “Filling the Evidentiary Gap in Climate Litigation.” *Nature Climate Change* 11, no. 8 (2021): 651–55.

Sulyok, Katalin. “Science, Epistemology and Legitimacy in Environmental Disputes—The Epistemically Legitimate Judicial Argumentative Space.” *Leiden Journal of International Law* (2023): 1–28. https://doi.org/10.1017/S0922156523000559.

Taebi, Behnam, Jan H. Kwakkel, and Céline Kermisch. “Governing Climate Risks in the Face of Normative Uncertainties.” *Wiley Interdisciplinary Reviews: Climate Change* 11, no. 5 (2020): e666.

Weaver, R. Henry, and Douglas A. Kysar. “Courting Disaster: Climate Change and the Adjudication of Catastrophe.” *Notre Dame Law Review* 93 (2017): 295–356.

Zahar, Alexander. “Human Rights Law and the Obligation to Reduce Greenhouse Gas Emissions.” *Human Rights Review* 23, no. 3 (2022): 385–411.

Zahar, Alexander. "The Missing Relational Element in Tort Cases on Greenhouse Gas Emissions." *Climate Law* 12, no. 3–4 (2022): 216–41.

Zhu, Mingzhe. "The 'Bitcoin Judgements' in China: Promoting Climate Awareness by Judicial Reasoning?" *Review of European, Comparative & International Environmental Law* 32, no. 1 (2023): 158–62.

Part II

An epistemology of historical injustice adjudication

Questioning *how* legal decision-makers justify their conclusions in legal cases has been one of the major objects of inquiry in legal studies. One has to concede, however, that legal adjudication process is not an easy task. On many occasions, legal decision-makers are hesitant, doubtful and even bewildered. The daunting process of adjudication, so to speak, is always situated under the judge's epistemic capacity. Moreover, institutional pressures expect them to resolve matters according to the institutional rules and deficits—up to a point where these may become institutional memories, to borrow from Siegel.[1] The judges' alignment and compromise force them to run the machinery of adjudication through an objective and rational measurement. Nevertheless, as our case-studies in Part I have suggested, this kind of objective measurement cannot be adequately achieved (or, in our part, evaluated) through some formulaic modes of reasoning—e.g., one may refer to statutory interpretation, analogy, public policy-oriented argument or principle and custom based-reasoning, or, talking about *-isms* in legal reasoning, one can point out formalism, analogy or realism.

Three points stand out at the moment to reflect our findings in Part I. *First*, transition (Chapter 1), trauma (Chapter 2) and uncertainty (Chapter 3) are subject-matters that prompt judges' hesitation, doubts or even bewilderment. These narratives insist on the judges to encounter the passage of time as an object to reason about. The three narratives compel judges to reconsider how and to what extent law and legal reasoning interact with the elusive idea of time and temporality. *Second*, transition, trauma and uncertainty are arguably the underlying phenomena of expectable mass human suffering—as reflected in our case studies, we have seen three inquiries of racial discrimination, post-colonial extractivism and climate crisis. In these narratives, the judges encounter the unexpected, something that is distinct from their past encounters. *Third*, by examining transition, trauma and uncertainty we have

1 Reva Siegel, "The Politics of Constitutional Memory," *Georgetown Journal of Law & Public Policy* 20, no. 1 (2022): 19–58.

DOI: 10.4324/9781003518693-6

thus far arrived at a novel perspective on how to understand the process of legal reasoning and how the practice of judgment is capable of capturing the multiplicity of lived experiences resulting from past injustices. Arguably, this methodological approach is one of the contributions of intuition to the ethics of adjudicative reasoning, from which judges can perceivably capture (or even disrupt!) persistent injustices at a micro-level.

Building on these findings, Part II embarks on the questions: what does intuitive judgment tell us about legal reasoning and the temporalities of injustice? And how should judges, within their epistemic capacity, understand legal inquiry and collective responsibility in historical injustice adjudication? In this part, we will examine (and somehow reconstruct) an epistemological dimension of historical injustice adjudication. It stands on a basic premise that if temporalities are inherent in legal reasoning, there should be an alternative way of explaining how judges understand legal inquiry and collective responsibility in historical injustice adjudication. Part II thus seeks to draw an alternative framework for *what* and *how* judges know about historical injustice adjudication through the lens of legal temporalities. As briefly mentioned in the introductory chapter, temporalities play a fundamental role in conceptualizing the judges' reasoning process that guides them in finding and selecting any justifying reasons. As a follow up, in Chapter 4 we will initially sketch a phenomenological understanding of legal decision-making as an internal experience that is always evolving and in the process of becoming. Suffice it to say that, as our case-studies have also suggested, a discussion about temporalities brings to the fore the significance of judicial intuition in guiding judges to infer their conclusion from the multiplicity of experiences of injustice. In this regard, we will later claim that judicial intuition is valuable for judges in selecting justifying reasons insofar as it allows them to signal creative and experimental legal inquiries into the multiplicity of experiences of injustice (Chapter 6). As a result, legal techniques and concepts employed by intuitive judges, as part of their reasoning procedure, are *processed* virtually through intuition, which is seen as an immediate method that conflates the modalities of time (i.e., the past, present and future of injustice). This proposition will be fundamental for us in building an (alternative) epistemology of historical injustice adjudication which is comprised of untimely legal inquiry (Chapter 5) and time-mindful legal responsibility (Chapter 7).

Chapter 4

Legal reasoning as a creative process

As contemporary legal systems develop over time, theories explaining judicial reasoning simultaneously flourish to inform and shape legal institutions. In our common understanding, legal practitioners grasp legal reasoning as rule-based argumentation: any conclusions are drawn primarily from what a given rule says about a certain fact pattern. Such a deductive logic is what we often call mechanical reasoning. It focuses on the semantic meaning and linguistic interpretation of legal texts and expressions. However, this kind of approach is not adequate to be applied in all types of cases, specifically when it is shown by the plurality of solutions to the so-called 'hard' cases. As a result, some argue that legal reasoning should rather be dialectical in nature. In this sense, legal reasoning is not exclusively deduced from rules because any reasoner must also be attentive to the context of the argument at hand. Rather than focusing on the semantic meaning of rules, the dialectical approach emphasizes the pragmatic element of legal terms in a communicative context. To contrast, the mechanical encompasses the individual, rational agent pursuing personal goals, while the dialectical embraces the collective features of agents and goals.

As part of this study's main objective—i.e., to formulate the methodological underpinning toward the active feature of adjudicative judgment in capturing the multiplicity of experiences of past injustices—we need to initially instill the concept of legal reasoning that serves as the foundation for our later analysis. In doing so, this chapter attempts to synthesize the ground for a temporal approach to legal reasoning. This ground is based on the following theoretical propositions: *First*, legal reasoning is a justification for the representation of the virtual into the actual. It should be understood as a process of justification based on a scheme of intelligibility applied by legal decision-makers (i.e., judges) in a legal case that represents the virtuality of norms and facts in the actual case. *Second*, legal reasoning is a process of unfolding practical reasons. This view helps us draw on the phenomenological understanding of legal decision-making as an internal experience that is always evolving and in the process of becoming. *Third*, legal time-mindfulness asserts a temporal ontological foundation of law and

DOI: 10.4324/9781003518693-7

legal reasoning. In this respect, we would be able to address some reflective deliberations and transformative potentials of legal reasoning *within* a community over time.[1] By juxtaposing this series of theoretical propositions, we may infer three main claims from this chapter: (1) legal reasoning as a *process* of justification based on a scheme of intelligibility that represents the virtuality of norms and facts into the actual;[2] (2) the representation of the virtual into the actual essentially signifies that time is *inherent* in law and legal reasoning and (3) such temporality *in* legal reasoning is fundamental in recognizing the role of experience in facilitating judges' creative mind and transformative capacity.

Legal reasoning as justification of the virtual

Does legal reasoning *actually* exist? If so, is it value-based or is it merely instrumental? Are legal norms and principles determining factors in judicial decision-making? On the contrary, if it does not exist, what would it say about law's epistemology and method? These questions have been pervasive in debates and conversations among legal theorists, and admittedly, addressing them requires a detailed and comprehensive analysis. For the purpose of the present chapter, our response to these questions can be concluded by capturing the (de-)mystifying legal reasoning arguments between the two opposing claims, that is, on the one hand theorists claiming that legal reasoning is a special kind of (practical) reasoning with its own subject matter, and on the other hand those who declare that such a reasoning is not a special kind of reasoning since it is simply similar to other kinds of practical reasoning. This section specifically highlights the conversation between Alexander and Sherwin's *Demystifying Legal Reasoning* and Geoffrey Samuel's rebuttal of this demystification project. From the (de-)mystification conversation, we later argue that in the context of this study, legal reasoning should be grasped

1 Drucilla L. Cornell, "Institutionalization of Meaning, Recollective Imagination and the Potential for Transformative Legal Interpretation," *University of Pennsylvania Law Review* 136 (1987): 1135–229; Maksymilian Del Mar, "On the Hinges of History: For a Relational Legal Historiography," in *Searching for Contemporary Legal Thought*, ed. Justin Desautels-Stein and Christopher Tomlins (Cambridge, UK: Cambridge University Press, 2017), 61–79. Notably, Cornell argued that legal interpretation should be understood as recollective imagination.

2 Note that 'representation' here is not to be understood as merely an image but also an activity (of staging and performing the law). See Shaunnagh Dorsett and Shaun McVeigh, *Jurisdiction* (Oxon & New York: Routledge, 2012); Edward Mussawir, *Jurisdiction in Deleuze: The Expression and Representation of Law* (London: Routledge, 2011), 138–39. In this regard, Mussawir suggests from a Deleuzian point of view that jurisdiction is a matter of expression rather than representation. Expression, he argues, rather accommodates the active feature of jurisdiction by which the procedure of jurisdiction constitutes creativity and innovation of the practice of judgment. To avoid further confusions, however, this study will use the terms representation and expression interchangeably.

as a *process* of justification based on a scheme of intelligibility applied in an actual case, which represents the virtuality of norms, principles and facts.

The demystifying legal reasoning argument claims that "legal reasoning is ordinary reasoning applied to legal problems."[3] It is basically a rejection of lawyer's traditional understanding of how they do their work; for instance, judges are applying deductive reasoning or case-based analogy in order to justify rules based on facts in a given case. It denies the presumption that how to think like a lawyer is indeed a lawyer's special (or different) "mastery of an array of talents in argument and decision-making."[4] According to the demystification claim, such a specialty (or difference) is not necessarily special at all to any other reasoners in decision-making contexts. Instead of grasping their way of thinking as a specialized form of reasoning, lawyers rather "explain these techniques as ingrained practices that may have instrumental value for imperfect reasoners."[5] Simply put, according to Alexander and Sherwin, legal reasoning is nothing more than "ordinary moral, empirical, and deductive reasoning."[6]

Suggested by common law practices, the demystification view considers a problem in legal decision-making, in which "courts often insist that they are reasoning in ways that we say they are not."[7] This view maintains that courts in practice are facing a series of epistemic knowledge and institutional constraints based on which the judges are apparently not applying certain judicial techniques as decision-making tools, but rather, their reasoning is seen as "indirect strategies to avoid the disadvantages that judges face in their dual capacities as adjudicators and lawmakers."[8] Moreover, this view demonstrates that analogy, known to be a lawyer's basic way of thinking in a case, is not a form of reasoning, since it can be explained in terms of rule-based reasoning. Alexander and Sherwin claim that

> there is no such thing as analogical decision making, case to case. Judges who resolve disputes by analogy either are acting on a perception of similarity that is purely intuitive and therefore unreasoned and unconstrained, or they are formulating and applying rules of similarity through ordinary modes of reasoning. To the extent that judges base analogies on "legal

3 Larry Alexander and Emily Sherwin, *Demystifying Legal Reasoning* (New York: Cambridge University Press, 2008), 3.

4 Frederick Schauer, *Thinking Like a Lawyer: A New Introduction to Legal Reasoning* (Cambridge, MA & London: Harvard University Press, 2009), 1; Shidarta, *Multisentrisme Humaniora Digital: Filsafat Hukum Masa Depan Dan Masa Depan Filsafat Hukum* (Jakarta: Universitas Bina Nusantara, 2022).

5 Alexander and Sherwin, *Demystifying Legal Reasoning*, 4.

6 Ibid., 130.

7 Ibid., 4.

8 Ibid.

> principles," the principles on which they rely either are indistinguishable from moral principles or are nonsensical constructs designed to accommodate morally incorrect prior results. "Interpretations" of legal texts that deviate from the lawmaker's intent are not interpretations, but independent exercises of lawmaking authority.
>
> *Judges, in other words, have no special decision-making tools. To answer legal questions, they must either follow rules posited by others or rely on ordinary moral and empirical reasoning to reach their own conclusions.* Their "craft" consists, at best, of their knowledge of posited rules and legal procedures, their familiarity with the reasoning of past judges on questions of social importance, and a set of conventional practices that enlarge their perspective beyond the exigencies of the case before them and incline them to caution in making rules and altering established law.[9]

Contrary to this view, Geoffrey Samuel argues that the demystification claim falls short in its understanding of ordinary and empirical reasoning.[10] Legal reasoning is not only a matter of induction, deduction or analogy. Against Alexander and Sherwin's view claiming that analogy is a method of searching for similarities, Samuel argues that analogy is "about the extension of relations between objects in one domain to objects in another domain."[11] In this sense, reasoning operates in terms of factual images being constructed by the court in a legal case. That is, he claims, "the reasoning functions at the level of factual image and the decision arrived at by the judge flows by way of analogy from the way this factual image was constructed by the reasoner."[12]

As a scientific reasoning method, the way lawyers think involves a more complex epistemological network with a scheme of intelligibility, structure and paradigms. And, still according to Samuel and considering the incomplete argument posed by Alexander and Sherwin, such epistemological networks are as necessary as the general analysis and synthesis reasoning. To support this claim, three arguments should be highlighted here, namely about the applicability of schemes of intelligibility, the relationship between the virtual and the actual and the lawyer's paradigm orientation.

Let us first observe what we mean by *the schemes of intelligibility* of legal reasoning. The schemes can be described simply as the way judges perceive the factual image of a case. Samuel borrows the schemes of intelligibility from a French science epistemologist, J. Berthelot, who identified six schemes

9 Ibid., 234. (emphasis added)
10 Geoffrey Samuel, "Can Legal Reasoning Be Demystified?" *Legal Studies* 29, no. 2 (2009): 181–210; Geoffrey Samuel, *Epistemology and Method in Law* (London & New York: Routledge, 2016).
11 Samuel, "Can Legal Reasoning Be Demystified?" 189.
12 Ibid., 190.

in scientific inquiry, including causality, functionalism, structuralism, hermeneutics, actionalism and dialectics. A brief description of each scheme is as follows:

a. The causal scheme simply means that fact A causes fact B to happen, and without fact A, fact B would not exist;
b. The functional scheme shows that reasoners (i.e., judges) take fact A into account in terms of its function, which is fact B;
c. The structural scheme demonstrates that "one fact (A) results from a system of relations with other facts (facts B, C and so on) in which the fact A is not only an element in the structure but is also defined by its relationship with the other facts (A, B, etc.);"[13]
d. The hermeneutical analysis captures a deeper relationship between facts, that is, fact A (the signifier) signifies fact B (the signified);
e. An actional scheme construes images of facts based on the construction of individual actors and their mental attitude;
f. Last, the dialectical scheme understands that one fact A is the resultant of contradictory images of facts ('fact B versus fact B').

Samuel then applies these epistemological schemes to the analysis of legal reasoning in such a way that we are actually attempting to *understand* as much as *explain* the way judges think. He contends that "[o]ne is not talking here of searching out rules of law and mechanically applying them to a set of facts in a syllogistic fashion."[14] Instead, as he furthermore asserts,

> [t]he importance of these schemes is the way they 'insert' themselves so to speak within the actual facts and thus, depending on the scheme being employed, construct a factual situation which of itself suggests the legal result that ought to follow.[15]

What is important at this point, at a metaphysical level, is the refutation of the idea of separation between the world of rules and the world of facts that the demystification project claims. In that sense, Alexander and Sherwin argue for the autonomy of rules as a reason for agents to act, and that these rules "pick out the important features of individual cases."[16] Samuel, however, insists on the inseparability of rules and facts, because in a legal case the latter (fact pattern) and the former (rules) are mediated through the schemes of intelligibility. He furthermore claims that the problem of rule

13 Ibid., 194.
14 Ibid., 195.
15 Ibid.
16 Alexander and Sherwin, *Demystifying Legal Reasoning*, 22.

indeterminacy and the ambiguity of interpretation are all "differences in how the facts are perceived as a result of the differing schemes of intelligibility."[17] That being said, it can be inferred that, following Samuel, "it is the way facts are perceived via schemes of intelligibility (and as will be seen, institutional structures and paradigm orientations) that pick out the important features of rules."[18]

Second, another important element against the demystification claim would be the *virtuality* and *actuality* of facts within the scheme of intelligibility.[19] That is, if a reasoner takes the hermeneutical scheme seriously, she might be able to "alter the factual model without having to worry about any correspondence with an external reality, since the apparently descriptive notions of 'damage', 'thing' and 'person' are as much 'virtual' fact as 'actual' fact."[20] Cautiously applying the logic philosophy of science, legal reasoning could benefit from the logic that "[t]hese *virtual facts* are different from *actual facts* in that they are idealized: their connection with actual reality is not complete because they are deliberately 'simplified' by the process of schematization itself."[21] According to Samuel, this kind of logic in understanding legal facts is more convincing compared to rule-based reasoning because, in this way, "lawyers can construct situations of 'social reality' without having to concern themselves too closely with the reality to which this construction supposedly corresponds."[22] This view therefore denies the semantic autonomy of rules, from which alone the judges pick out the relevant features of the case.[23] Facts, in this sense, are not institutionally constructed by rules, as they are fabricated, instead, by reasoning that "can only takes place in a world of virtual fact."[24]

17 Samuel, "Can Legal Reasoning Be Demystified?" 201.

18 Ibid.

19 From a cognitive science lens, see Marek Jakubiec, "Legal Concepts as Mental Representations," *International Journal for the Semiotics of Law-Revue Internationale de Sémiotique Juridique* 35, no. 5 (2022): 1837–55.

20 Samuel, "Can Legal Reasoning Be Demystified?" 202; Carel Smith, "The Vicissitudes of the Hermeneutic Paradigm in the Study of Law: Tradition, Forms of Life and Metaphor," *Erasmus Law Review* 4 (2011): 21–38. Quoting from Smith, "The concern of legal hermeneutics is not how the judge ought to understand the law, but the act of understanding itself. It does not offer a particular methodology, neither does it prescribe which interpretive standards have priority in law, nor does it hold a hierarchy of legal values. Instead, it examines the conditions of understanding in general and of understanding the law in particular." (22)

21 Samuel, "Can Legal Reasoning Be Demystified?" 202. (emphasis original)

22 Ibid., 203.

23 Linda Tvrdíková, "Vagueness and Indeterminateness in Law: Are Judges Humpties Dumpties?" *International Journal for the Semiotics of Law-Revue Internationale de Sémiotique Juridique* (2022): 1–22.

24 Samuel, "Can Legal Reasoning Be Demystified?" 203; Cass R. Sunstein, "On Analogical Reasoning," *Harvard Law Review* 106, no. 3 (1993): 741–91. Relevant to this we can make a reference to Sunstein's argument about analogical reasoning. According to Sunstein,

Finally, lawyers' (i.e., the judges) reasoning is isolated by the authority paradigm. In that way, they are not interested in models or methods on how to reason to the extent that such models "*correspond* to some external reality."[25] What is important for the epistemological validity of lawyers' reasoning is not the testability or refutability of their legal-scientific inquiry but instead the paradigm of authority. To put it simply, their reasoning orientation relies on the logic of authority rather than inquiry. In legal cases, lawyers (i.e., judges) "feel little intellectual need to justify their empirical assertions and this is . . . because actual social reality is not really the object of legal 'science'." The object in this sense is understood as

> a set of 'virtual' facts governed not so much by correspondence with an external object but by the categories, concepts, institutions (person and thing), and 'descriptive' notions (damage, fault and the like) all of which construct a world as sealed as the rules themselves.[26]

It does not mean, however, that the judges' reasoning is taken off of the (objective, empirical) reality so that one will find a rather absurd, farcical decision. But instead, what we are seeing here is the 'absoluteness' of authority that typifies the peculiarity of legal reasoning.[27]

Addressing the three points generates our initial view about the particularities of legal reasoning. From Samuel's responses to the demystification claim, we may also argue that legal reasoning is a *process* of justification based on the plurality of schemes of intelligibility that represent the virtuality of norms and facts into the actual. In such a process, legal reasoning is seen to be epistemologically valid insofar as the schemes of intelligibility applied internally are coherent within the system, rather than corresponding with external reality. But how should we understand such (internal) coherence? Also, how does coherence contribute to our understanding of the process of creation in legal reasoning?

"The critics of analogical reasoning sometimes act as if analogies were 'things,' which either resolve or do not resolve contested cases. If they do resolve contested cases, they are not mere analogies but genuine rules; if they do not, they are nothing at all. But analogies should not be seen in this way. Their meaning lies in their use. They are not simply unanalyzed fact patterns; they are used to help people think through contested cases and to generate low-level principles. In this way they have a constitutive dimension, for the patterns we see are a product not simply of preexisting reality, but of our cognitive structures and our principles as well. The principles and patterns we develop and describe are in turn brought to bear on, and tested through confrontation with, other cases." (citation omitted) 779.

25 Samuel, "Can Legal Reasoning Be Demystified?" 210.

26 Ibid., 206.

27 G. Alexander Nunn and Alan M. Trammell, "Settled Law," *Virginia Law Review* 107, no. 1 (2021): 57–117.

Creativity in legal reasoning

The matter of a legal decision-maker's capacity to represent or express any legal realities is inescapably rendered by her theoretical orientation.[28] Thus, when we spoke earlier about the process of justifying the representation of the virtual into the actual, we were simultaneously questioning the theoretical underpinning of such a particular process. In this context, as probably the most dominant theoretical paradigm pervading legal science, legal positivism has faced many challenges. Specifically relevant to this study is the view that claims legal positivists are dogmatic in the sense that they narrowly frame the legal representation of reality as a matter of subsumption. That is, as Alex Lefebvre submits, we need to examine the way dogmatism inadequately accommodates the so-called 'activism' and 'accident' in judicial decisions.[29] The former asserts that judges are taking extra-legal considerations into account in deciding a case, and the latter claims that judges' law creation, instead of applying it, only happens by mistake. Importantly, these assertions appear to set creativity external to law and legal practice—we are cursed to *un*change.[30]

Meanwhile, Lefebvre advocates for the law's inherent creativity. Creativity, in his view, is "a fundamental, necessary capacity of judgement . . . it is an inescapable aspect of judgement, one we must come to terms with if we are to understand law and adjudication."[31] In constructing his theoretical account of adjudicative decision, Lefebvre relies on Gilles Deleuze's philosophical concept, which is deemed to be useful in exploring "ways of seeing how judges create law, why it is necessary, and how, given this necessity, it must be affirmed."[32] Such a kind of work *with* Deleuze brings us to understand some of the Deleuzian progenitors, such as Bergson and Spinoza. By suggesting the law's image of creativity, Lefebvre attempts to reject some major views on legal positivism. He argues that some positivistic theories—ranging from Hart's *concept of law*, Dworkin's *law of integrity* and Habermas's *communicative functions of law*—have been dogmatic insofar as they are suggesting legal judgments as a matter of subsumption. In this perspective, judges are simply *applying* what is known from the past (i.e., rules and principles) to the present factual pattern of a case. The dogmatics, claimed Lefebvre, perceive

28 Neil MacCormick, *Legal Reasoning and Legal Theory* (New York: Oxford University Press, 1978); Maksymilian Del Mar, "The Spatio-Temporality of Objectification in Legal Theory: Concepts of Legality between Theory and Practice," *Problema* 2 (2008): 127–55.

29 Alexandre Lefebvre, *The Image of Law: Deleuze, Bergson, Spinoza* (Stanford: Stanford University Press, 2008); Alexandre Lefebvre, "A New Image of Law: Deleuze and Jurisprudence," *Telos* 130 (2005): 103–26.

30 This expression was intended to emphasize Deleuze's philosophy of change and becoming. Deleuze once wrote that "we are cursed to change."

31 Lefebvre, *The Image of Law: Deleuze, Bergson, Spinoza*, vii.

32 Ibid., xiii.

legal reasoning under an 'image' of subsumption, that is, recognizing cases as simply instances of rules. By encompassing 'recognition' instead of 'creation,' the dogmatists have consequently put creativity aside and outside law and legal reasoning.

At the moment, we may submit that law's image of creativity is composed of three main components: (1) creative legal pragmatism; (2) the nexus of the concept of Encounter and law's internal time; and (3) the creation of legal concepts by judges. Let us examine each of these components.

First, the common law pragmatism, aspired from several pragmatists' thoughts, claims that the image of law is *necessarily creative*. Interestingly, Lefebvre reaches this premise by juxtaposing legal pragmatism with Bergson's theory of duration. Bergson is invaluable in this context since his philosophy of time allows for recognition of unpredictability and inventiveness. According to Bergson, "[t]ime is invention or it is nothing at all,"[33] and by that, we may claim a nondogmatic image of thought that rejects the predictable and foreseeable future mechanism and finalism.[34] Creativity and time in law, borrowing from Bergson's concept theory of *Creative Evolution*, comprise two concepts: internal difference and differentiation. That is, according to Lefebvre, "[t]he first of these concepts shows the identity between subject and alteration; a subject is a continuous multiplicity, and the true subject of Bergson's text is not a state or a product but a movement or a tendency."[35] Meanwhile, the second concept asserts that "tendencies are differentiated into new and inventive lines according to problems encountered and the corresponding solutions engendered."[36] While Bergson situates his philosophy in the context of life and living organisms, we can use such an image of thought in the so-called law's life, which is famously depicted in Oliver Wendell Holmes's pragmatic reflection of law. In this context, Holmes's philosophy of law proclaims that "[t]he life of the law has not been logic; it has been experience."[37] From this line, Holmes furthermore argued that

[t]he felt of the time, the prevalent moral and political theories, *intuitions* of public policy, avowed or unconscious, even the prejudices which judges share with their fellowmen, have had a good deal more to do than the syllogism in determining the rules by which men should be governed. The law . . . cannot be dealt with as if it contained only the axioms and corollaries of a book of mathematics.[38]Reading Holmes's rejection of logic through Berg-

33 Henri Bergson, "Creative Evolution," in *Henri Bergson: Key Writings* (Bloomsbury Publishing, 2002), 341.
34 Lefebvre, *The Image of Law: Deleuze, Bergson, Spinoza*, 88–92.
35 Ibid., 96.
36 Ibid.
37 Oliver Wendell Holmes, "The Common Law," in *The Common Law* (Harvard University Press, 2009), 1.
38 Ibid. (emphasis added)

son's temporal pragmatism could yield three indications: (1) logic serves calculation and prediction of law; (2) logic is atemporal; and (3) logic forecloses life's creativity.[39] At the same time, this is the point where experience takes part in law and legal reasoning. We can synthesize the law's *cross-temporally projectable shape* to Bergson's duration in that legal decision-makers purport adjudicative decisions as a sub-species of duration, that is, an anticipation of the unknown and to understand a legal event as unique in itself or as an unrepetitive experience.[40] However, such a shape is not to suggest that the judges ought to break with legal tradition but rather to treat judgments as a way to "actualize a temporally mobile basis of interest and desire in conjunction with tradition."[41] Or, in Holmes's words, in adjudicative judgments, "the rule adapts itself to the new reasons which have been found for it, and enters on a new career."[42]

Second, law's internal time views judges as institutional memory-being.[43] This claim asserts that judges exist within the *pure past of the law*.[44] That is, "this past of the law is virtual; it is the past in general (the pure past) in which all the rules for judgment are found."[45] Here, we found two important Bergsonian terms used to explain the 'double existence' of rules; that is, "on the one hand, they fill and are found in the books (they are *actual*); on the other hand, they exist in or as a pure past (they are *virtual*)."[46] This perspective insists on two important features of what we mean by **case** and **judgment**. Related to the former, two points are important to highlight: (1) perceiving an event as a legal case involves the role of memory to prescribe or inform law to the event; and (2) for a certain rule to be *actual*ized in a legal

39 Lefebvre, *The Image of Law: Deleuze, Bergson, Spinoza*, 98.

40 Jingjing Wu, "Justifying Particular Reasoning in a Legal Context," *Informal Logic* 40, no. 3 (2020): 423–41. This statement might lead us to question the coherency of the particularity in legal reasoning (as opposed to the general universal legal reasoning). As we would argue later, the experiential temporalities reasoning is applicable in the context of universalizable particular reasoning. In this sense, we may agree with Wu who outlines that "only particulars that are universalizable are justifiable particulars." 428. Thus, thinking about rules and fact situations in terms of temporality suggests that "the justification rules of particular reasoning only articulate the salient feature(s) that make the case sufficiently particular to be excluded or allowed to deviate from universal rules or principles." 432.

41 Lefebvre, *The Image of Law: Deleuze, Bergson, Spinoza*, 101.

42 Holmes, "The Common Law," 5.

43 See Reva Siegel, "The Politics of Constitutional Memory," *Georgetown Journal of Law & Public Policy* 20, no. 1 (2022): 19–58; Joachim J. Savelsberg and Ryan D. King, "Law and Collective Memory," *Annual Review of Law and Social Science* 3, no. 1 (2007): 189–211, https://doi.org/10.1146/annurev.lawsocsci.3.081806.112757.

44 Lefebvre, *The Image of Law: Deleuze, Bergson, Spinoza*, 144.

45 Ibid.

46 Ibid., 145.

case, we should presuppose the rule to exist in the *virtual*.[47] In relation to the latter, this nexus develops judgments as "a connection or a composition of perception and memory; it is not a subsumption of perception by memory."[48] Such a position depicts what Lefebvre claims to be our elision from the lame debate between physical versus dynamic conception of time in theories of adjudication, since "there is only a single time to law [that is] the actualization of the virtual."[49]

Third, as suggested by Deleuze's (and to some extent Spinoza's) philosophy, the creation of legal concepts by judges is seen as the answer to some *enacted* legal problems. By combining Deleuze with Spinoza, we can obtain three different terms in a legal judgment, including Encounter, problem and concept. In this context, Encounter is understood as an *interruption*—it is "unrecognized" and "singular"; it forces (judges) to think; and it is "*transcendental* condition for thought, that which breaks thought away from routine recognition."[50] That being the case, the Encounter interrupts "the links between perception and recollection in inattentive judgment; it interrupts that smooth process whereby a percept immediately calls to mind a recollection to recognize it."[51] It interrupts the so-called easy cases or quick judgments, the predetermined ones that work under a simple formula of [Situation Action Modified Situation]. Providing reference to the *Delgamuukw* case dealing with indigenous people's rights claims in Canada, which is regarded as a hard or difficult case (as opposed to a predetermined, easy case), Lefebvre weaves the relationship between the three composites: "[a]n encounter spurs the judge toward the formulation of a problem able to create concepts to adjudicate the encounter." That is, in this case,

> [t]here is an encounter with an aboriginal land claim (as unrecognizable to the common law, sui generis); there is the problem of aboriginal title (how to achieve reconciliation and live together); and there is the concept of aboriginal title (which spells out its precise content).[52]

To put it simply, we have a new formula for adjudicative creation at the moment: [Encounter → Problem → Concept].

47 Ibid., 146; Jakubiec, "Legal Concepts as Mental Representations." Notably, Jakubiec categorizes three levels of explanation of a legal concept, namely cognitive level, legal history conceptualization and conceptualization from a whole legal system framework. Based on these epistemological categories, Jakubiec adds another branch in the dichotomy of law in books, law in action and law in mind.

48 Lefebvre, *The Image of Law: Deleuze, Bergson, Spinoza*, 169.

49 Ibid., 142. (emphasis added)

50 Ibid., 174–75. (emphasis original)

51 Ibid., 175.

52 Ibid., 210.

Following Lefebvre, we can furthermore identify five features of this so-called attentive judgment.[53] First, judgment is a process of dwelling on the encounter. Second, judgment reveals itself in time; that is, it involves a "prolonged search of memory," "enter[ing] into sustained exploration of the (pure or virtual) past."[54] This temporal modality should not be understood chronologically since, following Bergson, it is an ontological leap into the virtual (pure past). Third, judgment is experimental in the sense that we choose to recollect one image over another for the perception. Fourth, judgment is an accumulation of the experimentation process. In making sense of the encounter, we are ceaselessly making recollections to the deep and distant pure past, which "illuminate its previously unperceived and ignored aspects; and these new discoveries in turn incite more leaps and continued exploration of the pure past, bringing to light new memories, and so on."[55] Fifth, attentive judgment is creative in the sense that it always creates singularity. According to Lefebvre,

> [j]udgment has a one-track mind; it always takes on a pragmatic orientation of recognition in the service of action. Only the encounter frustrates this activity and interrupts its linkages . . . In striving toward recognition, an experimental and cumulative process is initiated wherein perception and recollection shuttle back and forth and, in this activity, create a composite singularity.[56]

Since Lefebvre's objective is to canvass a Deleuzian image of creativity in law, his theory of adjudication does not considerably yield an adequate explanation of *how* the theory of attentive adjudication practically translated into the criteria of *practice* of legal reasoning. It appears that Lefebvre has attempted to detach the practice of adjudication from political affairs, granting law's objectivity as such.[57] As a result, since we are attempting to argue for legal adjudications *in* time, one might plausibly ask, for instance, about the extent to which judges' practical reasoning might be implicated

53 To a certain degree, attentive judgment could be read along with Amalia Amaya's virtue-based theories of judgment. See Amalia Amaya, "Virtue and Objectivity in Legal Reasoning," in *Objectivity in Jurisprudence, Legal Interpretation and Practical Reasoning* (Edward Elgar Publishing, 2022).

54 Lefebvre, *The Image of Law: Deleuze, Bergson, Spinoza*, 182.

55 Ibid., 183.

56 Ibid., 183–84.

57 Kyle McGee, "Creation, Duration, Adjudication: A Review of Alexandre Lefebvre's The Image of Law: Deleuze, Bergson, Spinoza," *Law & Literature* 21, no. 3 (2009): 480–91.

in their explanatory views when *encountering* the burden of proof (or judicial evidence) and the applicability of legal principles as justifying reason.[58]

Relevant to this question, we can benefit from MacCormick's institutional theory of law (ITL) which claims that the process of argumentation is a process of justification guided by the coherence principle.[59] It is from ITL that we may perceive temporalities in legal reasoning as a matter of how judges establish past events in an actual case, in which they would simply fetch the rules under the logic: if *p* then *q*. However, as MacCormick noted, "[t]he process of legal proof—even when based on parties' admissions—is obviously not guaranteed always to establish the truth. The memories and perceptions of honest people can be false."[60] In the face of such an epistemic situation, MacCormick went on, arguing that

> [t]he best kind of reason we can ever have for believing some proposition about the past to be true is that it is *more coherent* than any other with our general beliefs about cause and effect and the motivation of human actions, and with a series of other particular propositions of fact which are themselves coherent inter se, and which include some propositions founded on present sensory perceptions.[61]

Conflict of evidence, as MacCormick put it, creates "the construction of two rival coherent versions of the past."[62] He furthermore contends that

> [t]he common response of legal systems, of course, has been not to abandon the attempt to establish the truth about the past, but to regulate it, ordinarily by way of adopting, at least formally, a stance of moderate scepticism. Whatever is asserted about the past is to be disbelieved unless either admitted by those against whom it is alleged, or supported by coherent evidence up to a stipulated standard of proof. This may be the 'intimate conviction of the trier of facts; or proof on the balance of probabilities', or proof 'beyond reasonable doubt'.[63]

58 Claudio Michelon, "Legal Inquiry and Legal Arguments," *Netherlands Journal of Legal Philosophy* 2, no. 51 (2022): 170–78; Claudio Michelon, "The Inference to the Best Legal Explanation," *Oxford Journal of Legal Studies* 39, no. 4 (2019): 878–900. Further examination in Chapter 5.
59 MacCormick, *Legal Reasoning and Legal Theory*.
60 Ibid., 87.
61 Ibid., 90–91. (emphasis added)
62 Ibid., 92.
63 Neil MacCormick, *Rhetoric and the Rule of Law: A Theory of Legal Reasoning* (Oxford: Oxford University Press, 2005), 228.

Through MacCormick's ITL, we can discover that law's creativity is *actually* guided by the principle of coherence, within which time and temporalities play a fundamental role—which is found in narratives. Furthermore, McCormick also asserts that essential to temporal narrative is the coherence of both causal and motivational explanations:

> Yet always a key element in intelligibility is temporal ordering. Always, we want to know why things happened as they did, and at least a part of the answer to the 'Why?' question is a causal explanation. Causes cannot succeed effects, so we need to know, within the given framework of explanation, which events were earlier, which later, which simultaneous. Another aspect of explanation is not causal but motivational, indeed, practically oriented. We give reasons for events in terms of the principles and values acted upon, or the purposes or plans being pursued, by persons both as individuals and as members of groups and organizations, or leaders of them. People acting in real time have reasons for acting, be they principles, values, plans, or purposes. These reasons of theirs become, in narrative, reasons why they did things, thus reasons why things happened, even when that which happened is not exactly the same as was planned. Once we bring in motivational explanation, it adds a certain complexity to causal sequencing, because the future as an agent has envisaged it will have formed an essential part of that agent's deliberation about the action now to be explained. Looked at in simple causal terms, it is the agent's present mental state (present although in its content future-oriented) that prompts A to act, and the act in turn produces whatever effects it does. (If A is lucky or skilful or whatever, the act will bring about the planned outcome.) *But in terms of A's own practical reasoning, A comes to a decision only by forming an intention about the future and the values A thinks achievable or realizable in it.* In this sense, the future can have present effects. This has important implications for our approach to explaining the human world.[64]

One should not forget that ITL—and so does Lefebvre's creative image of law—understands law's objectivity and legal adjudication's pursuit of it. From both lenses, however, we have been informed of the necessity of judges to attend to hard cases (as opposed to plain cases). Two follow-up questions can be raised at this point: the first is about how judges account for the criteria of hardness, and the second is about how the process of finding justifying reasons is implicated by such criteria of hardness. The latter issue, however,

64 Ibid., 217. (emphasis added)

will be thoroughly discussed in Chapter 5, and for the purpose of this chapter we are going to walk only through the former.[65]

Complexity and coherence

As we have observed in the introductory chapter, the judges' cognitive dilemma is essentially a matter of their epistemic capacity to represent the law in their legal reasoning, in which time and temporality play a fundamental role in the process of providing and selecting *justifying reason*. The dilemma of representation requires them to encapsulate justifying reason as their way of seeing the world.[66] In this section, there are two related notions pertaining to the way judges conceive of justifying reason in legal cases: the complexity of a case and a virtue-based reasoning. In that regard, such a problematization of justifying reason was the point of departure of James Maclean's theory of law in a processual worldview. Criticizing the variety of theories of practical judgment, Maclean argues that

> [e]very attempt to offer *justifying* reasons for legal decisions appears at best to register only at the level of *explanation*. Why? I suggest that perhaps part of the problem may be that our inherited conceptual framework is tied to a 'static' way of thinking that is now outmoded. We try to understand by objectifying reality, analysing what we objectify. But reality is not static; it only conveniently appears that way. It is not, in fact, composed of simply locatable, separate 'entities' but is more akin to a continuous flux, where things merge into each other and the essential qualities seem to be more correctly describable in terms of relatedness than separateness. So any articulation of the problem of finding justifying reasons for decisions conceived in static terms may be misconceived in law. In other words, a decision cannot be 'caught' because once a decision is made, it is gone: it is momentous, and all that we observe of it is its trace.[67]

Maclean's discussion is about the contention between universal versus particular ways of finding justifying reasons, in which he claims that law and

65 Nathan Moore, "Icons of Control: Deleuze, Signs, Law," *International Journal for the Semiotics of Law-Revue Internationale de Sémiotique Juridique* 20, no. 1 (2007): 33–54. I think it is worth noting here that from a Deleuzian point of view, the hard case can be framed as "something that must be argued through, cannot indicate a proper outcome at its beginning, by reference to law and the laws, but is in fact a singular problem that calls the current allocation of the law and laws into question." 43

66 Ronald Dworkin, *Law's Empire* (Cambridge, MA & London: The Belknap Press of Harvard University Press, 1986).

67 James MacLean, *Rethinking Law as Process: Creativity, Novelty, Change* (Oxon & New York: Routledge, 2012), 3.

legal institutions are always, in fact, in a state of perpetual change.[68] This concept of perpetual change implies that the persistent dichotomies in legal theory, i.e., universal vs. particular, legislation vs. adjudication, law-applying vs. law-making, are only intended to present an *appearance* of institutional stability.[69] Maclean argues that law is essentially a process of becoming, always ever-changing, situated by new experiences and facts.[70] Under this framework, we may come to understand that

> [l]egal decisions are unfolding processes, in which judges interact with unavoidably local conditions through recourse to rules, etc. What, from an external observation point, seems like decision-making controlled by legal rules and other norms is, in fact, *experienced internally* as a subtle yet dynamic succession of finely tuned actions and interactions in a continuously evolving realisation of what is really happening and being made to happen.[71]

Seeing law-as-process invites us to think in a narrative mode instead of the traditional propositional one. The essential matters in such narrative mode of thinking are "not those which we entertain on account of their propensity to predict a certain future but which will act as *signposts*, pointing out a way forward by disclosing hitherto hidden associations and suggesting novel relations and connections."[72] As already mentioned in the previous description, this view concerns pushing the limits of law and searching for any potentials and possibilities through "the operation of a narrative view-point and a metaphorical use of the idea of complexity."[73]

68 Bartosz Brożek, "The Architecture of the Legal Mind," in *Law and Mind: A Survey of Law and the Cognitive Sciences* (Cambridge University Press, 2021), chap. 4.

69 MacLean, *Rethinking Law as Process: Creativity, Novelty, Change*, 182; Harry H. Bash, "A Sense of Time: Temporality and Historicity in Sociological Inquiry," *Time & Society* 9, no. 2–3 (2000): 187–204. In discussing about the so-called structure versus process, quoting from Bash's sociological notes, it is important to highlight that "if what we 'observe' depends on the vantage point that is offered by a particular conceptualization or perspective through which we approach the phenomenal world, then whether we 'see' structural (static) or processual (dynamic) features of that world *turns crucially on the time-frame through which we choose, consciously or not, to conduct our analysis*. For example, the assumption of an instantaneous, snapshot-like, here-and-now temporal frame that is essentially ahistorical, will convey to us an impression of 'structure'. In contrast, adopting a more commodious time-frame that admits of duration and fully accommodates priority, sequence and subsequence—one that is imbued with a sense of historicity—would convey to us the appearance of 'process'" (emphasis original). 193.

70 MacLean, *Rethinking Law as Process: Creativity, Novelty, Change*, 182–83.

71 Ibid., 183. (emphasis added)

72 Ibid., 154. (emphasis added)

73 Ibid.

It is important to note at the moment that complexity in this paradigm is framed under the so-called difficult or hard cases. In this frame, complexity can be read in two accounts. First, complexity has something to do with

> the ease or difficulty with which information that conveys a sufficient and correct account of an experience of some phenomenon can be transmitted; it is linked directly to the subject experiencing the phenomenon, dependent on their ability to represent it.[74]

Second, complexity deals with "the compressibility of information, so that information that can be condensed into short, sharp phrases will be less complex."[75] Such compressibility of information is the essence of the distinc tion between the propositional from the narrative mode of thinking. The former, supported by ITL, appears poised to reduce any empirical observations, while the latter is trying to be attentive to stories and anecdotes. According to Maclean, the propositional form of knowledge, while being compressible, fails to enable judges to capture or accommodate complex experiences, and, arguably, such a deficit should be overcome by the narrative mode of thinking. That being the case, for the quest for objectivity in adjudicative decision-making in ITL, the complexity of a case should be algorithmically compressed. Thus, the question that follows would be: how could this narrative mode of reasoning provide objectivity to legal judgment? One primary assertion is that this rather methodical mode of thinking should initially be freed from the burden of achieving an objectively correct decision.[76] Such a need to overcome the reductionistic mode of thinking is what Maclean refers

74 Ibid., 155.

75 Ibid.

76 Amaya, "Virtue and Objectivity in Legal Reasoning," 271–92. According to Amaya, "the acknowledgment that methods do not suffice to provide the needed guidance in a substantial number of cases does not show that objectivity should be expected of some judgments but not others, to deny its limitations, or to conclude that it should be abandoned. Instead, one might want to question whether the fact that a conception of objectivity is unattainable should not tell against that claim that it provides an appropriate standard for guiding and evaluating legal judgements. In other words, that there are different (and important) types of cases in which the methodological rules do not lead to objectively correct results does not show the limits of objectivity, but rather the inappropriateness of a conception that makes such rules the site of objectivity. Furthermore, once we free methods from the burden of furnishing a full-blown conception of objectivity, we may come to envisage that perhaps some of the alleged imperfections of methodological rules, from which the supposed limits of objectivity derive, may turn out to be features that are necessitated by the very nature of the decision-making task, as a cognitive activity that is meant to satisfactorily respond to the plurality of value as well as complex (and unexpected) configurations of facts. Thus, the suggestion is that the limits of methods provide an argument not for the limits of objectivity in legal reasoning but rather for the need to articulate an alternative conception of objectivity." 11.

to as *second-order complexity*; that is, "by moving from a position where every focus is on the system's reductionistic tendency to one where we can entertain descriptions of the system as complex."[77] Reading along the line of the virtue-based theory of judgment, such second-order complexity implies an acknowledgement that the method and the agency are both imperfect, which then insists on us putting the objectivity of legal judgment partly in the subject rather than detaching the self from judgment.[78] In that sense, subjectivity is the pedigree of objectivity in legal judgment, which can generate objective standards of correctness. Related to this, we can bring virtue-based theory into conversation in such a way that, according to Amaya,

> [t]he virtue standard of objectivity is agent-dependent, in that properties of agents are relevant to determining the objectivity of judgments. It is critical to note that in this approach, as in methodical objectivity, objectivity is still claimed to be a property of objects, rather than persons.[79]

The narrative mode of reasoning, as one can understand from Maclean, presupposes our awareness toward the matter of judge's own complexity, from which we could extrapolate this idea into Amaya's virtuous judges. In a way, narrative mode should be seen as a sort of *virtue* in judge's effort to achieve objectivity in legal judgment. According to Maclean,

> Narrative thinking discloses a legal decision delivered by a legal decision-maker in a particular legal position, interpreted by others, some of whom are legal practitioners in the same sense, who are also occupied collectively in the narrative act. Sequences of events, relationships, persons, etc., are contextualized by legal decision-makers whose positions as legal decision-makers offer the context by means of the insight that operates within the context of the legal decision- making process. To the extent then that a legal decision-maker's thinking is part of the situation to which the decision relates, a decision-maker who is aware of this interaction and dependence between their thoughts and decisions will be able to generate more descriptions of that situation.[80]

That said, it is fair to say the narrative mode of reasoning is more interested in time than truth. Through the concept of *emplotment*, this mode of reasoning seeks to find justifying reason from a coherent plot or story, that is, "its sequential ordering of component parts."[81]

77 MacLean, *Rethinking Law as Process: Creativity, Novelty, Change*, 157.
78 Later discussion about intuition-based judicial discussion is explored in Chapter 5.
79 Amaya, "Virtue and Objectivity in Legal Reasoning."
80 MacLean, *Rethinking Law as Process: Creativity, Novelty, Change*, 163.
81 Ibid., 166; Paul Ricoeur, *Time and Narrative, Volume 2*, vol. 2 (Chicago: The University of Chicago Press, 1985); Andrew Benjamin Bricker, "Is Narrative Essential to the Law?

Through the power of plot or story, temporalities, as lived experience, are produced by memory, expectation and attention, in which

> the past that is memory and the future that is expectation interact to produce the present, and this coming together of the past and the future in the present means that memory and expectation can potentially reach across time to bring to consciousness in the present those things that belong to both memory and expectation.[82]

Cross-temporal justification

Two important features of legal reasoning have been glossed so far after reading Lefebvre and MacCormick in the previous section. These include law's inherent creativity (and inventiveness), and the creativity of law should be guided by the principle of coherence. In this section, as this chapter attempts to propound a time-based epistemological frame of legal reasoning, we can extend the two features into the discourse of normativity. That is, one might ask, of what value does cross-temporal justification—as a normative claim—have in our larger conversation about judges' cognitive dilemma in historical injustice adjudication?

Our normativity discourse will be glossed into two fundamental criteria: deliberative agents and transformative experience. The argument proposed by this normativity claim is that the image of legal reasoning as a process of justification of the virtual into the actual fundamentally demonstrates an inherent temporal dimension of law which entwines individual and social experiences. This argument is grounded in Postema's time-based jurisprudential vision, which claims that law fundamentally orders time in such a way that, in our striving to understand law, theory of law should engage with human temporal experiences.[83] Examining from the common law tradition, theories of law, *pace* Postema, have been describing law and legal system as time-slice. Against this view, we may contend that law is intrinsically temporal, or, as we later suggest, law is a time-mindful normative order.[84]

Precedent, Case Law and Judicial Emplotment," *Law, Culture and the Humanities* 15, no. 2 (2019): 319–31.

82 MacLean, *Rethinking Law as Process: Creativity, Novelty, Change*, 166; Jenann Ismael, "Temporal Experience," in *The Oxford Handbook of Philosophy of Time* (Oxford University Press, 2011).

83 Gerald J. Postema, "Time in Law's Domain," *Ratio Juris* 31, no. 2 (2018): 160–82.

84 Gerald J. Postema, "Melody and Law's Mindfulness of Time," *Ratio Juris* 17, no. 2 (2004): 203–26; David Luban, "Time-Mindedness and Jurisprudence," *Virginia Law Review* 101, no. 4 (2015): 903–17.

From integrity to fidelity

Speaking about temporality and legal reasoning, one might view that the best way to elucidate the relationship between the two is through the practice of precedent. Mostly flourishing in common law tradition, the practice of precedent embarks on the claim that there is a moral ground to follow. This moral ground pertains to the court's way of understanding and accounting for the normative relevance of the past to the decisions in present cases.[85] According to Postema, there are two ways of describing this normative relevance: external and internal justification. On the one hand, the former appears to be content-dependent, refusing to acknowledge "entirely the merits or normative grounds of the decisions."[86] On the other hand, the latter "takes into account the fact of the past decision and its causal or external consequences, but it also looks to the reason or rationale of the decision."[87] It is worth noting that in explaining the internal justification, Postema, while departing from Dworkinian original notions of *integrity* as a political value, takes a somewhat different route from Dworkin. Thus, before we delve into Postema's own route, it would be helpful to sketch Dworkin's integrity principle briefly. According to Dworkin, law as integrity "insists that legal claims are interpretive judgments and therefore combine backward- and forward-looking elements; they interpret contemporary legal practice seen as an unfolding political narrative."[88] Distinct from conventionalism and pragmatism, the integrity paradigm offers a more interpretive program, and it is "both the product of and the inspiration for comprehensive interpretation of legal practice."[89] Through this paradigm, history matters insofar as it avows law to pass on the narrow content of past decisions along with the principle that justifies them[90]—that is, *the* principle that "both fits and justifies some complex part of legal practice, that it provides an attractive way to see, in the structure of that practice, the consistency of principle integrity requires."[91] That said, law as integrity essentially exhorts legal practice to be coherent in terms of action and principle.

85 See generally Nina Varsava, "How to Realize the Value of Stare Decisis: Options for Following Precedent," *Yale Journal of Law & the Humanities* 30 (2018): 62–120; Nina Varsava, "Stare Decisis and Intersystemic Adjudication," *Notre Dame Law Review* 97 (2021): 1207–64.

86 Gerald J. Postema, "Integrity: Justice in Workclothes," *Iowa Law Review* 82, no. 3 (1997): 822.

87 Ibid.

88 Dworkin, *Law's Empire*, 225.

89 Ibid., 226; Tvrdíková, "Vagueness and Indeterminateness in Law: Are Judges Humpties Dumpties?"; Raff Donelson, "Describing Law," *Canadian Journal of Law & Jurisprudence* 33, no. 1 (2020): 85–106.

90 Dworkin, *Law's Empire*, 227.

91 Ibid., 228.

Instead of resorting to a certain political paradigm, a reinforcement of group relationships is in fact needed to understand the normative character of precedent. In this regard, according to Postema, Dworkin's integrity is "simply justice situated in politics, keeping the essential tension between the ideal and consensual dimensions of justice clearly in sight."[92] Integrity, he says, is a complex moral standard that calls for "a proper and defensible balance of respect and regret regarding past rules and decisions of a polity."[93] In fact, in defending its moral force, integrity should approximate justice by *justifying* the historical character of law that rests on the link between integrity and fidelity. In this understanding, fidelity is built upon interpersonal relationships rather than theories, rules and events. Fidelity is "a matter of keeping faith with our common past as the appropriate mode of keeping faith with each other as co-members of the community to which we are committed."[94] Postema asserts that what he meant "[b]y keeping faith with each other" is that we are "interacting on terms and in ways appropriate to the moral nature of the relationship among us."[95]

One might wonder how the idea of fidelity is constructive to the temporal configurations of law and legal practice. Relevant to this question, we need to view fidelity as a reflection in relationships, be it friendship, familial linkage, or loyalty—as an expression of relationship that wields complex links between interpersonal experiences and the value they share and appraise. According to Postema, the nexus between integrity and fidelity thus extends such value *cross-temporally*, which is grasped as a connection between past, present and future. Therefore, time and temporalities extend the value of relationships, and in such temporally extended values, time has a multi-direction and a mutually multi-dimension. Justice as a normative value, as a result, can (or maybe ought to) be viewed as a temporally extended value. Read in that way, positing justice in the communal sense shall bring the community's historical character to the fore; that is, "a function of self-conscious common memory framed and informed by a sense of significance that gives the historical events a distinctively human value."[96] From this historical lens, there is a sense of mutual dependency amongst generations that is built up in a society—i.e., the present generation inherits their predecessor for what they consider materially, culturally and morally valuable. Justice thus gives moral shape to this extended temporality of a society, which then predicates fidelity to the past in the service of justice. In a vivid statement, Postema claims that "fidelity takes the shape of integrity in a community bound to

92 Postema, "Integrity: Justice in Workclothes," 843.
93 Ibid., 854.
94 Ibid., 845.
95 Ibid.
96 Ibid., 849; Stanley Fish, "Working on the Chain Gang: Interpretation in Law and Literature," *Texas Law Review* 60 (1981): 551–67.

the pursuit of justice in the circumstances of integrity."[97] Law, in this sense, plays a role as "a natural medium in which to seek justice in the way integrity prescribes."[98] That being the case, the link between integrity and law invites a practical deliberation that understands legal reasoning in two senses. *First*, it grasps legal reasoning as "a framework of practical reasoning that anchors the public justification of decisions and actions to past communal decisions and actions,"[99] and *second*, this type of reasoning is seen as "an evaluatively informed assessment of the normative significance of the past decision for the instant case, as well as of the significance it might hold for the future."[100]

This sort of time-taming legal reasoning could be seen as a complete rejection of the sociability of law resulting from the separation mentality of jurisprudence, which can be traced back to Austin's most quoted phrase: "[t]he existence of law is one thing; its merit and demerit is another."[101] This has been translated by other positivists (from Austinian to Hartian) as the bedrock of the current analytical jurisprudence. Thus, following Postema, we can argue for a broader conception of jurisprudence as *vera philosophia*, with the term 'broader' in this sense being understood as a search for "a comprehensive understanding of law and its place in human experience, anchored in robust philosophical engagement in the history of that search."[102] Such a course of searching could be resolved by inspecting or paying attention to history, and relevant to this, we can equate the term 'history' with 'time' by asserting that "[t]ime is not only among the conditions of the existence of law, but (if we are willing to put it this way) it is of its essence."[103] In this respect, law is similar to melody in a way that "like melody, law not only exists in time and persist[s] over time, but it orders time."[104] From this argument, we can trace back to Postema's assertion in *Melody and Law's Mindfulness* that treats melody (*melos*) as the third model of law's normativity (other than *nomos*

97 Postema, "Integrity: Justice in Workclothes," 851.
98 Ibid.
99 Ibid.
100 Ibid.; Carlo Focarelli, *International Law as Social Construct: The Struggle for Global Justice* (Oxford University Press, 2012). Importantly, from a social constructionism point of view, Focarelli addresses that "Practical reason is, therefore, here defined as reason operating in society, counting as 'reason' to society and capable of guiding daily social action enabling people to live together. Thus defined, practical reason is not necessarily what is true to one or a few scholars, logicians, theorist, or outsiders. Practical reason amounts to what 'works in practice' within the community, whatever its theoretical or logical soundness from the perspective of the single observer." 72.
101 Gerald J. Postema, "Jurisprudence, the Sociable Science," *Virginia Law Review* 101, no. 4 (2015): 875.
102 Ibid., 883.
103 Ibid., 885.
104 Ibid.

and *thesmos*).[105] He claims that "musical thinking is a kind of rule-following: To grasp a melody *in medias res* is to project the direction of musical movement on the basis of what is sounding and has already sounded."[106] As we make sense of the past, present and future through the flows of music, we may find a rather similar temporal coherence and normativity in law's narrative. Musical phrases, he explains, order time, within which three interrelated governing norms of harmonic field, metrical field, rhythmic pattern and melodic field interplay and manifest into the tone sequence. In this duration of tone sequence, we may find "multiple, emerging, and maturing patterns" of music.[107] This melody model of law's time-mindfulness is therefore, quoting from Postema, "essential to its fundamental modus operandi, that of providing normative guidance to deliberative agents who must act in a social space consisting of other deliberative agents interacting with them."[108]

The coherent self

The idea of legal time-mindfulness requires us to embrace the particular importance of deliberative agents. It asks us to see that law guides agents by positing "present choice in a trajectory from past actors into a meaningful future,"[109] which in turn intersects one over another, creating an overlapping trajectory, which Postema calls a "polyphony of public actions."[110] Postema elaborates these arguments more thoroughly in *Time in Law's Domain*, in which he argues that law is "a discursive, argumentative discipline: it is a practice of giving, taking, assessing, and tracing out the implications of reasons for propositions of law."[111] Furthermore, from this perspective, law is fundamentally and reflectively recursive and has public and temporal dimensions. We can understand that law shapes and is shaped by the practices of the public. Consequently, since public practices intrinsically have temporal character, "the understanding [of law change] must reflect in its content and structure the time-mindfulness of law and the necessary role of law in providing the ballast of continuity for the political community it seeks to order."[112]

The concept of deliberative agents necessitates thinking about the sociability of law and legal reasoning. Based on Alexander Peirce's synechism, philosophical jurisprudence is sociable in two ways: first, it is externally sociable in the sense of "its openness to interaction and partnership with other modes

105 Postema, "Melody and Law's Mindfulness of Time."
106 Ibid., 208.
107 Postema, "Time in Law's Domain," 162.
108 Postema, "Jurisprudence, the Sociable Science," 885.
109 Ibid., 886.
110 Ibid.
111 Postema, "Time in Law's Domain," 165.
112 Postema, "Jurisprudence, the Sociable Science," 887.

of inquiry," and second, it is internally sociable, referring to "its synechist methodological orientation or mentality."[113] Contrary to the separation mentality of jurisprudence (that distinguishes law from non-law, positivist from naturalist), synechists seek to bring a phenomenon into a broader context of continuity that enables them to understand the content in a networked and integrative manner. However, as Luban argues, the idea of synechism is rather unconvincing.[114] Placing this idea in historiographic discourse, such a continuity understood by synechists is inclined to include discontinuity, something that Luban describes as a hockey stick-shaped function;[115] this might be seen as continuity but then swerving off in a different direction. In line with such a proposition, Drucilla Cornell argued from Peircean readings on the inherent ethical basis of reason to develop a novel understanding of the process of interpretation as recollective imagination. Cornell contended that "[t]here can be no final culmination of the interpretive process."[116] In that sense, claimed Cornell, "legal interpretation is never *just* exposition of an 'existing' principle; it is also a *positing* of the very principle it reads into the case law through the enunciation of the 'should be' inherent in the justification of principle."[117]

Normativity and experiential time

We need to extend the discussion about the rational role of human agency in its relationship to time. At the basic level, we may claim that human experience in time is subjective time or time sense.[118] Human brains process information as representational wholes that encompass *cross-temporal dimensions* and yields *significances* to present experience.[119] It certainly does not align with objective or physical time, given that human brains structure subjective time into patterns, and, importantly, it is subject to revision.[120] According to Postema, only by positing humans as *temporally extended* or enduring selves can we grasp time as neither static nor possessed, but rather

113 Ibid., 895.
114 Luban, "Time-Mindedness and Jurisprudence."
115 Ibid., 916.
116 Cornell, "Institutionalization of Meaning, Recollective Imagination and the Potential for Transformative Legal Interpretation," 1229.
117 Ibid., 1144.
118 Holly K. Andersen and Rick Grush, "A Brief History of Time-Consciousness: Historical Precursors to James and Husserl," *Journal of the History of Philosophy* 47, no. 2 (2009): 277–307; Holly Andersen, "The Representation of Time in Agency," in *A Companion to the Philosophy of Time*, ed. Heather Dyke and Adrian Bardon (Oxford: Wiley Blackwell, 2013), 470–85.
119 Bartosz Brożek, "Legal Interpretation: Towards a New Paradigm?" *Teoria Polityki*, no. 4 (2020): 79–92.
120 Postema, "Time in Law's Domain," 168.

as experienced. Such (temporal) experience might eventually be transformative in the sense that it could be disruptive or discontinue the past—it simply goes off course from our plan.[121] Bearing that in mind, we may need to understand that the idea of an enduring self is not an attempt to seek out a certain pattern but rather, we could argue, a plausible way to experience the untimely and unpredictable future.

Consequently, it is suggested that transformative experience is part of the life of the enduring self. Such experience is a reflection of time dilation, read in the sense that

> what we have done and what has happened to us in the past not only shape the circumstances and options we face in the present, but they also engage us as persons and agents; they cast us into a future already populated by our incomplete selves.[122]

As agents, every practical experience we have is presupposed (and shaped) by "deliberation and action in a world of other agents who are also deliberating and acting."[123] This deliberation among agents is always improvisational rather than scripted, as it might be equally converged and self-disclosing.[124] As a consequence, other than having a public character modeled in generalized directives, in order to be capable of providing normative guidance to the public, laws must also have a cross-temporally projectable shape, that is, a state in which each of the members of the public could "mesh their own deliberative point of view with that offered by law."[125] Moreover, the element of discipline is also temporally embedded in this deliberative practice of reasoning, insisting on "practical coherence over time," as much as is reflected in common law jurisprudence.[126]

Our line of argument pertaining to the time-ordering legal reasoning embraces its evaluative aspect through the lens of substantive rationality as sort of ideal standards in the community.[127] It is worthy to note that the essential matter in this evaluation is the communities' commitment to substantive rationality, understood as an iterative interaction both in terms of process as well as end, and their commitment to society's cross-temporal self-formation

121 Filip Vostal, "Slowing down Modernity: A Critique," *Time & Society* 28, no. 3 (2019): 1039–60.

122 Postema, "Time in Law's Domain," 170; Laurie Ann Paul, *Transformative Experience* (Oxford: Oxford University Press, 2014); Petronella Randell, "Familiar Transformative Experiences," *Synthese* 202, no. 45 (2023): 1–16.

123 Postema, "Time in Law's Domain," 171.

124 Ibid., 172.

125 Ibid., 175.

126 Ibid., 175–76.

127 Brożek, "The Architecture of the Legal Mind," chap. 5.

and re-formation within the idea of fidelity. As a result, we can say that fidelity is the keyword to understanding society's past wrongdoings or failures. The call for self- and re-formation of society is therefore to seek "responsibility for the failure, repair of the damage done, and restructuring of one's attitudes, motivations, and practices to avoid repeating them."[128]

Conclusion

In this chapter, we have made three main claims. First, as a form of practical reasoning, legal reasoning is a *process* of justification based on a scheme of intelligibility that represents the virtuality of norms and facts into the actual. Second, the representation of the virtual into the actual essentially signifies that time is *inherent* in the domain of law and legal reasoning. And third, such temporality *in* legal reasoning is fundamental to recognizing the role of the experiential temporal frame in facilitating a judge's creative and transformative capacity. This chapter is a springboard to further examine some epistemological implications regarding the intersection between legal reasoning and temporality. This implication includes an investigation into some interrelated aspects in the adjudicative process, namely that if legal reasoning is a process of justification of the virtual, how does it shape the way legal decision-makers find and select justifying reasons?

Reference list

Alexander, Larry, and Emily Sherwin. *Demystifying Legal Reasoning*. New York: Cambridge University Press, 2008.

Amaya, Amalia. "Virtue and Objectivity in Legal Reasoning." In *Objectivity in Jurisprudence, Legal Interpretation and Practical Reasoning*, 271–92. Edward Elgar Publishing, 2022.

Andersen, Holly K. "The Representation of Time in Agency." In *A Companion to the Philosophy of Time*, edited by Heather Dyke and Adrian Bardon, 470–85. Oxford: Wiley Blackwell, 2013.

Andersen, Holly K., and Rick Grush. "A Brief History of Time-Consciousness: Historical Precursors to James and Husserl." *Journal of the History of Philosophy* 47, no. 2 (2009): 277–307.

Bash, Harry H. "A Sense of Time: Temporality and Historicity in Sociological Inquiry." *Time & Society* 9, no. 2–3 (2000): 187–204.

Bergson, Henri. "Creative Evolution." In *Henri Bergson: Key Writings*. Bloomsbury Publishing, 2002.

Bricker, Andrew Benjamin. "Is Narrative Essential to the Law? Precedent, Case Law and Judicial Emplotment." *Law, Culture and the Humanities* 15, no. 2 (2019): 319–31.

Brożek, Bartosz. "Legal Interpretation: Towards a New Paradigm?" *Teoria Polityki*, no. 4 (2020): 79–92.

128 Postema, "Time in Law's Domain," 178.

Brożek, Bartosz. "The Architecture of the Legal Mind." In *Law and Mind: A Survey of Law and the Cognitive Sciences*. Cambridge University Press, 2021.

Cornell, Drucilla L. "Institutionalization of Meaning, Recollective Imagination and the Potential for Transformative Legal Interpretation." *University of Pennsylvania Law Review* 136 (1987): 1135–229.

Donelson, Raff. "Describing Law." *Canadian Journal of Law & Jurisprudence* 33, no. 1 (2020): 85–106.

Dorsett, Shaunnagh, and Shaun McVeigh. *Jurisdiction*. Oxon & New York: Routledge, 2012.

Dworkin, Ronald. *Law's Empire*. Cambridge, MA & London: The Belknap Press of Harvard University Press, 1986.

Fish, Stanley. "Working on the Chain Gang: Interpretation in Law and Literature." *Texas Law Review* 60 (1981): 551–67.

Focarelli, Carlo. *International Law as Social Construct: The Struggle for Global Justice*. Oxford University Press, 2012.

Holmes, Oliver Wendell. "The Common Law." In *The Common Law*. Harvard University Press, 2009.

Ismael, Jenann. "Temporal Experience." In *The Oxford Handbook of Philosophy of Time*. Oxford University Press, 2011.

Jakubiec, Marek. "Legal Concepts as Mental Representations." *International Journal for the Semiotics of Law-Revue Internationale de Sémiotique Juridique* 35, no. 5 (2022): 1837–55.

Lefebvre, Alexandre. "A New Image of Law: Deleuze and Jurisprudence." *Telos* 130 (2005): 103–26.

Lefebvre, Alexandre. *The Image of Law: Deleuze, Bergson, Spinoza*. Stanford: Stanford University Press, 2008.

Luban, David. "Time-Mindedness and Jurisprudence." *Virginia Law Review* 101, no. 4 (2015): 903–17.

MacCormick, Neil. *Legal Reasoning and Legal Theory*. New York: Oxford University Press, 1978.

MacCormick, Neil. *Rhetoric and the Rule of Law: A Theory of Legal Reasoning*. Oxford: Oxford University Press, 2005.

MacLean, James. *Rethinking Law as Process: Creativity, Novelty, Change*. Oxon & New York: Routledge, 2012.

Mar, Maksymilian Del. "The Spatio-Temporality of Objectification in Legal Theory: Concepts of Legality between Theory and Practice." *Problema* 2 (2008): 127–55.

Mar, Maksymilian Del. "On the Hinges of History: For a Relational Legal Historiography." In *Searching for Contemporary Legal Thought*, edited by Justin Desautels-Stein and Christopher Tomlins, 61–79. Cambridge, UK: Cambridge University Press, 2017.

McGee, Kyle. "Creation, Duration, Adjudication: A Review of Alexandre Lefebvre's The Image of Law: Deleuze, Bergson, Spinoza." *Law & Literature* 21, no. 3 (2009): 480–91.

Michelon, Claudio. "The Inference to the Best Legal Explanation." *Oxford Journal of Legal Studies* 39, no. 4 (2019): 878–900.

Michelon, Claudio. "Legal Inquiry and Legal Arguments." *Netherlands Journal of Legal Philosophy* 2, no. 51 (2022): 170–78.

Moore, Nathan. "Icons of Control: Deleuze, Signs, Law." *International Journal for the Semiotics of Law-Revue Internationale de Sémiotique Juridique* 20, no. 1 (2007): 33–54.

Mussawir, Edward. *Jurisdiction in Deleuze: The Expression and Representation of Law*. London: Routledge, 2011.

Nunn, G. Alexander, and Alan M. Trammell. "Settled Law." *Virginia Law Review* 107, no. 1 (2021): 57–117.
Paul, Laurie Ann. *Transformative Experience*. Oxford: Oxford University Press, 2014.
Postema, Gerald J. "Integrity: Justice in Workclothes." *Iowa Law Review* 82, no. 3 (1997): 821–55.
Postema, Gerald J. "Melody and Law's Mindfulness of Time." *Ratio Juris* 17, no. 2 (2004): 203–26.
Postema, Gerald J. "Jurisprudence, the Sociable Science." *Virginia Law Review* 101, no. 4 (2015): 869–902.
Postema, Gerald J. "Time in Law's Domain." *Ratio Juris* 31, no. 2 (2018): 160–82.
Randell, Petronella. "Familiar Transformative Experiences." *Synthese* 202, no. 45 (2023): 1–16.
Ricoeur, Paul. *Time and Narrative, Volume 2*. Vol. 2. Chicago: The University of Chicago Press, 1985.
Samuel, Geoffrey. "Can Legal Reasoning Be Demystified?" *Legal Studies* 29, no. 2 (2009): 181–210.
Samuel, Geoffrey. *Epistemology and Method in Law*. London & New York: Routledge, 2016.
Savelsberg, Joachim J., and Ryan D. King. "Law and Collective Memory." *Annual Review of Law and Social Science* 3, no. 1 (2007): 189–211. https://doi.org/10.1146/annurev.lawsocsci.3.081806.112757.
Schauer, Frederick. *Thinking Like a Lawyer: A New Introduction to Legal Reasoning*. Cambridge, MA & London: Harvard University Press, 2009.
Shidarta. *Multisentrisme Humaniora Digital: Filsafat Hukum Masa Depan Dan Masa Depan Filsafat Hukum*. Jakarta: Universitas Bina Nusantara, 2022.
Siegel, Reva. "The Politics of Constitutional Memory." *Georgetown Journal of Law & Public Policy* 20, no. 1 (2022): 19–58.
Smith, Carel. "The Vicissitudes of the Hermeneutic Paradigm in the Study of Law: Tradition, Forms of Life and Metaphor." *Erasmus Law Review* 4 (2011): 21–38.
Sunstein, Cass R. "On Analogical Reasoning." *Harvard Law Review* 106, no. 3 (1993): 741–91.
Tvrdíková, Linda. "Vagueness and Indeterminateness in Law: Are Judges Humpties Dumpties?" *International Journal for the Semiotics of Law-Revue Internationale de Sémiotique Juridique* (2022): 1–22.
Varsava, Nina. "How to Realize the Value of Stare Decisis: Options for Following Precedent." *Yale Journal of Law & the Humanities* 30 (2018): 62–120.
Varsava, Nina. "Stare Decisis and Intersystemic Adjudication." *Notre Dame Law Review* 97 (2021): 1207–64.
Vostal, Filip. "Slowing down Modernity: A Critique." *Time & Society* 28, no. 3 (2019): 1039–60.
Wu, Jingjing. "Justifying Particular Reasoning in a Legal Context." *Informal Logic* 40, no. 3 (2020): 423–41.

Chapter 5

Historical injustice as temporal legal inquiry

This chapter explores various temporal approaches to inquiry into historical injustices. Our epistemological examination will focus on the ways legal decision-makers *conceive of* a certain legal problem involving historical injustice as a particular kind of inquiry. We will portray the conception of historical injustice from an otherwise mundane perspective on the role of time and temporality in understanding wrongdoings that occurred in the past. Considering historical injustices from a temporal perspective requires a reevaluation of a range of temporalities inherent in legal inquiry. In that case, rather than viewing past injustices as a *historically given* condition in a legal inquiry, they can be seen as a perception of legal actors (i.e., judges). Reading in this manner, legal decision-makers are expected to be more attentive to the *historical* dimension of inquiries into past injustices.

This chapter argues for an investigation of historical injustice as a temporal legal inquiry. In this context—and as our case studies in Chapters 1 through 3 have described—temporal legal inquiry is understood as an investigation into the interaction between historical processes and legal temporalities. Such an interaction results in what we called the Encounter in Chapter 4. The Encounter is a set of categorical temporalities constructed in accordance with some dynamic criteria, attention to which would allow legal decision-makers (i.e., judges) to engage in the process of meaning-making a legal concept. The overarching argument in this chapter builds upon a range of literature discussing the precarious intertwinement between historical injustices or wrongdoings and their persistence or continuation in the present time. The argument calls for a thorough reading of some theoretical works in the fields of jurisprudence, political philosophy and legal history. These works later allow us to distinguish between two main approaches to investigating historical injustice adjudication, which we may call timelessness and timeliness approaches. Within these approaches, the intricate temporalities of historical injustice have been underpinned by the incessant dilemmas between time and justice. These dilemmas suggest a necessity for a more accurate temporal-analysis framework, because none of the existing approaches seems adequate to capture the multiplicity of injustice experiences. This chapter

DOI: 10.4324/9781003518693-8

later suggests an alternative approach developed from Grosz's philosophical approach to the untimely.[1]

This chapter is divided into four sections. *First*, it describes the idea of the 'historical' of injustice, drawing from two contentious perspectives: supersession and reconciliatory thesis. The contention between the two perspectives intelligibly sets grounds for our understanding of the 'historical' *of* injustices. *Second*, according to the contemporary debate on historical injustice, the current tension has been mostly framed under the traditional, while easily confused, legal relations between entitlement and obligation. To wit, historical injustices are, legally speaking, structured within the relational correlative functions of the present's claim-right (i.e., to remedy) and the past's duty (i.e., to repair). At the same time, this function tends to compel judges to focus on the legal 'positions' within the structure of injustices, in which the term 'position' itself is fundamentally a *spatial* metaphor that minimizes the role of *time* within the structure. *Third*, it addresses the significance of the role of time in historical injustice structure by reframing our theoretical orientation through Shklar's theory of injustice.[2] It is suggested that in talking about 'the kind of history' *of* injustices, our investigation should pivot on the situatedness of its context, which is, borrowing from Shklar, unpredictable and contingent. Therefore, historical injustice should be seen as a form of temporal legal inquiry. This viewpoint would allow us to sketch the contestation between timeliness and timelessness approaches to an inquiry into the past. *Fourth*, the idea of temporal encounter in historical injustices is emphasized by encapsulating the function of (immanent) time within the historical injustice inquiry. Given the variety of forms of temporal encounters, as shown in Chapters 1 through 3, we can later argue that the debate over timeliness versus timelessness of a claim of historical injustice has been unable to consider the ever-expanding perspectives related to the dilemma between time and justice in numerous jurisdictions around the world.

The historical of injustices

Historical injustice is rudimentarily grasped as a society's past problematic situation. In its application, the analysis of this kind of injustice involves a wide spectrum of implications ranging from individual, communal, national and even transnational levels. We may, for instance, easily discover the legal implications of injustices resulting from the legacy of colonialism,[3] authori-

1 Elizabeth Grosz, *The Nick of Time: Politics, Evolution, and the Untimely* (Durham & London: Duke University Press, 2004).

2 Judith N. Shklar, "The Faces of Injustice," in *The Faces of Injustice* (Yale University Press, 1990).

3 Tom Bentley, "Colonial Apologies and the Problem of the Transgressor Speaking," *Third World Quarterly* 39, no. 3 (2018): 399–417, https://doi.org/10.1080/01436597.2017.140192

tarian ruling,[4] mass atrocity,[5] industrialization[6] and war.[7] Widely used in the context of atrocious and discriminatory past of a society, historical injustice is also used or perceived through some other terms; for instance: historical wrongs, past injustices, past wrongdoings, or perhaps in some technical terms such as past atrocity, past gross violation of human rights and until quite recently, climate crisis temporalities.

This section exhibits two ways in which we can situate or perceive the 'historical' of injustice, including superseding and reconciliatory theses. Our examination of the 'historical' *of* injustices can be found in the differing views over past injustices between James Waldron, who argues for the former, and Janna Thompson, the latter. In grasping the past, Waldron took account of the supersession of historical injustice thesis. This thesis says that any claims of historical injustices should be responsive to what he calls "changes in circumstances."[8] Changes in circumstances are to be understood as a situation that occurred between points *of* time, for instance, from T_1 to T_2, which could transform the contour of (in)justices. In Waldron's words, "an act which counted as an injustice when it was committed in circumstances C_1 may be transformed, so far as its ongoing effect is concerned, into a just situation if circumstances change in the meantime from C_1 to C_2."[9] This super-

2; Gyan Prakash (ed.), *After Colonialism: Imperial Histories and Postcolonial Displacements* (Princeton, NJ: Princeton University Press, 1995); Larissa Van den Herik, "Addressing 'Colonial Crimes' through Reparations? Adjudicating Dutch Atrocities Committed in Indonesia," *Journal of International Criminal Justice* 10, no. 3 (2012): 693–705, https://doi.org/10.1093/jicj/mqs033.

4 Mark J. Osiel, *Mass Atrocity, Collective Memory and the Law* (Routledge, 2017); Joachim J. Savelsberg and Suzy McElrath, "Crime, Law, and Regime Change," *Annual Review of Law and Social Science* 10, no. 1 (2014): 259–79, https://doi.org/10.1146/annurev-lawsocsci-110413-030555; Andreas Langenohl, "Memory in Post-Authoritarian Societies," in *Cultural Memory Studies: An International and Interdisciplinary Handbook*, ed. Astrid Erll and Ansgar Nünning (Berlin: Walter de Gruyter, 2008).

5 Rachel Lopez, "The (Re)Collection of Memory after Mass Atrocity and the Dilemma for Transitional Justice," *International Law and Politics* 47 (2015): 799; Louise Mallinder, "Atrocity, Accountability, and Amnesty in a 'Post- Human Rights World'? Political Settlements Research Programme," *Political Settlements Research Programme, Working Paper 09/2017*, no. 18 (2017), www.politicalsettlements.org.

6 Nicole Rogers, *Law, Fiction and Activism in a Time of Climate Change* (Routledge, 2019); Ulrich Beck, "Emancipatory Catastrophism: What Does It Mean to Climate Change and Risk Society?" *Current Sociology* 63, no. 1 (2015): 75–88.

7 Mark J. Osiel, *Making Sense of Mass Atrocity* (New York: Cambridge University Press, 2009); Mark A. Drumbl, "Collective Responsibility and Postconflict Justice," in *Accountability for Collective Wrongdoing*, ed. Tracy Isaacs and Richard Vernon (New York: Cambridge University Press, 2011), 23–60; Daniel Butt, "Historic Injustice and the Inheritance of Rights and Duties in East Asia," in *Inherited Responsibility and Historical Reconciliation in East Asia*, ed. Jun-Hyeok Kwak and Melissa Nobles (Routledge, 2013), 42–59.

8 Jeremy Waldron, "Superseding Historic Injustice," *Ethics* 103, no. 1 (1992): 4–28.

9 Ibid., 24.

session thesis is seemingly a refutation of the directness of perception toward an unjust situation that says it must be right to give back something that was wrongly taken. It does not mean that history is absent in this thesis, since Waldron acknowledges the role of history as a lesson in the virtual that we recollect to "bringing to imaginative life the full implications of principles to which we are already in theory committed."[10] By attending to the importance of history recollection to identity and contingency, the supersession thesis is primarily underpinned by two major premises: (1) the claim that entitlements (i.e., to property, in Waldron's frame) can fade with the passage of time, and (2) any counterfactual reasoning would be hard to verify due to the enormous number of possibilities that might happen in the passage of time.

While Waldron sought to emphasize the importance of individualistic property-based rationale, Thompson offered a different view by taking a rather communitarian view in explaining the historical injustices. Thompson defended what she calls a reconciliatory approach to reparation that focuses on rectifying broken *relationships* in the past. In constructing this reconciliatory approach, Thompson interestingly made a clear distinction between history as a series of events and history as a narrative—something that is apparently missed in Waldron's supersession thesis. Thompson suggests that "[a] history that connects earlier and later injustices is not merely a chronicle of events. It is a narrative that makes sense of events at a particular time by reference to later or earlier happenings."[11] Her view seems to invite our attention to the lived experience that contains (and even preserves) the inherent nature of memory to some harmful historic events through the narrative of the past. By arguing that "[p]eople are caused to suffer not merely by the events themselves, but by the ideas they get into their heads about these events," Thompson seems to make her case a clear rejection of Waldron's supersession thesis.[12] She dismissed the common view that contrasts ancient and recent injustices. This view shows the latter has always been more significant than the earlier circumstances. Instead, she claimed that the important aspect of the reconciliatory point of view is whether there exist any attitudes, interests or policies that caused injustice during the passage of time—that is, the duration from C_1 to C_2.[13] In this passage of time, we ought to reckon that historical evidence is also being interpreted within a context in which nothing is objectively neutral. Thus, through a reconciliatory lens, according to Thompson, the 'historical' of injustice puts equal importance on

10 Ibid., 5.
11 Janna Thompson, *Taking Responsibility for the Past: Reparation and Historical Injustice* (Cambridge, UK: Polity Press, 2002), 82.
12 Ibid., 84.
13 Ibid.

both the attitude toward historical dialogue and the reassessment of present relationships.[14]

From a broader perspective, the two differing views between the supersession thesis and the reconciliatory approach highlight the tension between the liberal conception of distributive justice and the communitarian-relational concept of reparative justice.[15] Such a tension intelligibly sets the groundwork for our understanding of the 'historical' *of* injustices. Because the aim in this section is to posit (historical) time in a phenomenological understanding of injustice inquiry—rather than synthesizing our own thesis regarding historical injustices—it would be reasonable to indicate some overlapping elements between the two theories, including (1) historical injustice is a kind of community's past problematic event(s), (2) such problematic events should be situated within the passage of time and (3) the historical of injustice is taking place in the process of 'recollection' and 'interpretation' of historical evidence. But when we see historical injustice as an 'event,' we are bracketing it within certain time boundaries rather than in an otherwise-dynamic temporal flux.[16] Thus, how can we foreground the significance of temporality in understanding the 'historical' of injustice?

A kind of legal inquiry

Although the 'historical' of injustice has been temporally situated, it remains to be seen what *kind* of inquiry we are in when we make an inquiry into historical injustices. This question seems plausible given the various forms of claims, perspectives, and approaches practiced by many societies dealing with their past. By framing the examination from a legal epistemology perspective, we can understand that when judges make an inquiry into (historical) injustices, they are fundamentally augmenting knowledge about the tangled elements of space and time imagination into a legal relationship.[17]

Before we delve into the substantial elaboration of injustice, at this initial stage, it is important to explain what we mean by the term 'inquiry.' As a general notion, inquiry is a common, practical activity to know or think about

14 Ibid., 86.

15 Michael Freeman, "Historical Injustice and Liberal Political Theory," in *The Age of Apology: Facing up to the Past* (Philadelphia, PA: University of Pennsylvania Press, 2008), 45–60.

16 Harry H. Bash, "A Sense of Time: Temporality and Historicity in Sociological Inquiry," *Time & Society* 9, no. 2–3 (2000): 187–204.

17 Maksymilian Del Mar, *Artefacts of Legal Inquiry: The Value of Imagination in Adjudication* (Bloomsbury Publishing, 2020). Implicit in this proposition are Del Mar's four features of legal inquiry, claiming that inquiry is a normative, social, diachronic and experimental activity.

certain knowledge.[18] As a way of knowing, inquiry traditionally involves two overlapping processes of discovery and justification. In legal adjudication theories, the two express a stark distinction: that is, on the one hand, discovery deals with the procedural dimension of the ways judges reach their decision, and on the other hand, we are dealing with the way they justify their decision or conclusion. Evaluation of legal decisions, commonly exercised in legal science, is based on the latter since justification produces some evaluative criteria. Meanwhile, approaching discovery in legal adjudication mostly takes place in the empirical science field.

Nonetheless, we need to follow Del Mar's suggestion regarding the exigency of revising our orientation on the dichotomy (between discovery and justification) to the extent that we would be able to capture some aspects of mental processes left unexamined in legal adjudication theories.[19] There are at least two important matters to highlight at this point. First, the dichotomy restricts our way of examining the role of mental processes, such as imagination and emotion, in legal decisions.[20] Strict dichotomy treats mental processes in discovery as mere 'hunches' or 'premonitions,' whereas toward justification, we tend to separate reason and rationality from feelings, imaginations and embodiment. Second, and this is equally significant to our investigation, the dichotomy takes place in a narrow and simplistic temporality; that is, "first we discover, then we justify."[21] In this sense, as Del Mar submits, the temporality of mental process in legal reasoning is far more complex than such a simple view as inquiry (1) "occurs both in the immediate, real time of a present case as well as over extended periods of time;" and (2) "involves balancing past-oriented, present-oriented and future-oriented concerns, with its future-oriented aspect being particularly important and also largely neglected."[22]

Despite the term used or the avenues observed in inquiring historical justice, the ways in which scholars—legal scholars in particular—view historical injustice claims as past problematic legal events are fundamentally framed through a correlative functional framework. That is, historical injustice

18 In a Foucauldian sense, the term 'inquiry' is distinguished from 'test' in judicial judgments. The 'test' here reflects a battle for victory, encompassing strength in a conflict between parties (A versus B). It therefore interests in achieving justice through a somewhat localized conflict. The 'inquiry', nonetheless, puts a different procedural mechanism by canvassing the conflict (of A versus B) into a broader public matter. See Michel Foucault, "Truth and Juridical Forms," *Social Identities* 2, no. 3 (1996): 327–42.

19 Del Mar, *Artefacts of Legal Inquiry: The Value of Imagination in Adjudication*, 33–36.

20 Sharyn Roach Anleu and Kathy Mack, *Judging and Emotion: A Socio-Legal Analysis* (Oxon & New York: Routledge, 2021); Emily Kidd White, "On Emotions and the Politics of Attention in Judicial Reasoning," in *Virtue, Emotion and Imagination in Law and Legal Reasoning*, ed. Amalia Amaya and Maksymilian Del Mar (Oxford: Bloomsbury Publishing, 2020), 101–20.

21 Del Mar, *Artefacts of Legal Inquiry: The Value of Imagination in Adjudication*, 37.

22 Ibid., 48.

claims are framed as past legal events (or series of events) that entail, on the one hand, correlative historical entitlement and historical obligation on the other hand.[23] Through this rather liberal framework, historical injustice cannot be envisaged as factual or historic premises independent from the correlative concepts of right and duty.[24] That said, historical injustice inquiry is more often than not demonstrated through the lens of the right-holder (or legitimate claimant) and/or duty-bearer. Nevertheless, a clear distinction is not drawn between the civil and criminal nature of such injustices. Suffice it to say at this point that as a discourse, historical injustice inquiry has always been approached through the analogous correlational architecture of legal concepts.

The complexity of historical injustice inquiry has been thoroughly discussed in Janna Thompson's works on the theory of reparation.[25] She draws her theory by extrapolating Edmund Burke's relational identity concept to the right-obligation relationship. Notwithstanding the types of injustices under examination, Thompson clearly wrote that the reparation theory she builds must be seen as "an alternative to the 'legalistic', or 'restorative', approach to reparation for historical injustices."[26] Important for our discussion, however, is the way Thompson frames her moral inquiry of past injustices as "a systematic inquiry into the existence, nature and extent of historical obligations and entitlements."[27] In her view, historical obligation is understood as "a moral responsibility incurred by individuals as citizens, owners or executives of corporations, or members of some other transgenerational association or community, as the result of the commitments or actions of their predecessors."[28] Furthermore, it is argued that

> [t]he past is a source of obligation not merely because of the effect of past deeds on present conditions . . . [but also] by past happenings—by the fact that a treaty was signed or an unjust deed done.[29]

23 John Rawls, *A Theory of Justice* (Cambridge, MA: Belknap Press, 1999).

24 Diego M. Papayannis, "The Morality of Compensation through Tort Law," *Ratio Juris* 36, no.1 (2023): 3–25. Papayannis supports the unity thesis in tort law, which sees a sort of 'continuation' between the rights initially violated and the remedies later recognized by tort law. Papayannis wrote that "The unity thesis makes it clear that the restrictions the law imposes on our behavior before the injustice and the remedy awarded by law after the injustice share the same justification. In other words, the reasons that justify the remedy are the same reasons why we consider that the causative event constitutes an *injustice*." 9 (emphasis original).

25 Thompson, *Taking Responsibility for the Past: Reparation and Historical Injustice*; Janna Thompson, *Should Current Generations Make Reparation for Slavery?* (Cambridge, UK: Polity Press, 2018).

26 Thompson, *Taking Responsibility for the Past: Reparation and Historical Injustice*, xi.

27 Ibid., ix.

28 Ibid.

29 Ibid., x.

Since Thompson's work aims at forming a comprehensive theory, it seems reasonable for her to have such sweeping conditions of the past. In every inquiry, correspondingly, it also appears natural to argue that a certain historical obligation should entail historical entitlement that belongs to certain right holders who later claimed to be the victim. In Thompson's intelligible assertion, "[e]ntitlement is the logical flip side of obligation, and from the specification of an obligation we can derive a statement about the corresponding entitlement."[30] As a kind of legal inquiry based on this theory, historical injustice inquiry is fundamentally an examination of and a navigation toward legal positions.

Arguably, we can draw a critical view on Thompson's view on the correlative right-duty of investigating historical injustices. Specifically, our argument is addressed to this Hohfeldian scheme-alike, which seemingly pervades our (i.e., legal scholars) understanding about the issue.[31] Our critiques against this liberal correlative scheme are not necessarily peculiar to historical injustice adjudication to the extent that they are in fact trying to situate some of the existing critiques of the Hohfeldian symmetrical scheme in the context of the 'obligation-entitlement flip' of historical injustice inquiry.[32] Three points of critique particularly stand out. *First*, the obligation-entitlement flip is inadequate to capture the nonrelational legal positions of historical injustices. The correlativity implied in the issues of historical injustice reparations arises from the temptation to reduce legal relations into rights and duties (or a situation that Hohfeld calls jural relations). This relation is fundamentally functional: A has a claim-right over ø, while at the same time ascribes B some duties to ø toward A.[33] In the context of historical injustices, however, this relation is insufficient to accommodate the nonrelational 'necessities' to condemn great or radical evil, mostly discussed by international criminal lawyers. Take, for instance, Mark Drumbl's argument that exhibits the universality of condemnation against the repugnance of extreme evil. Drumbl also argued for "the universality of the condemnability of the underlying substantive harm" and "the universality of the notion that victimizers are to

30 Ibid.

31 Wesley Newcomb Hohfeld, *Fundamental Legal Conceptions as Applied in Judicial Reasoning: And Other Legal Essays* (New Haven: Yale University Press, 1923); L. H. LaRue, "Hohfeldian Rights and Fundamental Rights," *The University of Toronto Law Journal* 35, no. 1 (1985): 86–93; Vivienne Brown, "Rights, Liberties and Duties: Reformulating Hohfeld's Scheme of Legal Relations?" *Current Legal Problems* 58, no. 1 (2005): 343–67.

32 Elizabeth Kahn, "Beyond Claim-rights: Social Structure, Collectivization, and Human Rights," *Journal of Social Philosophy* 52, no. 2 (2021): 162–84; Onora O'Neill, "The Dark Side of Human Rights," *International Affairs* 81, no. 2 (2005): 427–39.

33 J. E. Penner, *Hohfeldian Liberties, Property Rights: A Re-Examination*, Online ed. (Oxford: Oxford Academic, 2020), https://doi.org/10.1093/oso/9780198830122.003.0003.

be held to account."[34] In addition to that, we might also want to refer to the 'epistemic moral elitism' that took place in post-war trials. In such instances, past injustices are construed upon individual reflection, meaning that any condemnations imposed on them "will result in the optimal balance between different moral values."[35] All these instances try to say that historical injustice inquiries ought not to be canvassed exclusively as relational legal relations, because they can also happen to be nonrelational.[36]

Second, the 'obligation-entitlement flip' is also unable to cover some of the undirected duties toward the past—for instance, as shown in our case studies in Chapters 1 through 3, the duty: to compensate or repair, to revoke unfair past legal agreement and to mitigate further future crisis. Relevant to this, Thompson situated these relational positions into theories of reparation, which she divided into two approaches: rights-centered and obligation-dependent reparation. Encompassing the latter approach, she then advocated reconciliatory reparation. At this moment, based on Thompson's thesis, it is important to note that the forward-looking reconciliatory approach to reparation is confined by certain directed duties that existed trans-generationally. In this sense, we recognize A's duty toward B to compensate B, while in a slightly different statement, we cannot deny that there also exists A's (indirect) duty to compensate.[37] This can be reflected in the growing number of laws and regulations enacted to allocate compensation for victims of past injustices. In such situations, historical injustice cannot be simply considered an event that generates directed duties to compensate.[38]

Third, the obligation-entitlement flip as a way of describing historical injustices inquiry entices us to engage in a generic representation of temporalities that conflates any causal relationships from past events into a certain mental and social state of the people in the present. Meanwhile, quoting from Jon Elster, we must also be appreciative of

> states that are essentially by-products, [which] can only come about as the by-product of actions undertaken for other ends. They can never, that is,

34 Mark A. Drumbl, *Atrocity, Punishment, and International Law* (Cambridge: Cambridge University Press, 2007), 183.

35 Carlos Santiago Nino, *Radical Evil on Trial* (New Haven & London: Yale University Press, 1996), 159.

36 Jan-Christoph Heilinger, "Individual Responsibility and Global Structural Injustice: Toward an Ethos of Cosmopolitan Responsibility," *Journal of Social Philosophy* 52, no. 2 (2021): 185–200.

37 See also Joseph Mazor, "On Environmental Justice, Part II: Non-Absolute Equal Division of Rights to the Natural World," *Economics & Philosophy* 39, no. 2 (2023): 256–84.

38 For instance, see California Task Force to Study and Develop Reparation Proposals for African Americans, "Interim Report," 2022, accessed April 17, 2023, https://oag.ca.gov/system/files/media/ab3121-reparations-interim-report-2022.pdf.

be brought about intelligently or intentionally, because the very attempt to do so precludes the state one is trying to bring about.[39]

From Elster's individualization method,[40] we can extrapolate the idea of states of by-products by suggesting that there are multiple temporal possibilities that can explain a particular condition. This requires us to be aware of the *process*ual dimension of a legal claim of injustice.[41]

Based on those three criticisms, the 'obligation-entitlement flip,' exhibited as a common denominator in construing historical injustice inquiries, understands the pasts as *moments* that took place in particular *space*. Such a flip derives from the metaphor of legal *position*, which exclusively spotlights the spatial element of an event in the past. In a way, my speculative guess is that d'Almeida shared the same view when claiming that "[legal] '[p]osition' is a convenient spatial metaphor: a person's position is where she normatively stands—another spatial metaphor—relative to some other person, and to some type of action or omission by one of them."[42] The 'flip' simply (or maybe even intuitively) considers legal relations (between subjects) within the past injustices from a spatial lens—as if it were *posited* somewhere—while disparaging its temporal aspect. Or, to be precise, such a view tends to consider time as something external, yet given to this historical event. From this lens, historical injustice essentially remains to be understood as an *atemporal* inquiry into the past, which is reducible to an exclusive *spatial* investigation of legal position.

The way of understanding historical injustice that can be reduced to (spatial) events is somewhat incomplete, if not problematic. It fails to accommodate the temporal element of legal relation, which is known to be the 'ballast' of law and legal systems.[43] This kind of (spatial) inquiry is inadequate to capture the unpredictability and contingency of the 'recollection' and 'interpretation' of historical evidence. As a response, the current temporal turn in law and legal studies might be beneficial for us in exploring a more nuanced conversation into the role of time in historical injustices inquiry, and in doing so, it is important to reexamine what we mean by injustice in this inquiry.

39 Jon Elster, *Sour Grapes* (Cambridge University Press, 2016), 43.

40 Jon Elster, "The Case for Methodological Individualism," *Theory and Society* 11, no. 4 (1982): 453–82.

41 See Chapter 4 on the discussion about law-as-process approach.

42 Luís Duarte d'Almeida, "Fundamental Legal Concepts: The Hohfeldian Framework," *Philosophy Compass* 11, no. 10 (2016): 556.

43 Niklas Luhmann, *A Sociological Theory of Law* (Oxon & New York: Routledge, 2014); Niklas Luhmann, "The Future Cannot Begin: Temporal Structures in Modern Society," *Social Research* (1976): 130–52; Dan Priel, "Analytic Jurisprudence in Time," in *Philosophy of Law as an Integral Part of Philosophy: Essays on the Jurisprudence of Gerald J. Postema*, ed. Thomas Bustamante and Thiago Lopes Decat (Oxford: Hart Publishing, 2020), 213–41.

Taking injustice seriously

While there is a considerable array of literature that discusses the idea of justice, the theoretical conversation about 'injustice' is pretty scarce among philosophers, political scientists and lawyers. Such is also the initial criticism expressed by Judith Shklar in her seminal *The Faces of Injustice*. In this book, Shklar points out that the concept of injustice has been left aside in many political theories, implying its insignificance. Many political theories traditionally claim that injustice is reducible to the 'normal model' of justice.[44] Normal mode renders that every political society is governed by rules, and the rules are seen just insofar as "they correspond to the most basic ethical beliefs of the society."[45] These theories frame injustice mostly as the absence of this normal model of justice, as something that is not just or unlawful, and this model is "taken implicitly to be adequate to the task of controlling [injustice] in practice and understanding it in theory."[46]

As a response, Shklar built her theory from the experience of victims of injustice, in which she made a distinction between active and passive injustice. The former is seemingly clear: if a person inflicts injury or acts driven by greed (or any other ominous emotional phenomena), then she is actively performing unjust action.[47] It would be clear that this kind of injustice invokes our normative judgment toward a certain event or action. The latter is about those "who turn away from actual and potential victims [and] contribute their share to the sum of iniquity."[48] Such inactivity of agents, claimed Shklar, should be regarded as a deficit in the normal model of justice. This is arguably a significant contribution to her theory of injustice. Shklar wittingly expressed that

> [t]he passively unjust man is not accused of failing to go beyond duty, but of not seeing that citizenship involves more than normal justice demands. The normally unjust man is guilty of falling below law and custom by actively violating them and also by being unfair. The passively unjust man, however, does something different; he is simply indifferent to what goes on around him, especially when he sees fraud and violence. His failure is specifically as a citizen. It is not a matter of lacking general human goodness. When he sees an illegal action or a crime, he just looks the other way. If he is a public official his offence is very grave. He is a tyrant who condones injustice by ignoring it or a negligent official who does nothing to mitigate

44 Rawls, *A Theory of Justice*, 251–58.
45 Shklar, "The Faces of Injustice," 17.
46 Ibid., 19.
47 Ibid., 30–31.
48 Ibid., 40.

> and prevent social and natural disasters. It is he who is always the first to say, "life is unjust" and forget the victims.[49]

Shklar's victim-centered approach to understanding (in)justice emphasizes the normative character of injustice. The significant moral and political consequences of the theory of injustice are that it enables us to portray a wider frame of victim's experience of injustices, particularly in the face of powerful groups in society. Arguably, the notion of power groups in society is imperative, since, as Yack pointed out,

> [s]uch groups, not surprisingly, have a strong interest in diminishing the importance of passive injustice, because the greater the attention paid to claims about passive injustice, the greater the demands that can be made on their resources and attention. Once we take this interest into consideration, it becomes clear that the normal model's restricted understanding of injustice not only fails to capture the full range of phenomena surrounding our sense of injustice, but that it also tends to reinforce the authority of the powerful and further disempower the potential victims of their arrogance, insensitivity, and indifference.[50]

There are three points to highlight from Shklar's approach to injustice. *First*, it opens a view toward the asymmetry of power acting as the structural underpinning that enables cruelty to result from "oppression and prevarication, and the fear they create."[51] *Second*, it pays attention to the so-called phenomenology of victimhood that could guide us to circumvent the questions of justification that permeate the traditional liberal theories.[52] In this sense, as Gatta suggested,

> [w]hile justificatory projects have engaged in a bracketing of reality for the sake of normative construction, Shklar draws her normative commitments from an observation of the pervasive cruelty and injustice present in the world and from a wish to affirm the rebellion of individuals to them for the sake of their safety and freedom.[53]

49 Ibid., 41–42.

50 Bernard Yack, "Injustice and the Victim's Voice," *Michigan Law Review* 89, no. 6 (1991): 1339.

51 Giunia Gatta, "Liberalism for Dark Times: Judith Shklar versus Populist Constituencies," *Global Intellectual History* 7, no. 4 (2022): 3.

52 Natascha Mueller-Hirth, "Temporalities of Victimhood: Time in the Study of Postconflict Societies," in *Sociological Forum*, vol. 32 (Wiley Online Library, 2017), 186–206; Cheryl Lawther, "'Let Me Tell You': Transitional Justice, Victimhood and Dealing with a Contested Past," *Social & Legal Studies* 30, no. 6 (2021): 890–912.

53 Gatta, "Liberalism for Dark Times: Judith Shklar versus Populist Constituencies," 3.

Third, such a phenomenological frame exhibits the complexity of political processes and decision-making and the extent to which agents are negotiating 'abstract moral assumptions' within the 'unpredictable and contingent' context.[54] It is important to note at this point that we do not attempt to equate 'political process and decision-making' with 'adjudicative process and decision-making.' Rather, we intend to underline the processual nature of both processes, which takes into account and acknowledges the unpredictability and contingency of a certain condition—as discussed in Chapter 4.

Having outlined our particular vision toward injustice, we may furthermore indicate some theoretical implications for the nexus between law and history, particularly in contexts related to past wrongdoings. At this point, it is important to note that if we take Shklar's discontent with liberal political theory seriously, we may need to assert that the justification framed in such liberal theories, whether utilitarian or natural-law theories, is fundamentally ahistorical.[55] This assertion implies that the concept of liberal justice is being generated *outside* of history because it seeks to exclusively create a just future rather than rectify the past. Furthermore, the existing viewpoint approaches justice, especially in the legal domain, solely through emphasizing individual liberalism while ignoring its communitarian element.[56] As a result, in a discussion about 'the kind of history' of injustices, we should focus on the situatedness of its context, which is, borrowing from Shklar, unpredictable and contingent. And for that reason, the nexus between law and history basically entails a dialogue between history's empirical and normative aspects.

The aforementioned criticisms draw our attention to shifting the historical investigation of injustices from an *atemporal* to a *temporal* legal inquiry framework. In this context, we should understand the term 'injustice' as experiences that occurred *in* time rather than simply in space. The underlying idea is that time pervades all aspects of our daily lives, including those of lawyers, and shapes how we see and understand the world. In that case, how do legal decision-makers (i.e., judges) approach historical injustice in a

54 Ibid., 5–6.

55 Berber Bevernage, "The Past Is Evil/Evil Is Past: On Retrospective Politics, Philosophy of History, and Temporal Manichaeism," *History and Theory* 54, no. 3 (2015): 333–52. Bevernage claimed that prevalent retrospective politics after the Cold War were underpinned by *post-histoire* ideology. As a consequence, this ideology "leads to a sort of temporal Manichaeism that can obscure the structural continuities between the chronological past and the chronological present and that, by means of its own version of *Ohnmachtsgarantie*, protects contemporary humanity from moral responsibility and blame leaking from the past into the present. Yet, as I noted, this same ideology also includes intellectual mechanics that extend this *Ohnmachtsgarantie* to evil and injustice happening in the (chronological) present. It does this by means of a specific politics of time that (performatively) historicizes parts of the chronological present on the basis of what one could call 'typological time.'" 15–16.

56 Rawls, *A Theory of Justice*, 153; Joel MacClellan, "How (Not) to Defend a Rawlsian Approach to Intergenerational Ethics," *Ethics & the Environment* 18, no. 1 (2013): 67–85.

temporal frame? In terms of time and temporality, how do they perceive past injustices?

We need to frame historical injustice as a form of *temporal legal inquiry*. Put another way, historical injustice involved in legal cases ought to be viewed as a form of inquiry that investigates the interaction between historical processes and legal temporalities. As our case studies in Part One have suggested, we can indicate the ways in which time, through the lens of historians, may interfere with time grasped by lawyers. This interference allows legal decision-makers to access (or imagine) the representation of historical injustice and to express the forms of lawful relations in a legal case. Two major approaches to historical inquiry are highlighted: timeliness and timelessness.

First, the common temporal approach in analyzing historical injustices is to ask whether the claim against an unjust event satisfies the *timeliness* approach; that is, a claim for remedy or reparation that is sufficiently timely in order to justify a practice of blaming and responsibility. This approach relies fundamentally on the temporal proximity principle, which is used as an effective legal tool to determine cause and effect over time.[57] Temporal proximity captures temporality as an interior part of the human mind capable of comprehending both tensed and tense-free temporality. This is, however, situated in an epistemic condition in the sense that, as Khan put it, "temporality is embedded in memorialized facts . . . yet the mind has the ability to misreport the temporal order of facts stored in memory."[58]

To make this proposition intelligible, let us cite again a passage from the *African American Slave Descendant Litigation* case filed by slaves' descendants in the United States. In this 2004 case, the District Court of Illinois dealt with a civil complaint of reparation resulting from chattel slavery centuries ago. Typically found in many other reparation claims, the primary legal challenge is about the feasibility of the Plaintiffs' claims.[59] The idea of *timeliness* of a complaint, as the Court argues, must satisfy at least three criteria: (1) the chronology of history that surmises the state of likelihood over time, either in terms of an individual's well-being or in terms of the diminishing properties; (2) the individual or group's self-identification as an extended character to represent harm, which can be seen from the Court's acknowledgment of the Plaintiffs' status as legal representatives of their slave ancestors and (3) the chronological temporal limit to legal doctrine and concepts. As seen from

57 Jeremy Waldron, "The Principle of Proximity," in *Public Law and Legal Theory Research Paper Series* (New York: New York University, 2011). A more elaborate critique against the proximity principle is provided in Chapter 7.

58 Liaquat Ali Khan, "Temporality of Law," *McGeorge Law Review* 40, no. 1 (2009): 77.

59 Nicole L. Immler and Stef Scagliola, "Seeking Justice for the Mass Execution in Rawagede/ Probing the Concept of 'Entangled History' in a Postcolonial Setting," *Rethinking History* 24, no. 1 (2020): 1–28.

these criteria, the timeliness approach is acting as a delimiting reason for the judges to justify the claimable damage or harm in the recent or distant past. This approach is consistent with Waldron's theory of supersession. Being agnostic toward the contour of injustice disputed, be it active or passive, the Court is capable of instrumentalizing time to contain what kind of event and whose experience is to be deemed as part of a legally valid claim.

Second, a distinct venture in legal scholarship has been trying to capture the epistemological features of continuity and persistence in historical injustice. Call this the *timelessness* approach. Contrary to the timeliness requirement, the timelessness of historical injustices sheds light on the idea of the perpetuity of injustices. Unlike the timeliness' basis of temporal proximity, this approach relies upon temporal correlation, which expounds that "law uses the correlation between temporality and change to determine legally significant relations."[60] In this sense, time correlates, rather than causes, change, while law itself "relies on temporal proximity to interweave events, draw inferences, and attach liability."[61] This kind of approach allows us to employ legal doctrines to portray the flexibility of fluid time. As a matter of semantic argument, we may again denote Justice Posner's argument invoking the tolling doctrine in order to 'extend the time' in the *African American Slave Descendant Litigation* case.

> *In all likelihood it would still be impossible for them to prove injury, requiring as that would connecting the particular slavery transactions in which the defendants were involved to harm to particular slaves.* But in any event, suits complaining about injuries that occurred more than a century and a half ago have been barred for a long time by the applicable state statutes of limitations. *It is true that tolling doctrines can extend the time to sue well beyond the period of limitations*—but not to a century and more beyond. Slaves could not sue, and even after the Thirteenth Amendment became effective in 1865 suits such as these, if brought in the South, would not have received a fair hearing.[62]

Forged by some authoritative legal practices and techniques, the persistence of past injustices in the present moment is deemed fundamental to understanding historical injustice as a temporal inquiry. The timelessness approach can be represented by the application of the legal imprescriptibility principle, which overcomes any temporal limitation in prompting historical inquiry in legal adjudication practices. This principle simply says that "[several] crimes have

60 Khan, "Temporality of Law," 69.
61 Ibid., 72.
62 7th Cir., In re African-American Slave Descendants Litig., 471 F.3d 754, 762 (2006). (emphasis added)

to be investigated, prosecuted, and punished regardless of the passage of time, that is regardless of time bars or statutes of limitations."[63] In practice, this principle precipitates a new right that accommodates the victim's right toward the principle, namely the right to the truth. This newly emerging right reads that

> victims of human rights violations and their families have the inalienable, non-derogable, and imprescriptible right to know the truth about the circumstances in which the violations have taken place and, in the event of death or disappearance, to know the victim's fate.[64]

As reflected by the legal imprescriptibility principle, the timelessness approach pivots on two principles. *First*, the inertia principle, which understands that "law maintains temporal inertia by resisting or refusing to acknowledge changes."[65] In brief, inertia implies that law maintains the status quo. Temporal inertia thus could be best understood as the law's core attribute, as it provides that "state rules that do not change over a period of time (Δt)."[66] It ensures the law's systemic, constant stability and continuity. In practice, inertia could also be reflected through the doctrine of precedent and remedy—through remedial injunction. *Second*, the principle of temporal triggers, which views a time-trigger as a point in time (t) that initiates or terminates a legal event.[67] In this view, time can allocate law, legal action, power, right or obligation into being, while at the same time, it can also bring legal concepts to an end.

The timelessness approach has been able to divulge the conversation beyond the timely justice upheld by legal formalism. For instance, Corrias and Francot have argued that there is an urgent need for legal scholars to read Radbruch's idea of justice, expediency and legal certainty in light of society's current challenges.[68] The contemporary societal challenge submits that we are living in an age of uncertainty that involves "all-pervasive contingency and structural process of acceleration."[69] This condition puts expediency trump over justice and legal certainty.[70] In that sense,

> [t]he past thus seems to last longer and longer, spilling over in the present and in the future. The temporal dimension . . . cannot be grasped by

63 Antoon De Baets, "Historical Imprescriptibility," *Storia Della Storiografia* 59 (2011): 129.
64 Ibid., 130.
65 Khan, "Temporality of Law," 80.
66 Ibid., 81.
67 Ibid., 87.
68 Luigi Corrias and Lyana Francot, "Temporal Boundaries of Politics and Law: Time Out of Joint," in *Temporal Boudaries of Law and Politics: Time Out of Joint*, ed. Luigi Corrias and Lyana Francot (Oxon & New York: Routledge, 2018), 1–12.
69 Ibid., 6.
70 Ibid.

> a conception of justice which takes its starting point in the situation of justice between equals living at (roughly) the same place and at the same time.[71]

In this kind of 'new order of historicity,' we may claim that there appears to be 'the past that does not pass.' Or, as Garapon suggested, there has been a 'new order of historicity' perceived as an assertion of attitude between politics and criminal justice in revising or purging history.[72] This new historicity was initially taking place in a post-war and transition-to-democracy context, in a society that mostly survived mass atrocities and grave violations of human rights. The present and future are viewed through the historic past, which is largely determined by a specific moment that traumatizes society (e.g., the Holocaust, the apartheid regime and so on). According to Garapon,

> [t]his new order of history seems characteristic of a time going in the opposite direction when compared to the normal flow of time. Rather than progressively moving towards oblivion by healing wounds, time seems to function exactly in the opposite way: resentment gradually grows as the event becomes more distant in time. Although the crimes may be declared imperceptible, they nonetheless seem less and less tolerable as time passes, like debt increases inexorably with interest over time.[73]

Consequently, what we are seeing is a tendency to incorporate the historic meaning of the past into the moral significance of a legal process. Such an incorporation of meaning is considered to be the foundation of timelessness of historical inquiries. To be timeless is thus about the way this new order of historicity "sets time aside to concentrate on the moment of the trial only."[74] The moment of trial, it is claimed, "suspends time," thus combining "two distinct and complementary temporalities: a past that is called upon (by way of discourse and the symbolic framework of the trial) and an all-powerful present (capable of acting in the past)."[75] Timelessness is understood not as an abolition of chronological time in our historical inquiry but rather to morally rectify the past "by adding moral consequences to material ones" (of the present)[76]—or "to undo the 'normalization' of the event which had

71 Ibid., 4.

72 Antoine Garapon, "Judging the Past: Three Ways of Understanding Time," in *Temporal Boundaries of Law and Politics: Time Out of Joints*, ed. Luigi Corrias and Lyana Francot (Oxon & New York: Routledge, 2018), 15–32; François Hartog, *Regimes of Historicity: Presentism and Experiences of Time* (New York: Columbia University Press, 2015).

73 Garapon, "Judging the Past: Three Ways of Understanding Time," 19. (citation omitted)

74 Ibid., 22.

75 Ibid.

76 Ibid., 23.

occurred with time."[77] This process is a reflection of what Garapon claims to be the dualistic "suspension/restoration" of time, and, from such assertions, timelessness can be characterized as: (1) insensitivity to the passage of time; (2) representing the multitude of (irreparable) experiences that have something to do with the idea of the victim's experiences; (3) reconciliatory beyond truth provided by the court of law and (4) transforming a double task that may appear contradictory; that is, to take note of evil while fighting against it at the same time.

The temporal encounter

The timeliness and timelessness approaches to historical injustice inquiry have arguably been helpful for legal practitioners and decision-makers to situate the interference between historical time and legal temporalities. Particularly, we have seen the ways in which time plays a role in justifying the forms of legal reasoning undertaken by legal decision-makers in cases involving historical injustices.[78] It suggests that the passage of time is undoubtedly fundamental in our effort to frame historical injustice as a form of temporal legal inquiry. In such instances, the interplay between historical time and legal temporalities yields what we may call *temporal encounter*, that is, a set of categorical temporalities based on dynamics criteria that enables legal decision-makers (i.e., judges) to participate in the meaning-making process of a legal relation. As a result, seeing historical injustices through the passage of time compels us to think about various temporal encounters that exist *within* every historical inquiry. Temporal encounter is simply understood as, to borrow from Grosz's term, a "nick of time" that the judges do not expect—it is something that insists they be creative in experimenting with the law in time.[79]

This final section explains the significance of temporal encounters in the historical injustice inquiry. The examination covers two critical matters: *first*, the importance of temporal encounter in our investigation of historical injustice as temporal inquiry, and *second*, several limitations of applying timeliness and timelessness to understand temporal encounter. Such limitations later invite us to seek out an alternative model or approach to inquire about historical injustices. We parse the concept of 'temporal encounter' by situating legal historian Antoon De Baets' principle of historical imprescriptibility and view this principle as an encounter in time. De Baets views historical imprescriptibility as an extension of the imprescriptibility principle

77 Ibid.
78 See Chapters 1 through 3.
79 Grosz, *The Nick of Time: Politics, Evolution, and the Untimely*; Elizabeth Grosz, "Bergson, Deleuze and the Becoming of Unbecoming," *Parallax* 11, no. 2 (2005): 4–13.

recognized primarily in international legal practice. De Baets argued for two types of elements that have stretched the imprescriptibility principle from the legal to the historical plane based on historical progress in the field of international (criminal) law. The first type is backward stretching. This type covers (1) the imprescriptibility discussed in the 1968 United Nations Convention on the Non-Applicability of Statutory Limitations to War Crimes and Crimes Against Humanity and (2) impressive pedigrees in the development of victim-centered right protection.[80] The second type is forward stretching, which includes (1) the perpetuity of a victim's right to invoke the right to the truth regarding human rights violations; (2) victims and their families have the right to the truth, which may extend to almost two centuries; and (3) the truth of past injustice has social significance that lasts even after the passing of perpetrators and victims.[81]

However, historical imprescriptibility does not diminish the importance of legal imprescriptibility exercised in legal adjudications (see e.g., de Baets' distinction between legal and historical imprescriptibility).[82] Rather, by juxtaposing the two, as de Baets suggests, we can obtain a more nuanced landscape of temporal legal inquiry. Some challenges certainly arise against this move. In that sense, we need to reframe our understanding of cognitive dilemmas (described in the introductory chapter) in light of the time versus justice conundrum related to this kind of legal inquiry. These conundrums include: (1) time and fair trial related to the perpetrators, in which imprescriptibility is concerned with the likelihood that those accused of the crime will receive a fair trial while, at the same time, it appears to be deteriorating as a result of diminishing evidence over time; (2) time and humanity to the victims, in which imprescriptibility put concerns more on the victim's predicament over rights of the suspects; (3) time and social importance to society at large, in which whether imprescriptibility hampers reconciliation or instead facilitates "continuity of obligations, public interest in the truth, and remembrance"[83] and (4) time and epistemology to the professionals (e.g., historian and lawyers) that puts imprescriptibility, on the one hand, running the risk of anachronism, and on the other hand, appealing to the principles of retrospection, comparability and consequentialism.[84]

We can classify the first two dilemmas as the dilemma of agency and the last two as the dilemma of structure.[85] In this sense, the dilemmas aimed at

80 De Baets, "Historical Imprescriptibility," 130.
81 Ibid., 131.
82 Ibid., 132.
83 Ibid., 145.
84 Ibid., 142.
85 Of course, we can expand discussion on these issues, particularly on the structural part. But it suffices to state here that the structure may cover matters addressed by some contemporary theorists. See in particular Iris Marion Young, *Responsibility for Justice* (New York: Oxford

indicating "the range of well-founded evaluations" toward responsibility for historical injustices underpin the way legal decision-makers craft a plausible interpretation of historical injustices.[86] These dilemmas are actually temporal Encounters, a 'nick of time' that the judges may not expect. As part of the process of inquiry, they are a set of categorical temporalities construed upon some dynamic criteria of agent and structure that enable legal decision-makers to participate in the process of meaning-making in legal relations. The critical question at this point is then what is the best way to approach these dilemmas? Specifically, one may ask, how do legal decision-makers need to think of the *quality* of time experienced within these dilemmas?

Accordingly, based on the said proposition, we can say that the dilemmas of imprescriptibility, as *the* temporal encounter, cannot be fully explained through the timeliness or the timelessness approaches. Both the timelessness and timeliness approaches appear to be restrictive in understanding the role of time in two senses, *at least* in their efforts to depict the two dilemmas of agency and structure. *First*, the two approaches fail to capture the structural dimension of injustice. The structure—something immaterial like 'societal discrimination'—would be too vague to understand by legal decision-makers because these approaches are simply dwelling into the temporalities of the past and the present.[87] Meanwhile, as suggested by Grosz's critical philosophy, the untimely approach advises us to get detached from the current structure that preserves (and sometimes prevails) injustices over time. *Second*, these approaches are inadequate insofar as they are unable to accommodate the question of the role of agency in temporal legal inquiry. That is, neither timeliness nor timelessness equips us with a view to accommodate the heterogeneous experiences of injustice.[88] Meanwhile, attending to the temporal encounter requires legal decision-makers to be sensitive to the actual-passive injustice, which compels them to employ a broader canvas in sketching historical injustice.

The *untimely* approach can be an appropriate framework of navigating the judge's cognitive dilemma between time and justice (i.e., transition, trauma and uncertainty in Part One). The term untimely here builds upon

University Press, 2011); Maeve McKeown, "Structural Injustice," *Philosophy Compass* 16, no. 7 (2021): e12757.

86 De Baets, "Historical Imprescriptibility," 149. A more detailed discussion about responsibility is provided in Chapter 7.

87 Yuvraj Joshi, "Affirmative Action as Transitional Justice," *Wisconsin Law Review*, no. 1 (2020): 1–48; Angela Onwuachi-Willig, "Reconceptualizing the Harms of Discrimination," *Virginia Law Review* 105, no. 2 (2019): 343–69.

88 Mueller-Hirth, "Temporalities of Victimhood: Time in the Study of Postconflict Societies." As an example, Mueller-Hirth sketched several areas of 'temporal conflicts' in a post-conflict society, including victimhood as temporary/victimhood as continuous; the pace of national reconciliation/the time(s) of individual healing; and the speed of a neoliberal economy/the pace of social transformation.

McNeilly's argument that grasps the field of international human rights law as the untimely.[89] Inspired by Elizabeth Grosz's political theory of the untimely, McNeilly argues that untimely thinking toward the law "requires abandoning commitment to linearity, progression, and predictability."[90] In contrast, she suggests that

> this area of law must be apprehended as operating via a conception of the future that does not necessarily follow progressively from the past or present, that is unknown and out of control of the present, and that better foregrounds the continual elaboration of the new.[91]

From a different point of view, as Bevernage rightly suggests, this approach may require us to "break with the idea of the fully contemporaneous present and instead embrace that of radical noncontemporaneity or noncoevalness."[92] Applying this approach to historical injustice inquiry requires legal decision-makers to acknowledge the unpredictability and contingency of such inquiry and be attentive to the multiplicity of injustice (e.g., as experienced by the victim-claimants).

Seeing through the lens of legal adjudication, the untimely approach emphasizes the need for legal decision-makers to recognize the transition from 'the regularity and expediency of adjudication'—i.e., recall the issues Corrias and Francot have emphasized in relation to Radbruch's theory—to a form of creative and experimental judgment.[93] By respecting the creative exploration toward the temporal encounter of a legal inquiry, the untimely approach may be able to provide legal decision-makers with a novel perspective on historical injustice. In that sense, as suggested by Grosz, the idea would be that the 'historical' of the (present time) injustice should be understood as "the persistence of the past in the present" [and] "the ongoing revision of the past in the light of its changing relevance to the present."[94] Moreover, seeing the untimely through the lens of Bergsonian theory of duration emphasizes

89 Kathryn McNeilly, "Are Rights Out of Time? International Human Rights Law, Temporality, and Radical Social Change," *Social & Legal Studies* 28, no. 6 (2019): 817–38, https://doi.org/10.1177/0964663918815729; Grosz, *The Nick of Time: Politics, Evolution, and the Untimely*; Christos Marneros, " 'It Is a Nomos Very Different from the Law': On Anarchy and the Law," *Acta Universitatis Lodziensis. Folia Iuridica*, no. 96 (2021): 125–39.

90 McNeilly, "Are Rights Out of Time? International Human Rights Law, Temporality, and Radical Social Change," 17.

91 Ibid., 2.

92 Bevernage, "The Past Is Evil/Evil Is Past: On Retrospective Politics, Philosophy of History, and Temporal Manichaeism," 19.

93 Alexandre Lefebvre, *The Image of Law: Deleuze, Bergson, Spinoza* (Stanford: Stanford University Press, 2008), 173–95. McNeilly, "Are Rights Out of Time? International Human Rights Law, Temporality, and Radical Social Change."

94 Grosz, *The Nick of Time: Politics, Evolution, and the Untimely*, 254.

the role of the past as "not only the condition of the present but also the condition of every possible future that may arise from or be made out of the present."[95] The past is infinitively reflective, demanding an active force for reactivating the past in the present. Importantly, and this is also relevant to our previous discussion about legal reasoning, following Grosz, we could infer that such an active force "is not simply the present seeking out past resemblances and relevancies, precedents; it is also the past seeking to extend itself and its potential into the present, waiting for those present events that provide it with revivification."[96]

Arguably, it also seems enticing to presume that the untimely approach has a similar understanding to the *de-temporalizing* injustice approach. As one of the few scholars who advocates the de-temporalizing approach, Alasia Nuti claims that de-temporalizing injustice is a matter of "showing that unjust history should be envisaged as present in a deep and dynamic way. In particular, it entails reconceptualizing history (and unjust historical events) as long-term structures."[97] Two elements are fundamental in this approach, namely: "(1) the relation between past and present injustice, and consequently (2) the complex interplay between persistence and change."[98] As a matter of underlying principles, the untimely bears some resemblance to Nuti's de-temporalizing approach in the sense that both approaches are attentive to the processual nature of injustice over time. Both suggest that past injustice is not a mere contained event but rather linked to the so-called long-term structure. Therefore, the two approaches refrain any inquiries into injustice from being reduced to a conversation (or even a debate) about historical demarcation of events.[99]

Nevertheless, as a matter of inquiry,[100] the untimely approach differs itself from the de-temporalizing injustice in two senses: *First*, the untimely is essentially a way to detach the historical inquiry from the present injustice—the present can be seen as Rainer Forst's space of justification.[101] It attempts to

95 Ibid.
96 Ibid.
97 Alasia Nuti, *Injustice and the Reproduction of History: Structural Inequalities, Gender and Redress* (Cambridge: Cambridge University Press, 2019), 13.
98 Ibid.
99 Emanuela Fronza, *Memory and Punishment: Historical Denialism, Free Speech and the Limits of Criminal Law, International Criminal Justice Series*, vol. 19 (The Hague: T.M.C Asser Press, 2018), www.tandfonline.com/doi/abs/10.1080/0731129X.2000.9992088.
100 Historical injustice could be also seen as a matter of conceptual discussion. Later in Chapter 7, we will address the concept of collective responsibility as the doctrinal object in the pursuance of historical justice.
101 Rainer Forst, *The Right to Justification: Elements of a Constructivist Theory of Justice*, trans. Jeffrey Flynn, vol. 46 (New York: Columbia University Press, 2011), 22. Space of justification, according to Forst, "is not a space that contains a stock of moral truths that are fixed once and for all, but one that must always be reactualized and newly validated

see the present as an extension of the past rather than treating the two as separate modalities of time or even othering the past from the present. That is, the conflating modalities of time (past, present and future) assert that the actual presence of injustice is rather a *result* of the virtual (past) injustice recollection. This assertion gives us more liberty to understand injustice compared with the structural interpretation of history proposed by the de-temporalization approach.[102] *Second*, the untimely appreciates the process of becoming within the domain of injustice. In this sense, while both approaches primarily affirm the reproduction and reactivation of past injustices into the present, the untimely yields a sort of mindfulness to any possibilities to explore and experiment with potentialities—in our case, the law's potential force—instead. The past is not seen as a 'pattern' for change but simply a 'model,' or rather 'a mask for innovation' that accelerates and transforms. The past in the untimely, therefore, "no longer expresses the repetition of what has gone before, but actions which are by definition different from those had gone before."[103]

To recapitulate, this section has described temporal encounter as a set of categorical temporalities construed by legal decision-makers, i.e., judges, in accordance with the dynamic criteria that allows them to participate in the process of giving a legal concept a certain meaning. We have seen that, either in the timeliness or the timelessness approaches, the linear, progressive and knowable future is the common structure of temporal frame in interpreting historical inquiries. Meanwhile, given the extent to which law has been stretched to encompass historical imprescriptibility, we may come to believe that time is fundamentally *ingrained* in the practice of law (and history, for

in concrete practices of justification. The members of this space recognize themselves as moral persons who owe one another mutually determined reasons for their actions; they understand themselves at the same time as reasonable, autonomous, and moral beings who must be able to account for their actions to one another. In this sense they are members of a common 'realm of reasons' that corresponds in moral respects to a 'realm of ends': a community of moral persons who make respect. for the fundamental right to justification the basis of their action." (citation omitted) 22.

102 It is important to note that Nuti also stresses that "recognizing the structural dimensions of history does not mean regarding the actual occurrence of an event (e.g., a wrong, crime or injustice) as fully determined by the long-term structures that ground its condition of possibility. It merely attributes 'explanatory autonomy' to long-term structures by arguing that how a particular event (and repetitions of analogous events) could happen in the first place remains unexplained without considering such structures. Moreover, long-term structures do not reproduce a historical injustice on their own; they are reactivated precisely by human agency." Nuti, *Injustice and the Reproduction of History: Structural Inequalities, Gender and Redress*, 28–29. (citation omitted)

103 Eric J. Hobsbawm, "The Social Function of the Past: Some Questions," *Past & Present*, no. 55 (1972): 6; Rainer Forst, "The Justification of Progress and the Progress of Justification," in *Justification and Emancipation: The Critical Theory of Rainer Forst*, ed. Amy Allen and Eduardo Mendieta (Penn State Press, 2019), 17–37.

obvious reasons). The fact that time and temporality are beyond judges' *actual* control compels them to pay close attention to the notion that historical injustices are *virtually* resulting or generating the so-called temporal encounters. Consequently, as also confirmed by our case studies in Chapters 1 through 3, legal decision-makers must alter their way of approaching the topic of historical injustice, or, to be precise, of elucidating the question pertaining to 'the historical' of injustice. Suggested by Grosz's untimely approach, we may therefore submit that in framing historical injustice as temporal legal inquiry, "[t]he past is our resource for overcoming the present, for bringing about a future."[104] The *historical*, within such a perspective, could enrich legal decision-makers with many possibilities of transformation as it can disrupt the present with resources that were unused by oppressed, disadvantaged people from the past.[105] Experiences stemming from the historical process of injustices, as a result of the Encounter, imply the idea of rendering injustices out of time, isolating judges' investigation from the context of the past and present, thus enabling them to see the novel and unknowable future becoming. The untimely brings to judges history into a novel form, that is, history in duration. It is, quoting from Zanfi's reading on Bergson's duration,

> a history in which there is no divorce from our living background, which does not believe us capable of completely abandoning our natural conditions, in which the "laws" of history reflect the movement of the evolution of life; and also, a history propelled by the actions of great human individuals as well as by non- human agents such as technical objects and conditions of access to natural resources.[106]

Conclusion

This chapter has delineated some fundamental, albeit general, roles of time and temporality in understanding historical injustices and depicted the spatiotemporal significance of historical injustice as proposed by theorists in the fields of philosophy and sociolegal jurisprudence. This study frames historical injustice as a form of temporal legal inquiry that examines the way in which the temporalities of law interact with the historical processes involved in legal inquiry. If Shklar's conception of injustice is to be taken seriously, we will need to further investigate the reality of change, contingency and

104 Grosz, *The Nick of Time: Politics, Evolution, and the Untimely*, 257.

105 Hobsbawm, "The Social Function of the Past: Some Questions," 10–14; Joseph Mazor, "On Environmental Justice, Part I: An Intuitive Conservation Dilemma," *Economics & Philosophy* 39, no. 2 (2023): 230–55; Mazor, "On Environmental Justice, Part II: Non-Absolute Equal Division of Rights to the Natural World."

106 Caterina Zanfi, "The Duration of History in Bergson," *Bergsoniana*, no. 1 (2021): 168.

context that underlie the ways and extent to which legal decision-makers frame (or express) such temporal legal inquiries. This kind of reality involves the intersection of historical time and legal temporality, which then generates a temporal encounter in the form of dilemmas of time and justice. Nevertheless, the two common approaches to describing temporal legal inquiry (i.e., timeliness and timelessness) have proven to be insufficient in meeting the contemporary need for jurisprudence to understand the question of the structure and agency of injustice. As this chapter has suggested, the untimely approach to historical injustice, as an approach to temporal legal inquiry, could address the dilemma of time and (in)justice. This approach underscores that an inquiry into the historical of injustice is fundamentally an experimental quest in law. Law (and legal reasoning) in this sense is a creative process of inventing, changing and transforming.

Seen through the untimely approach, legal decision-makers are able to perceive the temporal modalities of the past, present and future as reflections of life itself. And life, in that sense, is always political; to quote from Grosz's view on the critical movement,

> [i]t is an ongoing struggle, for it is the articulation of ways of living, an ongoing experiment in the attainment of maximal difference rather than the attainment of specific goals. It is an art more than a science, a mode of intuition rather than reflection, dealing with bringing into existence new social relations, distributions of force, theoretical models, concepts, and ethical values, the likes of which have never existed before.[107]

Reference list

7th Cir. In re African-American Slave Descendants Litig., 471 F.3d 754, 762 (2006).

Anleu, Sharyn Roach, and Kathy Mack. *Judging and Emotion: A Socio-Legal Analysis*. Oxon & New York: Routledge, 2021.

Baets, Antoon De. "Historical Imprescriptibility." *Storia Della Storiografia* 59 (2011): 60.

Bash, Harry H. "A Sense of Time: Temporality and Historicity in Sociological Inquiry." *Time & Society* 9, no. 2–3 (2000): 187–204.

Beck, Ulrich. "Emancipatory Catastrophism: What Does It Mean to Climate Change and Risk Society?" *Current Sociology* 63, no. 1 (2015): 75–88.

Bentley, Tom. "Colonial Apologies and the Problem of the Transgressor Speaking." *Third World Quarterly* 39, no. 3 (2018): 399–417. https://doi.org/10.1080/01436597.2017.1401922.

Bevernage, Berber. "The Past Is Evil/Evil Is Past: On Retrospective Politics, Philosophy of History, and Temporal Manichaeism." *History and Theory* 54, no. 3 (2015): 333–52.

107 Grosz, *The Nick of Time: Politics, Evolution, and the Untimely*, 260.

Brown, Vivienne. “Rights, Liberties and Duties: Reformulating Hohfeld’s Scheme of Legal Relations?” *Current Legal Problems* 58, no. 1 (2005): 343–67.
Butt, Daniel. “Historic Injustice and the Inheritance of Rights and Duties in East Asia.” In *Inherited Responsibility and Historical Reconciliation in East Asia*, edited by Jun-Hyeok Kwak and Melissa Nobles, 42–59. Routledge, 2013.
California Task Force to Study and Develop Reparation Proposals for African Americans. “Interim Report.” 2022. https://oag.ca.gov/system/files/media/ab3121-reparations-interim-report-2022.pdf.
Corrias, Luigi, and Lyana Francot. “Temporal Boundaries of Politics and Law: Time Out of Joint.” In *Temporal Boudaries of Law and Politics: Time Out of Joint*, edited by Luigi Corrias and Lyana Francot, 1–12. Oxon & New York: Routledge, 2018.
Drumbl, Mark A. *Atrocity, Punishment, and International Law*. Cambridge: Cambridge University Press, 2007.
Drumbl, Mark A. *Atrocity, Punishment, and International Law*. “Collective Responsibility and Postconflict Justice.” In *Accountability for Collective Wrongdoing*, edited by Tracy Isaacs and Richard Vernon, 23–60. New York: Cambridge University Press, 2011.
Duarte d'Almeida, Luís. “Fundamental Legal Concepts: The Hohfeldian Framework.” *Philosophy Compass* 11, no. 10 (2016): 554–69.
Elster, Jon. “The Case for Methodological Individualism.” *Theory and Society* 11, no. 4 (1982): 453–82.
Elster, Jon. *Sour Grapes*. Cambridge University Press, 2016.
Forst, Rainer. *The Right to Justification: Elements of a Constructivist Theory of Justice*. Translated by Jeffrey Flynn. Vol. 46. New York: Columbia University Press, 2011.
Forst, Rainer. “The Justification of Progress and the Progress of Justification.” In *Justification and Emancipation: The Critical Theory of Rainer Forst*, edited by Amy Allen and Eduardo Mendieta, 17–37. Penn State Press, 2019.
Foucault, Michel. “Truth and Juridical Forms.” *Social Identities* 2, no. 3 (1996): 327–42.
Freeman, Michael. “Historical Injustice and Liberal Political Theory.” In *The Age of Apology: Facing up to the Past*, 45–60. Philadelphia, PA: University of Pennsylvania Press, 2008.
Fronza, Emanuela. *Memory and Punishment: Historical Denialism, Free Speech and the Limits of Criminal Law. International Criminal Justice Series*. Vol. 19. The Hague: T.M.C Asser Press, 2018. www.tandfonline.com/doi/abs/10.1080/0731129X.2000.9992088.
Garapon, Antoine. “Judging the Past: Three Ways of Understanding Time.” In *Temporal Boundaries of Law and Politics: Time Out of Joints*, edited by Luigi Corrias and Lyana Francot, 15–32. Oxon & New York: Routledge, 2018.
Gatta, Giunia. “Liberalism for Dark Times: Judith Shklar versus Populist Constituencies.” *Global Intellectual History* 7, no. 4 (2022): 666–84.
Grosz, Elizabeth. *The Nick of Time: Politics, Evolution, and the Untimely*. Durham & London: Duke University Press, 2004.
Grosz, Elizabeth. “Bergson, Deleuze and the Becoming of Unbecoming.” *Parallax* 11, no. 2 (2005): 4–13.
Hartog, François. *Regimes of Historicity: Presentism and Experiences of Time*. New York: Columbia University Press, 2015.
Heilinger, Jan-Christoph. “Individual Responsibility and Global Structural Injustice: Toward an Ethos of Cosmopolitan Responsibility.” *Journal of Social Philosophy* 52, no. 2 (2021): 185–200.

Herik, Larissa Van den. "Addressing 'Colonial Crimes' through Reparations? Adjudicating Dutch Atrocities Committed in Indonesia." *Journal of International Criminal Justice* 10, no. 3 (2012): 693–705. https://doi.org/10.1093/jicj/mqs033.

Hobsbawm, Eric J. "The Social Function of the Past: Some Questions." *Past & Present*, no. 55 (1972): 3–17.

Hohfeld, Wesley Newcomb. *Fundamental Legal Conceptions as Applied in Judicial Reasoning: And Other Legal Essays*. New Haven: Yale University Press, 1923.

Immler, Nicole L., and Stef Scagliola. "Seeking Justice for the Mass Execution in Rawagede/Probing the Concept of 'Entangled History'in a Postcolonial Setting." *Rethinking History* 24, no. 1 (2020): 1–28.

Joshi, Yuvraj. "Affirmative Action as Transitional Justice." *Wisconsin Law Review*, no. 1 (2020): 1–48.

Kahn, Elizabeth. "Beyond Claim-rights: Social Structure, Collectivization, and Human Rights." *Journal of Social Philosophy* 52, no. 2 (2021): 162–84.

Khan, Liaquat Ali. "Temporality of Law." *McGeorge Law Review* 40, no. 1 (2009): 55–106.

Langenohl, Andreas. "Memory in Post-Authoritarian Societies." In *Cultural Memory Studies: An International and Interdisciplinary Handbook*, edited by Astrid Erll and Ansgar Nünning. Berlin: Walter de Gruyter, 2008.

LaRue, L. H. "Hohfeldian Rights and Fundamental Rights." *The University of Toronto Law Journal* 35, no. 1 (1985): 86–93.

Lawther, Cheryl. " 'Let Me Tell You': Transitional Justice, Victimhood and Dealing with a Contested Past." *Social & Legal Studies* 30, no. 6 (2021): 890–912.

Lefebvre, Alexandre. *The Image of Law: Deleuze, Bergson, Spinoza*. Stanford: Stanford University Press, 2008.

Lopez, Rachel. "The (Re)Collection of Memory after Mass Atrocity and the Dilemma for Transitional Justice." *International Law and Politics* 47 (2015): 799.

Luhmann, Niklas. "The Future Cannot Begin: Temporal Structures in Modern Society." *Social Research* (1976): 130–52.

Luhmann, Niklas. *A Sociological Theory of Law*. Oxon & New York: Routledge, 2014.

MacClellan, Joel. "How (Not) to Defend a Rawlsian Approach to Intergenerational Ethics." *Ethics & the Environment* 18, no. 1 (2013): 67–85.

Mallinder, Louise. "Atrocity, Accountability, and Amnesty in a 'Post- Human Rights World'? Political Settlements Research Programme." *Political Settlements Research Programme, Working Paper 09/2017*, no. 18 (2017). www.politicalsettlements.org.

Mar, Maksymilian Del. *Artefacts of Legal Inquiry: The Value of Imagination in Adjudication*. Bloomsbury Publishing, 2020.

Marneros, Christos. " 'It Is a Nomos Very Different from the Law': On Anarchy and the Law." *Acta Universitatis Lodziensis. Folia Iuridica*, no. 96 (2021): 125–39.

Mazor, Joseph. "On Environmental Justice, Part I: An Intuitive Conservation Dilemma." *Economics & Philosophy* 39, no. 2 (2023): 230–55.

Mazor, Joseph. "On Environmental Justice, Part II: Non-Absolute Equal Division of Rights to the Natural World." *Economics & Philosophy* 39, no. 2 (2023): 256–84.

McKeown, Maeve. "Structural Injustice." *Philosophy Compass* 16, no. 7 (2021): e12757.

McNeilly, Kathryn. "Are Rights Out of Time? International Human Rights Law, Temporality, and Radical Social Change." *Social & Legal Studies* 28, no. 6 (2019): 817–38. https://doi.org/10.1177/0964663918815729.

Mueller-Hirth, Natascha. "Temporalities of Victimhood: Time in the Study of Post-conflict Societies." In *Sociological Forum*, 32:186–206. Wiley Online Library, 2017.

Nino, Carlos Santiago. *Radical Evil on Trial.* New Haven & London: Yale University Press, 1996.
Nuti, Alasia. *Injustice and the Reproduction of History: Structural Inequalities, Gender and Redress.* Cambridge: Cambridge University Press, 2019.
O'Neill, Onora. "The Dark Side of Human Rights." *International Affairs* 81, no. 2 (2005): 427–39.
Onwuachi-Willig, Angela. "Reconceptualizing the Harms of Discrimination." *Virginia Law Review* 105, no. 2 (2019): 343–69.
Osiel, Mark J. *Making Sense of Mass Atrocity.* New York: Cambridge University Press, 2009.
Osiel, Mark J. *Mass Atrocity, Collective Memory and the Law.* Routledge, 2017.
Papayannis, Diego M. "The Morality of Compensation through Tort Law." *Ratio Juris* 36, no. 1 (2023): 3–25.
Penner, J. E. *Hohfeldian Liberties, Property Rights: A Re-Examination.* Online ed. Oxford: Oxford Academic, 2020. https://doi.org/10.1093/oso/9780198830122.003.0003.
Prakash, Gyan (ed.). *After Colonialism: Imperial Histories and Postcolonial Displacements.* Princeton, NJ: Princeton University Press, 1995.
Priel, Dan. "Analytic Jurisprudence in Time." In *Philosophy of Law as an Integral Part of Philosophy: Essays on the Jurisprudence of Gerald J. Postema*, edited by Thomas Bustamante and Thiago Lopes Decat, 213–41. Oxford: Hart Publishing, 2020.
Rawls, John. *A Theory of Justice.* Cambridge, MA: Belknap Press, 1999.
Rogers, Nicole. *Law, Fiction and Activism in a Time of Climate Change.* Routledge, 2019.
Savelsberg, Joachim J., and Suzy McElrath. "Crime, Law, and Regime Change." *Annual Review of Law and Social Science* 10, no. 1 (2014): 259–79. https://doi.org/10.1146/annurev-lawsocsci-110413-030555.
Shklar, Judith N. "The Faces of Injustice." In *The Faces of Injustice.* Yale University Press, 1990.
Thompson, Janna. *Taking Responsibility for the Past: Reparation and Historical Injustice.* Cambridge, UK: Polity Press, 2002.
Thompson, Janna. *Should Current Generations Make Reparation for Slavery?* Cambridge, UK: Polity Press, 2018.
Waldron, Jeremy. "Superseding Historic Injustice." *Ethics* 103, no. 1 (1992): 4–28.
Waldron, Jeremy. "The Principle of Proximity." In *Public Law and Legal Theory Research Paper Series.* New York: New York University, 2011.
White, Emily Kidd. "On Emotions and the Politics of Attention in Judicial Reasoning." In *Virtue, Emotion and Imagination in Law and Legal Reasoning*, edited by Amalia Amaya and Maksymilian Del Mar, 101–20. Oxford: Bloomsbury Publishing, 2020.
Yack, Bernard. "Injustice and the Victim's Voice." *Michigan Law Review* 89, no. 6 (1991): 1334–49.
Young, Iris Marion. *Responsibility for Justice.* New York: Oxford University Press, 2011.
Zanfi, Caterina. "The Duration of History in Bergson." *Bergsoniana*, no. 1 (2021): 155–71.

Chapter 6

Judicial intuition in time

In this chapter, we will argue for intuitive judicial reasoning as an aretaic model of judicial decision-making in time. Intuition is part of the judicial mode of thinking performed by legal decision-makers to express justifying reasons within their distinctive epistemic frame. It is a method to access normative arguments stemming from virtue. That said, intuitive judicial reasoning in this sense is a kind of judicial practice, a judge's mode of thinking that enables them to create and craft forms of lawful relations considering their epistemic justification toward the temporal experience of injustice. As part of this creative process, intuition is a basic form of legal knowledge through which legal institutions (i.e., the courts) shape the forms of lawful relations. Accordingly, we have argued in Chapters 4 and 5 that intuitive judicial reasoning is a method that generates access to (1) a kind of inquiry that does not follow progressively from the past or present, and (2) coherence that governs temporal patterns based on which a certain lawful relation may attain social purposes over time. Moreover, such intuitive judicial reasoning is part of the virtue approach to legal reasoning which can be found in empathy. To this extent, empathy needs to be seen as part of judicial intuitive methodology, as it provides a way to access creative minds.

This chapter consists of four sections. First, the structure of legal reasoning exercised by the courts, specifically through an explanatory view. This issue is addressed by borrowing from scholarly works working on the idea of inference to the best (legal) explanation (IBE). Second, this chapter delves into the discussion of Bergson's intuition as a method in a creative process and how intuition can be incorporated into the process of inference. To wit, rather than apprehending intuition as psychological instances, or 'hunch' as some scholars mentioned,[1] it is submitted that intuition is a systematic method

1 Joseph C. Hutcheson Jr, "Judgment Intuitive The Function of the Hunch in Judicial Decision," *Cornell Law Review* 14, no. 3 (1928): 274–88, http://scholarship.law.cornell.edu/clr/vol14/iss3/2; Chris Guthrie, Jeffrey J. Rachlinski, and Andrew J. Wistrich, "Blinking on the Bench: How Judges Decide Cases," *Cornell Law Review* 93, no. 1 (2007): 1–44; Diana Richards,

DOI: 10.4324/9781003518693-9

of knowledge production that can provide access to justifying reasons—considering a judge's epistemic justification toward the temporal experience of injustice. Simultaneously, the structure of legal explanation is refined by extrapolating Bergsonian intuition into the scheme of interference to the best legal explanation. Third, this chapter analyzes how intuition interacts with legal arguments, or, to be precise, how the legal inference corresponds with the rules of intuition in the process of crafting lawful relations. Fourth, this chapter ultimately examines the role of empathy as part of intuitive-based methodology, considering that it provides access to creative minds in order to craft lawful relations.

Justification and intuition

As previously investigated in Chapter 4, legal reasoning in its temporal sense primarily consists of (1) a process of justification based on a scheme of intelligibility, (2) a representation of the virtuality of norms and facts into the actual case and (3) an inherent temporal dimension in recognizing the role of narrative that mediates the judge's creative and transformative capacity. These propositions suggest that we need to reject the propositional explanation of legal reasoning and be inclined to support the narrative mode of thinking in legal reasoning. In the narrative mode of thinking, the central crux of legal decision-making is the process of justification, which in many circumstances is done through an inference to the best legal explanation. In this view, justification is a matter of arguments, a selection of the best explanation of a legal outcome.

At this point, one might seemingly consider a shift in observation: from legal reasoning to legal arguments or justification. To clarify, the two are evidently related to another in a way that, quoting Samuel,

> [t]he word 'reasoning' suggests a sophisticated activity where solutions are inferred from intellectual discourse systems whose paradigm example is mathematics and its deductive logic. . . . Reasoning may form part of argumentation inasmuch as inference is a form of argument; argumentation may form part of reasoning inasmuch as it is an intellectual activity based upon justifications.[2]

To put it otherwise, we may affirm that a legal argument is part of legal reasoning to the extent that it is justificatory in nature, whereas reasoning

"When Judges Have a Hunch: Intuition and Experience in Judicial Decision-Making," *ARSP: Archiv Für Rechts-Und Sozialphilosophie/Archives for Philosophy of Law and Social Philosophy* (2016): 245–60.

2 Geoffrey Samuel, *Epistemology and Method in Law* (London & New York: Routledge, 2016), 78.

can be part of argument to the extent that it is inferential. If we take this proposition into account, the idea would be that the process of representation of the virtual into the actual can be reflected in any explanatory modes undertaken by legal decision-makers.[3] One explanatory mode relevant to our present investigation is inference to the best legal explanation.

This section begins the discussion about justification and intuition with the assumption that in many circumstances judges infer the conclusion of their judgment. It has been claimed previously in Chapter 4 that a *logical* explanation of conclusion of a legal judgment is mostly derived from a truth-preserving inferential form, such as analogy and deduction. It is suggested that an acceptable conclusion is based on the truth of its premises. However, the judge's so-called *narrative* mode of thinking seems to suggest that the reached conclusion is actually 'truth-like,' particularly in hard cases. That is, it shows that a conclusion can be accepted even if it extends its premises. Such a mode of thinking is fundamentally underpinned by the inference to best (legal) explanation (IBE) to the extent that IBE is characterized as non-truth-preserving, ampliative and non-monotonic, as some scholars have claimed. In that sense, IBE can be seen as either a hypothesis-generating mechanism or an inferential form.[4] The former suggests that IBE is simply generating hypotheses in an investigative process, while the latter includes in IBE "a form of argument in which *the premises give support to the claim that the conclusion is true.*"[5]

One of the important works on IBE was written by Paul Thagard. Thagard claims that IBE "consists in accepting a hypothesis on the grounds that it provides a better explanation of the evidence than is provided by alternative hypotheses."[6] That is, "[w]e argue for a hypothesis or theory by arguing that it is the best explanation of the evidence."[7] According to Thagard, there are three important criteria for determining the best explanation: consilience, simplicity and analogy. The first two are particularly relevant at this point. First, consilience deals with measuring "*how much* a theory explains, so that we can use it to tell when one theory explains *more* of the evidence than another theory."[8] To wit, a theory is consilient if it is capable

3 Gilbert H. Harman, "The Inference to the Best Explanation," *The Philosophical Review* 74, no. 1 (1965): 88–95.
4 Claudio Michelon, "The Inference to the Best Legal Explanation," *Oxford Journal of Legal Studies* 39, no. 4 (2019): 878–900; Amalia Amaya, "The Role of Virtue in Legal Justification," in *Law, Virtue and Justice*, ed. Amalia Amaya and Hock Lai Ho (Oxford & Portland, OR: Hart Publishing, 2013), 51–66.
5 Michelon, "The Inference to the Best Legal Explanation," 5. (emphasis original)
6 Paul R. Thagard, "The Best Explanation: Criteria for Theory Choice," *The Journal of Philosophy* 75, no. 2 (1978): 77.
7 Ibid.
8 Ibid., 79.

of answering at least two classes of facts. The idea of *how much*, however, is not about "the sheer number of facts explained, but the variety, and variety [classes of facts] is not a notion for which we can expect a neat formal characterization." Second, a theory is simple to the extent that it explains classes of facts without resorting to reasoners making multiple "assumptions with narrow application."[9]

In legal science, IBE has been widely discussed in two main respects: (1) the way IBE is applicable in understanding the burden of proof and evidence in legal cases (hypothesis-generating mechanism), and (2) the way IBE as an inferential form supports legal principle.[10] The two, we may suggest, should not be treated exclusively. In that regard, we are particularly interested in the coherentist viewpoint advocated by Amalia Amaya. She calls this view a coherence-driven inference in IBE. Amaya suggests that we should see legal inference as coherence maximization in which, she says, "legal decision-makers generate a number of alternative explanatory and interpretative hypotheses and then select as justified the one that is best, that is, the one that best coheres."[11] In general, two stages are involved in legal inference, including the generation stage and the selection stage. In the first stage, suggests Amaya, "coherence with background beliefs helps restrict the set of alternative hypotheses to be further considered. Hypotheses that wildly *in*cohere with our empirical and normative beliefs are not considered plausible enough to make it to the selection stage."[12] Meanwhile, in the second stage, coherence can generate "standards of evaluation against which we may determine which, among a set of alternative explanations, is best."[13] And in that sense, "the suggestion is that the 'best' explanation in law is the explanation

9 Ibid., 87.

10 According to Michelon, IBE-Principle must fulfill five desiderata in that the judge's inference scheme departs from a certain set of items (the explanandum—or 'a set of rules' in Michelon's term) and then asks what the best normative explanation (explanans—or 'principles' in Michelon's term) for the items is. This best normative explanation is inferring from:(i) the truth of claims about the occurrence of the items;(ii) the explanatory relationship between them and the explanans;(iii) the truth of this explanation; and specifically in legal argumentations,(iv) that the items that constitute both the explanandum and the explanans are normative sentences;(v) courts are often creatively ambiguous about the type of conclusion they are arguing for, and an argument scheme for IBE-P should be able to explain that ambiguity. (6–7)Based on these desiderata, Michelon then draws the argument scheme of IBE-P as follows (p. 7)(1) Principle P1 explains Rules R1, R2, . . . , Rn.(2) No other principle explains each of R1, R2, . . . , Rn better than P1.(3) If P1 explains R1, R2, . . . , Rn and no other principle explains each of R1, R2, . . . , Rn better than P1, then there is a reason to act according to P1.Therefore, from (1)–(3), (4) There is a reason to act according to P1.

11 Amalia Amaya, "Legal Justification by Optimal Coherence," *Ratio Juris* 24, no. 3 (2011): 315.

12 Ibid.

13 Ibid.

that best satisfies a number of coherence constraints, as established by the principles of factual and normative coherence."[14] In a more detailed manner, according to Amaya, legal inference is a process of coherence maximization that has the following steps:

> (1) the identification of a "base" of coherence, that is, the set of elements upon which the coherence calculation is performed (Raz 1992); (2) the construction of a "contrast set," that is, the set containing a number of plausible decision alternatives; (3) the pursuit of the decision alternatives by means of a number of coherence-enhancing mechanisms; (4) the evaluation of the different decision alternatives against the criteria of factual and normative coherence; and (5) the selection as justified of the decision alternative that best satisfies the coherence constraints established by the theory of the relevant kinds of coherence, most importantly, explanatory coherence, in the case of reasoning about facts, and interpretative coherence, in the case of reasoning about norms.[15]

Inspired by this coherentism project, our narrative mode of thinking in legal reasoning—either in terms of *explaining* about factual questions or normative questions—is normatively guided by the principle of coherence insofar as this mode of reasoning fits with the so-called constraint satisfaction. From Amaya's coherence-based IBE, we can gather four ways in which coherence contributes to the generation of the best explanation. *First*, coherence enters implicitly in the process of generation of hypotheses via background (empirical or normative) knowledge.[16] *Second*, coherence also enters into the process of generation through a number of marshalling strategies, such as "'scenarios', 'schemata' and 'theories of the case'."[17] *Third*, generating new elements is sometimes driven by an effort after coherence.[18] And *fourth*, incoherence, such as emotional reactions, is also a driving force in hypothesis formation.[19]

For the purpose of the present chapter, we may highlight a twofold challenge against coherence-based inference. On the one hand, since our theoretical orientation necessitates a shifting view of the legal decision-makers from the regularity and expediency of adjudication to a form of creative and experimental judgment, a follow-up question would be about the way in which such legal inference, methodologically speaking, is able to provide

14 Ibid.
15 Ibid., 314–15.
16 Amalia Amaya, *The Tapestry of Reason: An Inquiry into the Nature of Coherence and Its Role in Legal Argument* (Oxford & Portland, OR: Hart Publishing, 2015), 506.
17 Ibid., 507.
18 Ibid.
19 Ibid., 508.

creative answers, particularly in responding to questions involving judges' cognitive dilemmas. On the other hand, since temporalities have been the main approach in this study, any explanations on temporal approaches to legal reasoning should be able to induce time's ontological role in law and legal reasoning. That said, to think of coherence-based legal inference in terms of time requires a judge's viewpoint that can unfold the way experience takes place and holds in a creative mind.[20]

Relevant to such challenges, some scholars have suggested that IBE as a mode of inference can enable reasoners to generate creative hypotheses that *explain* a theory. A few brief comments might be helpful at the moment to understand the extent to which the IBE can be viewed as a creative process. *First*, if we take the ampliative character of IBE seriously, we may come to view such explanatory inference as an eliminate mechanism that comprises a process of generation and, subsequently, a process of selection. It initially selects a full list of plausible theories and later selects the best theory from the list. It is 'eliminative' because, in order for the best explanation to emerge, one needs to eliminate the other possible alternatives in the list.[21] *Second*, coherence-based IBE deals with the contextualization of standards of legal justification. This suggests that the determination of the appropriate standards of justification may vary between legal systems, contingent upon some contextual factors that may be found within the three dimensions of "the domain of coherence, the constitution of the contrast set, and the degree of coherence required for justification."[22] *Third*, a question follows as to how we know that a justification comes from the best explanation. And how is the process of discovering the best explanations? Amaya responded to such questions by arguing that any set of explanations is constructed in an epistemically responsible way. Epistemic responsibility here is grasped as "a matter of fulfilling a number of epistemic duties and exercising a number of epistemic virtues in the course of legal inquiry and deliberation."[23] That said,

20 Marek Jakubiec, "Legal Concepts as Mental Representations," *International Journal for the Semiotics of Law-Revue Internationale de Sémiotique Juridique* 35, no. 5 (2022): 1837–55; Claudio Michelon, "Practical Wisdom in Legal Decision-Making," in *Law, Virtue and Justice*, ed. Amalia Amaya and Ho Hock Lai (Oxford & Portland, OR: Hart Publishing, 2013), 29–49. This could be seen as part of virtue to the extent that it contributes to the "necessary conditions to achieve excellence not in the decision-maker, but in the world beyond the self." 32.

21 Amaya, *The Tapestry of Reason: An Inquiry into the Nature of Coherence and Its Role in Legal Argument*, 504–5; Peter Lipton, "Inference to the Best Explanation," in *A Companion to the Philosophy of Science* (Wiley Online Library, 2017), 184–93, https://doi.org/10.1002/9781405164481.ch29.

22 Amaya, "Legal Justification by Optimal Coherence," 317.

23 Ibid., 316; Rima Basu, "What We Epistemically Owe to Each Other," *Philosophical Studies* 176 (2019): 915–31; Robert Carry Osborne, "What Do We Epistemically Owe to Each Other? A Reply to Basu," *Philosophical Studies* 178, no. 3 (2021): 1005–22.

Amaya's claim would be that "an interpretative/factual hypothesis in law is 'optimally coherent' and thus justified if it could be the outcome of an epistemically responsible process of coherence maximization."[24] One would furthermore ask about the kind of epistemic responsible behavior we think of in the context of legal inquiry. Three things particularly stand out, according to Amaya, which are "thoroughness, perseverance in following a line of inquiry, and open-mindedness in collecting and appraising evidence."[25] In the context of legal deliberation, the kinds of epistemic responsible behavior include "openness to new alternatives, readiness to consider objections to one's preferred alternative, and the ability to imagine how the different alternatives are likely to affect the parties involved."[26]

It seems plausible, based on this explication, that the coherence-based method provides conditions for creativity and transformation in such a way that it is non-foundational, dynamic and attentive to normative change. But what is the role of legal temporalities within this theory of legal justification? What drives reason to act according to a certain conclusion? At this point, Bergson's intuition may play a role in our attempt to generate a methodological foundation.

Intuition and the creative process of judgment

Our instant apprehension when discussing intuition is that it comes to us or emerges in our mind rather spontaneously. The immediacy of intuition is one of our basic assumptions that sets intuition apart from any other form of decision-making. In most cases, intuitive reasoning is seen as irrational and even arbitrary, as it does not involve adequate reflection in its process. The adequacy of reflection, particularly in decision-making, is essentially grounded in the passage of time; that is, the longer time flows, the more deliberate a decision is formulated.[27] Such a condition puts intuition primarily as a matter of psychology instead of grasped as a solid, systematic 'method' in the process of scientific inquiry.

Legal theorists, however, tend to sidestep the so-called intuition and intuitionism, particularly when discussing theories of legal justification and adjudication.[28] Every theorist has her own reason to escape from the intuitionist stream, but one fundamental ground for this bearing, we may presume, is that intuition has been widely perceived as the pronouncement of

24 Amaya, "Legal Justification by Optimal Coherence," 316.
25 Ibid.
26 Ibid.
27 Daniel Kahneman, *Thinking, Fast and Slow* (New York: Farrar, Straus and Giroux, 2011).
28 Richards, "When Judges Have a Hunch: Intuition and Experience in Judicial Decision-Making"; Neil MacCormick, *Rhetoric and the Rule of Law: A Theory of Legal Reasoning* (Oxford: Oxford University Press, 2005), 84–88.

the famous legal realist's saying "what the judge had for breakfast."[29] Intuition, as claimed by many, is not 'scientific' and may lead to 'unjustified' legal outcomes. Some claimed that legal scientists should be skeptical of intuition, as if legal reasoning is all about justification predetermined or predicated by judicial 'hunch.' Intuition thereby sets aside the significance of legal rules and principles, let alone positing law's capacity as a reason to act.[30]

Nonetheless, Hutcheson claims that intuition is not incompatible with legal reasoning *par excellence* since it, albeit unconsciously, may be legally well-informed.[31] Against anti-intuitionism, the following paragraphs will dig into the relationship between consciousness and intuition and the ways in which intuition plays a part in the creative process of judgment.[32] Within such a creative process, intuition can be viewed as an effort to place oneself in a movement of change that enables reasoners (i.e., legal decision-makers) to create and transform.[33] Following Bergson and Deleuze, intuition, as a method of inquiry, can provide an invaluable perspective on understanding the creative process in legal reasoning. It is a method in the sense that it directs a reasoner's sensory perception in *accessing* the production of an understanding.[34] The aim of intuition is, quoting Lawlor, "to experience directly or immediately the flow of my own interior life . . . of my own duration . . . to 'enlarge' consciousness to include the unconscious."[35] It is important to note here that intuition is properly suited to our theoretical underpinning that asserts knowledge in legal reasoning as a process. That said, the way intuition *accesses* the production of understanding is crucial for our methodological observation to the extent that such a process is understood as representing the virtual into the actual. Arguing from a Deleuzian perspective, we may view intuition as resulting from "a progressive reduction

29 Dan Priel, "Law Is What the Judge Had for Breakfast: A Brief History of an Unpalatable Idea," *Buffalo Law Review* 68 (2020): 899. Yet, according to Schauer, such reductionism of Frank's 'offhand oral quip' seems unfair, "because he believed that a large number of other less frivolous but still nonlegal factors typically determined judicial decisions. These might include, for example, the judge's political preferences, his views about litigants of certain races or religions or appearances, his views about the lawyers, his overall sense of which outcome would be fairer under the circumstances, and, perhaps most of all, the makeup of his personality." 129.

30 Richards, "When Judges Have a Hunch: Intuition and Experience in Judicial Decision-Making."

31 Hutcheson Jr, "Judgment Intuitive The Function of the Hunch in Judicial Decision."

32 R. George Wright, "The Role of Intuition in Judicial Decisionmaking," *Houston Law Review* 42 (2006): 1381; Mark Modak-Truran, "A Pragmatic Justification of the Judicial Hunch," *University of Richmond Law Review* 35 (2001): 55.

33 Pamela Sue Anderson, "Bergsonian Intuition: A Metaphysics of Mystical Life," *Philosophical Topics* 43, no. 1/2 (2015): 239–51.

34 Mark V. Tushnet, "Anti-Formalism in Recent Constitutional Theory," *Michigan Law Review* 83 (1984): 1502; Wright, "The Role of Intuition in Judicial Decisionmaking."

35 Leonard Lawlor, *The Challenge of Bergsonism* (A&C Black, 2003), 63.

of the separation between the virtual and the actual as the convergent movement of thought which brings together the ideal and the material in artistic practices as pure process."[36] Hence, as a method, intuition is not presupposed *a priori* in terms of common scientific procedure. It is rather construed simultaneously in the process of thought. Intuition is therefore best apprehended as "the reason a process acquires in its advance" inasmuch as it is "a difference discerned a posteriori."[37]

As in common adjudicative practices, the practice of augmenting knowledge in a legal inquiry is reckoned to be an iterative practice. At the same time, any legal decision-making process is institutionally restricted to the extent that justice must be expressed in any other cases following the established rules and principles (e.g., judges have been dealing with, say, racial discrimination-related matters in a number of civil suits in which similar rules and principles could and ought to be applied in reaching every conclusion). But, as is the case, in some instances they made a slightly different gesture, a deviation from the known repetitive practice of judgment. From there, what we are seeing is a process of 'creation'—not only that this answers or solves a particular legal problem—as it extends the problematization of a legal problem into a novel inquiry. Since the practice of legal judgment is an iterative gesture, such an extension of (legal) problem is not "the result of directed, programmed, systematic, methodical, conscious experimentation with technique or method," but rather

> a direct, non-conceptual, pre-scientific and pre-linguistic determination: the invention, the coming to discovery, is unmediated and unthought, but the result is clear, repeatable, and confirmable—it is a result of the going-with-it of practical insight into creative process: it is a solution to a problem we didn't even know was there since it comes to us from the future and not formulated in the past.[38]

Read in that way, intuition sets forth the straying from the accepted methodological path, paving ways to "the unexplored novelty of the 'what could

36 Felix Rebolledo Palazuelos, Tania Galli Fonseca, and Andreia Machado Oliveira, "A Philosophical Perspective on Intuition as a Method within Artistic Process," *Studies in Visual Arts and Communication: An International Journal* 5, no. 1 (2018): 2.

37 Ibid.

38 Ibid., 3; (citation omitted) See Costas Douzinas, Ronnie Warrington, and Shaun McVeigh, *Postmodern Jurisprudence: The Law of the Text in the Text of the Law* (Routledge, 1993). This proposition bears the sense of Kantian aesthetic judgment, in which it is rather reflective: "it functions in the absence of pre-existing rules. The aesthetic judgment is the application of a rule yet to come, an example in search of its own rule from which it derives. Subjective and individual, but in the service of a general and universal rule not yet determined, the aesthetic is a judgment of pure form, uncontaminated by ephemeral considerations of need or use." 163.

be done next'."[39] Intuition leads to an acknowledgment of a differential drift that took place between " 'the could' and the 'might', in the differentiation of the 'now' and the 'has- been'," or, in Deleuzian terms, "in the interval of difference and repetition."[40] Again, borrowing from an aesthetic prefiguration of intuition sketched by Palazuelos et al, we may therefore understand that,

> [t]he method of intuition when worked through iterative processes is akin to an attentive attunement to the event's immediation where focus is directly maintained on the sensory aspects of the interactive doing of the practice as opposed to the rationalizations around the what the work ought to or could be. Through the method of material intuition intrinsic to the iterative gesture, the artist can modulate the degree of turbulence that can be entrained into the habitually established as the regular, as the norm and the normalizing in a process.[41]

At this point, we may indicate the role of temporalities in such an intuitive judgment; that is, intuition is a practice-based habit or experience that is (1) temporally immediate and (2) progressively unmediated. It is temporally immediate in the sense that it involves instantaneous consciousness.[42] It is also unmediated since knowledge is seen as a direct comprehension through iterative practice. In this context, we can no longer see the way judges think of an inquiry independent from the inquiry (as an object) itself: the judge's reasoning is no longer regarded as her consciousness over 'something,' for instance, racial discrimination or climate crisis, but rather it is as "immanent becoming experiential."[43] Notably, experience of consciousness is fundamental at this point, since for Bergson it is the key portrayal of choice in social life.[44] Seeing intuition as a method from a legal perspective posits

39 Palazuelos et al., "A Philosophical Perspective on Intuition as a Method within Artistic Process," 3.

40 Palazuelos et al., "A Philosophical Perspective on Intuition as a Method within Artistic Process"; Gilles Deleuze, *Difference and Repetition* (Columbia University Press, 1994).

41 Palazuelos et al., "A Philosophical Perspective on Intuition as a Method within Artistic Process," 3.

42 This proposition takes into account Sinclair's categorizations of intuition, namely intuitive expertise, intuitive creation and intuitive foresight. See Marta Sinclair, "Misconceptions about Intuition," *Psychological Inquiry* 21, no. 4 (2010): 378–86.

43 See Introduction on Deleuzian jurisprudence.

44 Emmanuel Picavet, "Bergson and Our Understanding of Interaction, Constraints and Collective Aspirations," *Bergsoniana*, no. 1 (2021). Picavet notes that in *Mind-Energy Lectures*, Bergson "insisted that the most vivid parts of the experience of consciousness are only revealed on certain occasions, all of which are linked to decision-making; consciousness is indeed to be equated with choice in a certain sense." 127 While in *Creative Evolution*, consciousness is "portrayed as the light which is immanent to the area of possible actions. It is more precisely located in the interval between action and representation, and this leads to an "arithmetical" formula which describes the gap between virtual and real activity." 127–28.

judgments are no longer seen as following a predetermined procedure but rather as a 'subjective' way of inquiry. That said, intuition is rather absolute,

> since intuition is in the thing—here in this preposition (*en*) is immanence—and yet the thing given is a composite part that extends to infinity. Extending to infinity, the whole is never given, which implies that what is potential is literally unforeseeable.[45]

This would also mean that intuition is a-perspective and not relative. Related to that, claimed Lawlor, "[i]ntuition is a-perspectival for Bergson because the whole can never be turned into a spectacle. Intuition, therefore, in Bergson involves a kind of blindness."[46]

One might suggest that the *blindness* involved in intuition is highly indeterminate. Unavoidably, this sparks a follow-up question on how such a methodological multitude can be translated into methodological certitude. Deleuze's reading on Bergson's intuition can help us clarify this question. In *Bergsonism*, Deleuze delineates intuition as a method of sense-making in metaphysics.[47] This method unites the renowned distinction between intuition and analysis of science, which follows several fundamental rules. It is important to note, however, that those rules are not "a step-by-step protocol towards the correct use of intuition as method but an offering of strategies or possible approaches towards the positing of a precise and unambiguous problem through the almost formulation of its exacting and fitting solution."[48] Those rules are, therefore, simply a way for intuition to see things in a new way that is happening in the immediate experience.[49]

A bit of reflection on those three rules is of particular importance, and in doing so, we can borrow from Deleuze's reading on Bergson's method of intuition, which casts three rules of intuition in attending to the multiplicity of temporalities, namely *problematizing*, *differentiating* and *temporalizing*.[50]

45 Leonard Lawlor, "Intuition and Duration: An Introduction to Bergson's 'Introduction to Metaphysics'," in *Bergson and Phenomenology*, ed. Michael R. Kelly (New York: Palgrave Macmillan, 2010), 36.

46 Ibid.

47 Gilles Deleuze, *Bergsonism*, trans. H. Tomlinson and B. Habberjam (New York: Zone Books, 1991).

48 Palazuelos et al., "A Philosophical Perspective on Intuition as a Method within Artistic Process," 6.

49 Modak-Truran, "A Pragmatic Justification of the Judicial Hunch."

50 Anderson, "A Metaphysics of Mystical Life." Alternatively, as a method in metaphysics, Anderson draws roughly three steps involved in intuition. "(i) the first step of intuition is a kind of leap into pure duration; placing oneself in the heart of reality is distinguished from a twofold act of analysis (of breaking down and reconstituting); (ii) the second step of intuition is a dilation, or expansion, of one's own duration into a continuous heterogeneity; and (iii) the third step of intuition is the differentiation (of different kinds) which marks out the

Not much space is devoted here to elaborating on the metaphysical explanation of intuition.[51] Thus, we will instead directly situate the idea within the legal justification framework.

The *first* rule is the analytical stage of the experiential frame of time, which we may call problematizing. Problematizing deals primarily with the exactness or precision of an expression of a problem (or in our case, an expression of a legal inquiry). In that sense,

> [i]ntuition is productive, not in a haphazard manner, but through an exacting decisiveness: intuition is unhesitating, resolute and determined in its taking action—it is a threshold moment in the advance into novelty that is not chancy in itself but absolutely necessary in its outcome.[52]

Such an expression of an inquiry (or, for lawyers, a legal question) is "a unique, singular, coherent expression which encompasses being wide-open to experience and to interpretation."[53] That said, the solution of a problem could be expressed in the form of "a single, inevitable solution; a multiplicity of solutions; a non-solution as a paradox, enigma, or a confusing, improper formulation; or an open-ended iterative replication of its problematization."[54] Problematizing, however, is seen not as a way to delimit or constrain a problem or inquiry, but rather as a way of

> working with it to render the problem productive of a necessary, inevitable truth within and without—the truth is in the productivity of the operational coherence of the problem as a restatement of its premises, conditions, situation, implications, through to its possible outcomes and a decisive adequate solution.[55]

This rule can also be called *reflexive dualism*, that is, an intuitive strategy (of the judge's) to dissect the realities of a legal case between differences in degree and in kind, or, to make it germane to our present issue, between

extremes of this heterogeneity, even though the two extremes are knit together by memory in duration." 242.

51 For a general discussion about the role of intuition in the ethics of normative judgment, *See* Peter Singer, "Ethics and Intuitions," *The Journal of Ethics* 9 (2005): 331–52; Joakim Sandberg and Niklas Juth, "Ethics and Intuitions: A Reply to Singer," *The Journal of Ethics* 15 (2011): 209–26.

52 Palazuelos et al., "A Philosophical Perspective on Intuition as a Method within Artistic Process," 7.

53 Ibid.

54 Ibid.

55 Ibid.; Marcin Lewinski, "Practical Argumentation as Reasoned Advocacy," *Informal Logic* 37, no. 2 (2017): 85–113.

timeliness and timelessness of a legal claim.[56] Read through this intuitive proposition, such reflexive dualism involves a kind of 'preliminary sorting' that is carried out through legal perception aiming to search for salient properties of law (discussed in the next section).

The *second* methodological rule is differentiation, that is, a rediscovering of differences. As argued in Chapter 4, legal reasoning is rather interested in 'time' rather than 'truth,' and, as a consequence, reading legal inquiry as part of intuitive reasoning, we may also want to claim that legal inquiry is composed of "a repositioning of the problem from the normative moral logic of a problem's being true or false to the ethical knowledge of how things actually function coherently—of how the solution is territorialized functionally."[57] Arguably, through this function, we may arrive at a distinction between the difference of intensity and of innovation and inventiveness. To wit, we arrive at a reflective question: are judges in a legal case investigating some sustained, existing problems or rather opening a novel direction of a problem? That said, differentiation is primarily about *differentiating the Encounter* (note that virtue jurisprudence also upholds this idea, albeit with a different term).[58] In the context of this study's inquiry, the interplay between history and law's temporality engenders *a temporal Encounter* in legal reasoning.[59] The Encounter here is to be understood as something unanticipated or unrecognized past (cases, rules and principles) that forces judges to think and react in an atypical manner.[60] And by temporal Encounter, we are referring to a set of categorical—yet unexpected—temporalities construed upon memory and perception that enable legal decision-makers to engage in the meaning-making process of lawful relations.[61] Based on such a definition of

56 Deleuze, "Bergsonism (H. Tomlinson & B. Habberjam, Trans.)."

57 Palazuelos et al., "A Philosophical Perspective on Intuition as a Method within Artistic Process," 7–8.

58 See Maksymilian Del Mar, "Judging Virtuously: Developing an Empathic Capacity for Perceptual Sensitivity," *Jurisprudence* 5, no. 1 (2014): 196–208, https://doi.org/10.5235/20403313.5.1.196.

59 See Chapters 4 and 5.

60 Alexandre Lefebvre, *The Image of Law: Deleuze, Bergson, Spinoza* (Stanford: Stanford University Press, 2008), 72–73; Courtney M. Cox, "The Uncertain Judge," *University of Chicago Law Review* 90, no. 3 (2023): 739–811. Cox's problematization of normative uncertainty in adjudication to a certain degree can be viewed as an encounter.

61 Lawlor, *The Challenge of Bergsonism*. Notably, Lawlor's reading on Bergson suggests that the image of the encounter is always unpredictable and unforeseeable. The reason is twofold, argued Lawlor, "on the one hand, the past is spontaneously adding memory-images to the perceptual image, and, on the other, the coming moment is always adding different perceptual images to the whole of memory. If we keep this difference in mind between each coming moment being different in relation to the whole of the past and the spontaneous contributions of memory to the creation of the perceptual image, I think we can see that, in the passage between the past and the future, there are both quantitative differences and qualitative differences." 82.

temporal Encounter, three elements can be identified, namely categorical temporalities, memory and perception, and enablers for legal decision-makers to engage in the meaning-making process in legal inquiries. Each of these elements implies that any conversations about the Encounter entail a borderline between past wrongdoings as historical conditions and as collective responsibility which hinges upon how the court *instrumentalizes* time (of injustice) as collective experiences—rather than as mere acceptance of public historical understanding—in order to justify the applicability of norms and principles (i.e., justifying reasons).[62] As this study has asserted in the case-studies (Chapters 1-3), these exemplary legal cases imply that a case's historical inquiry is compounded by the interplay between historical processes (about what happened in the past and its relevance to the present) and legal temporalities (about how law—i.e., statutes, doctrine and principles—is applied considering the passage of time). Within such an interplay, the perceived temporal encounter is unequivocally disputable and in this critical moment, we can deduce the role of time and temporality in legal reasoning. Accordingly, the temporal encounter guides legal decision-makers to *create* the reality of injustices.

The *third* methodological feature suggests that judges' creativity to express the law is best reflected by any kind of intuition that *attentively* produces *generic dualism*, which is a capacity to state and solve problems in terms of time rather than space. Call this rule temporalization, implying that judge's intuition of objects takes place in duration. In duration, judges experience time passes as a dynamic flow, from which they can experience qualitative progress that involves "an unfolding of qualitative change as difference in kind."[63] Time, in this sense, is seen as the actualization of the virtual past.[64] Judges' creativity is therefore not about upholding one temporal approach while abandoning the other: it is not about selecting the right or desirable

62 Anderson, "Bergsonian Intuition: A Metaphysics of Mystical Life," 243; John Oberdiek, *Imposing Risk: A Normative Framework* (Oxford University Press, 2017). I am here suggesting that the fundamental challenge here is the predominant Kantian logic in law and legal reasoning. That is to say, for Kant, human's intellectual intuition is put under spatial time. Time in that sense is located in space. Meanwhile for Bergson, intuition takes place in duration, which understands time "flows as the virtual (past) accompanies the actual (present) as the present continually becomes (future). [That said,] Bergson treats pure duration as absolute, while intuition is "integral experience" (an open whole) in the sense that it is made up of an indefinite series of acts; and these acts are integrated into durations continual flow of time. Bergson's variation on a Kantian theme means that pure duration is real time; we *live*, not think (since the intellect solidifies), this time as fluid." Anderson, "Bergsonian Intuition: A Metaphysics of Mystical Life," 243.

63 Suzanne Guerlac, "Duration: A Fluid Concept," in *The Bergsonian Mind* (Routledge, 2021), 47.

64 Steven Wheatley, "Revisiting the Doctrine of Intertemporal Law," *Oxford Journal of Legal Studies* 41, no. 2 (2021): 484–509.

kind of time in each case. Temporalizing is about choosing the essence of a case by means of, as Lefebvre suggests,

> the relationship between perception and memory in its inattentive and attentive modes: from one where perception consistently actualizes recollections from the same plane of memory to provoke the same movements, to the other where a few aspects of a perception are dwelled on so as to elicit descriptions that, *once actualized together in the perception cohere as an essential singularity*.[65]

Related to this, the Bergsonian temporalization can situate the discussion of judges in a state of dynamic change or movement in the context of legal explanation and justification.[66] Suggested by the aforementioned IBE framework, this rule implies the ranking process of some possible explanations, with the first ranking deemed to be the best explanation. That is to say, legal decision-makers are always in the law's dynamic movement or in an active process reinventing *the unthinkable*.[67] Reading from Bergson's intuition, temporalization reflects an active life of law, which is "what erupts and flows in real time: the virtual past is intuited in the actual present, while the future gnaws into the past: 'duration . . . gnaws on things and leaves on them the mark of its tooth.'"[68]

Lest we forget: explanation is always a pragmatic project.[69] At the same time, the legal inference observed here is indubitably a pragmatic project of selecting the best legal explanation. Since the previous proposition is highly analytical, we need to extend such an explanatory concept into a phenomenological realm, specifically one that pertains to temporal experience. In

65 Lefebvre, *The Image of Law: Deleuze, Bergson, Spinoza*, 181. (emphasis added)

66 Simon Prosser, "Why Does Time Seem to Pass?" *Philosophy and Phenomenological Research* 85, no. 1 (2012): 92–116. Borrowing form Prosser, we must keep in mind that "the representation of something enduring through a change is a key element in the phenomenology of temporal passage." 113.

67 Adriana Alfaro Altamirano, *The Belief in Intuition: Individuality and Authority in Henri Bergson and Max Scheler* (Philadelphia: University of Pennsylvania Press, 2021). I suggest that such an active process reinventing 'the unthinkable' resembles what Altamirano wrote as 'calibrating our agency.' In this sense, such dynamic change or movement insists a reasoner, quoting Altamirano, "in contrast to the categorical imperative's invitation to subsume the maxim of our actions under the universal law, [to] [proceed] case by case, constantly adjusting our agency—more assertive at times, less so in others—to meet the requirements of the circumstances that we face." 56.

68 Anderson, "Bergsonian Intuition: A Metaphysics of Mystical Life," 248.

69 Thagard argued that "The presence of pragmatic elements does not imply that theory choice is subjective: theory choice is historically relative only in the benign sense that the application of objective criteria such as consilience presupposes a given scientific-historical context. It can be shown that this concern with the pragmatic translates into the avoidance of the notorious paradoxes of confirmation." 92.

that regard, a rather similar pragmatic project has actually been propounded by our main theory of time as duration. In duration, judges select virtually any relevant past moments and bring them to our actual precept in the present, or in Bergson's words, "[t]he essence of the general idea, in fact, is to be unceasingly going backwards and forwards between the plane of action and that of pure memory."[70] In his metaphor of inverted cone of memory (with layers AB, A"B" and A'B') that meets a plane at its summit (S), Bergson prescribes that

> [a]t S is the present perception which I have of my body, that is to say, of a certain sensori-motor equilibrium. Over the surface of the base AB are spread, we may say, my recollections in their totality. Within the cone so determined, the general idea oscillates continually between the summit S and the base AB.[71]

From this viewpoint, duration is essentially reflected in memory, which conflates the modalities of time: past, present and future. As already examined in Chapter 4, in duration judges are attentive to both the *singularity* of time that views the passage of time as unique and the *heterogeneity* of time that asserts our differing views on the past, present and future, thus recognizing the reality of each modality. How do the two intertwine? And how does such intertwining generate novelty and creativity in the process of reasoning and inference?

Legal perception and intuition

We have argued thus far how intuition *orders* experience through directing legal decision-makers' sensory perception in *accessing* the production of understanding. Our subsequent analysis is about how intuition interacts with legal arguments, or, to be precise, about how the rules of intuition correspond with the aforementioned legal inference in the process of crafting lawful relations.[72] In that context, the two can make a sort of connection in terms of the reasoner's capacity for perceptual sensitivity, in which one of the

70 Henri Bergson, *Matter and Memory*. Trans. N. M. Paul and W. S. Palmer (New York: Zone Books, 1911), 161.

71 Ibid.

72 At the moment, one might be tempted to bring the discussion into types of probative reasoning, such as legal probabilism. Such a line of idea, however, may lead us back to the propositional mode of thought, whereas in Chapter 4 we have described some difficulties in such a mode of thought in dealing with the multiplicity of experiences. For an overview of legal probabilism, see Rafał Urbaniak and Marcello Di Bello, "Legal Probabilism," in *Stanford Encyclopedia of Philosophy* (2021), https://plato.stanford.edu/entries/legal-probabilism/.

underlying aspects would be empathy towards injustice.[73] However, before delving into the idea of empathy towards injustice, a clear comprehension of perception should be put to surface, that is: Is perception similar to intuition? How is perception-intuition guided by coherence? Ultimately, we might want to ask, in short, is it possible for intuition to be normative (i.e., intuition as a normative argument)?

At this point, our analysis begins with the conversation about perceptual sensitivity. It is important to note that the discussion about perceptual sensitivity has been mostly grounded in the distinction between an investigation over the aspect of the reasoning agents' qualities and the quality of reasoning of a decision. Contrary to that view, the argument we made earlier has claimed that our phenomenological apprehension puts forward the proposition that we can no longer see the way judges think in an inquiry separated from the inquiry (as an object) itself.[74] On that account, legal reasoning *in* time means that it is internally experienced (by the judges), as Maclean suggested, "as a subtle yet dynamic succession of finely tuned actions and interactions in a continuously evolving realization of what is really happening and being made to happen."[75] Seeing through such an internalist lens, it would then be problematic to distinguish the two qualities (of reasoning agents and of reasoning/justification) as separate entities, and, bearing that in mind, it is plausible to claim that an investigation into the way intuition interacts with legal arguments through perception needs to be situated under this kind of epistemology.

A brief note regarding the difference between perception and intuition might be rewarding to highlight at the moment. From Bergson, we can understand that intuition speaks about mind and consciousness rather than an external observable object, which belongs to the domain of perception. Accordingly, Guerlac observes that "perception, analysis and measurement give us knowledge of material things, which we know from the outside; intuition is appropriate for inner experience, for dynamics of consciousness that tell us how things feel, and how they become."[76] That said, perception, in Bergsonian terms, should be seen as action, that is, "an action that prepares

73 Del Mar, "Judging Virtuously: Developing an Empathic Capacity for Perceptual Sensitivity."
74 Relatedly, one might also want to consult the idea of phenomenological conception of perceptual justification (PCPJ) coined by Berghofer. See Philipp Berghofer, "Motivating and Defending the Phenomenological Conception of Perceptual Justification," *Inquiry* 66, no. 6 (2023): 947–64. PCPJ mainly asserts that "Perceptual experiences have a distinctive, justification-conferring phenomenology, and if a perceptual experience E has such a justification-conferring phenomenology with respect to proposition p, E, by virtue of its phenomenology, provides immediate prima facie justification for believing that p." 90.
75 James MacLean, *Rethinking Law as Process: Creativity, Novelty, Change* (Oxon & New York: Routledge, 2012), 183. See Chapter 4.
76 Guerlac, "Duration: A Fluid Concept," 46.

another action, not one that operates in the service of knowledge."[77] Guerlac further notes that "[p]recisely because they have memory, however, living beings do not react automatically to external stimuli."[78] Through Bergson's intuition, Guerlac rightly suggests that

> [a]ctual perception . . . takes time (especially in higher animals) because memory has to coordinate complex sensory apparatuses (hearing, sight, touch, etc.) which operate through different rhythms. The interval of time required for memory to support perception by coordinating sensory input introduces a moment of indeterminacy into what would otherwise be an automatic circuit of stimulus and response. It produces a kind of disjunction in that mechanism, a hesitation which opens up an opportunity for choice, such that voluntary action occurs instead of automatic reaction.[79]

We can, however, take a rather moderate view of such a distinction. That said, we can submit intuition as a method that accounts for perception as an active force in the search for salient legal properties. As part of intuition, (legal) perception is always conceptual. Legal perception can be perceptually loaded through inner senses that organize data into several discrete unites or *gestalts*, as Michelon claims borrowing from Aquinas.[80] As we can also understand from Michelon, gestalts at this moment can be regarded as memory in the Bergsonian sense, as they are in charge of storing both evaluative and non-evaluative properties. That is, according to Michelon,

> [w]hen practical perception is engaged in the search for salient properties, what it produces is the perception of something *qua* something. In other words, as part of the production of practical arguments, practical perception is always conceptual: it is the perception of an object x possessing a property F. It is always predicated on the possession by the perceiving subject of concepts of x and F, and on the fact that she deploys those concepts in the experience.[81]

Reading (legal) perception from Bergsonian intuition makes a clear sense about the possibility of non-conceptual perception (i.e., perceptions that do not meet the conditions of possession and deployment of concepts), which

77 Ibid., 48.
78 Ibid.
79 Ibid.
80 Claudio Michelon, "Lawfulness and the Perception of Legal Salience," *Jurisprudence* 9, no. 1 (2018): 47–57.
81 Ibid., 4; Matthew William McKeon, "Argument, Inference, and Persuasion," *Argumentation* 35, no. 2 (2021): 339–56.

is to a certain extent illustrated as "legal peripheral perception."[82] The way Bergsonian intuition (i.e., perception-memory) operates in legal reasoning is feasibly complementary to the way legal perception develops in an agent's legal conceptual framework, as suggested by Michelon. In that sense, intuition supplants legal perception by underscoring (1) the reliance on memory prompts, (2) the undoing of separation between form and content, thus focusing on the quality of experience and (3) reality as a continuity of the process of becoming in a way that perception prolongs the past into the present through memory partaking. From those notions, we may understand the workings of perception within intuition, in that

> Memory implies an absorption of time, which remains virtually active. Our memory images become enlivened—actualized as images—when new perceptions occur that in some way resemble them; the new perceptions solicit the memory images to participate in their activity. Through this engagement, which Bergson calls attentive recognition, memory images inform how we parse raw sensory data and delineate the objects of our perception. They also inform how we decide to act in response to our perceptions. This is how our past is said to act on our present.[83]

Such an explanation is useful for us to clearly understand the flow of legal perception. It would be helpful to quote Michelon's exemplary depiction of this particular assertion as follows:

> An experienced lawyer, who engages appropriately with her experience, develops a complex framework of gestalts through which her inner senses organize the world. Those gestalts are formed as the answer-driving properties that were incorporated into successful legal arguments in previous cases accumulate in the *imaginatio* and in the sense-memory. The answer-driving properties are the properties in previous cases that attracted the relevant legal rules to resolve the legal dispute in that case. Such answer-driving properties, however, are always drawn from a much more complex set of properties belonging to each case. So in each case the lawyer would have learned both about properties that are immediately legally relevant and about properties that are not immediately legally

82 Michelon, "Lawfulness and the Perception of Legal Salience," 5. Michelon's example on perception in searching for physical object can be helpful in understanding this proposition. Michelon explains that "If someone fails to see an object he is looking for in a drawer, even though the object is in the drawer, in a relatively prominent place, but after closing the drawer, recalling its contents, realises that the object was among them, it seems that there was something like perception going on about the 'contents of the drawer,' and even about specifically the object that is been sought, *before the deployment of the concept*." 5.

83 Guerlac, "Duration: A Fluid Concept," 48.

> relevant. As a result, the lawyers experience will also generate a peripheral legal perception inhabited by properties that were not explicitly learned qua legally relevant, but might turn out to be so.[84]

From Michelon's depiction, it is suggestive that intuition is a kind of practical wisdom.[85] In that sense, practical wisdom can be seen as "the intellectual virtue that allows one to identify in an instant case the reasons that justify the actions a virtuous agent is inclined to perform in certain virtues-specific contexts."[86] And for that reason, Michelon furthers, "it is fidelity to those underlying reasons that ultimately constitutes virtue, and it is the possibility of deliberating about what those reasons require in the instant case that makes practical wisdom the touchstone of all virtue."[87] As a result, we may want to claim that intuition is an act of virtue to the extent that virtue is understood as direction rather than trajectory. In the former sense, virtue is simply grasped as acting well on continuing something that one has learned, that is, on applying a rather similar way of doing things in the past. Meanwhile, the latter sense of virtue asserts "an inclination towards performing the action that is required *by the correct appreciation of the reasons which underlie the virtues bearing on the situation.*"[88] It is thus reasonable to indicate a clear nexus between perceptual sensitivity and virtue in a way that, as Amaya has rightly suggested,

> the virtuous decision-maker has a perceptual sensitivity which, precisely, enables him to discern the reasons for his decision in the particular case and to provide the corresponding justifications. This perceptual sensitivity,

84 Michelon, "Lawfulness and the Perception of Legal Salience," 8.

85 Gary Klein, "Expert Intuition and Naturalistic Decision Making," in *Handbook of Intuition Research*, ed. Marta Sinclair (Cheltenham, UK & Northampton, USA: Edward Elgar Publishing, 2011), 69–78; William Duggan and Malia Mason, "Strategic Intuition," in *Handbook of Intuition Research*, ed. Marta Sinclair (Cheltenham, UK & Northampton, USA: Edward Elgar Publishing, 2011), 79–87. Suggested by cognitive sciences discipline, there are two major kinds of intuition, that is, expert and strategi intuition. Quoting from Duggan and Mason, "In *expert* intuition, recall comes quickly, without conscious thought, by drawing from direct experience. In *strategic* intuition, recall includes the experience of others learned through reading, seeing or hearing, which explains why it features slower recall from a wider range of weaker memory. But in both forms of intuition, the mechanism of recall is generally the same." 71 (emphasis original) Intuition in the context of this study, however, does not make such strict distinction (and separation). It is argued that, if we carefully read Michelon's claims, the kind of intuition that accounts for legal perception can be seen as both expert and strategic intuition.

86 Michelon, "Lawfulness and the Perception of Legal Salience," 11.

87 Ibid.

88 Ibid.; Ho Hock Lai, "Virtuous Deliberation on the Criminal Verdict," in *Law, Virtue and Justice*, ed. A. Amaya and Ho Hock Lai (Oxford & Portland, OR: Hart Publishing, 2013), 241–63. (emphasis original)

as it were, makes visible to the virtuous agent what are the relevant reasons or justifications in the particular case, and hence, what it is that, in the case at hand, virtue requires.[89]

Intuiting the time of injustice

So far, it has been argued that intuition is a kind of judicial practice—a judge's mode of thinking that enables them to create and craft forms of lawful relations. In this study, it is critical to emphasize that intuition must be juxtaposed with so-called historical injustice inquiries. Arguably, historical injustice should be demonstrated as a form of temporal legal inquiry (i.e., an investigation into how the temporalities of law and historical processes interact in legal problems). In that regard, legal decision-makers should investigate historical injustice through an untimely approach, meaning that they need to devise injustice within "a conception of the future that does not necessarily follow progressively from the past or present, that is unknown and out of control of the present, and that better foregrounds the continual elaboration of the new."[90] Experiences stemming from the historical process of injustices, as a result of the Encounter, implies the idea of rendering injustices out of time, thus isolating the investigation from the context of the past and present, and enabling judges to see the novel and unknowable future becoming.[91]

89 Amaya, "The Role of Virtue in Legal Justification," 59–60; Aulis Aarnio, "On Rational Acceptability: Some Remarks on Legal Justification," in *Law, Interpretation and Reality: Essays in Epistemology, Hermeneutics and Jurisprudence*, ed. Patrick Nerhot (Dordrecht: Springer, 1990), 73–83. Again, perceptual sensitivity does not necessarily undermine the idea of legal certainty. According to Aarnio, legal certainty (*Rechtssicherheit*) covers two elements of adjudication, namely: avoidance of arbitrariness and fulfillment of axiological (moral) criteria. 80.

90 Kathryn McNeilly, "Are Rights Out of Time? International Human Rights Law, Temporality, and Radical Social Change," *Social & Legal Studies* 28, no. 6 (2019): 2, https://doi.org/10.1177/0964663918815729; Jenny Wüstenberg, "Toward Slow Memory Studies," in *Critical Memory Studies: New Approaches*, ed. Brett Ashley Kaplan (London, New York & Dublin: Bloomsbury Publishing, 2023), 59–67.

91 Further examination, see previously in Chapters 4 and 5. See also Maksymilian Del Mar, *Artefacts of Legal Inquiry: The Value of Imagination in Adjudication* (Bloomsbury Publishing, 2020), 74; Simon Prosser, *Experiencing Time* (Oxford: Oxford University Press, 2016), Chap. 7. Del Mar contends that "[i]nsofar as our access, as persons, to normative objects is via our experiences as embodied, sensory and affective creatures, then that which we have access to has to be such as to be capable of being experienced by us as creatures of that kind. In other words, we *encounter* phenomena that we experience as a value, vulnerability or interest in a certain way, i.e., precisely as embodied, sensory and affective beings. In everyday life, many of these experiences will involve direct personal involvement, as when we interact with our fellows, and experience the variety and intensity of emotions those interactions bring: from love to hate, from indignation to pride, from sadness to joy, and so on." 74.

Historical injustice adjudication ought to be intuited by the legal decision-makers through the three rules of problematization, differentiation and temporalization. In the first rule, the problem of the 'historical' of injustice should be stated precisely as, to reiterate, "a unique, singular, coherent expression which encompasses being wide-open to experience and to interpretation." The second rule asserts the moment when a distinction is made, that is, differentiating between the knowledge of the difference in intensity and the difference in terms of innovation and inventiveness. That is, the judges ought to ask themselves whether they are investigating some sustained, existing problem, or instead opening a novel direction of a problem. Last, historical injustice will be explained in terms of time. Here, legal decision-makers are choosing the essence of a case by means of the interaction between perception and memory up to a point where, to reiterate Lefebvre, "a few aspects of a perceptions are dwelled on so as to elicit descriptions that, *once actualized together in the perception cohere as an essential singularity*."[92]

Through such a reading on intuition, we can find a more nuanced apprehension towards legal justification. That is, in intuiting the time of historical injustice, these rules should be read along with the coherence-based legal inference.[93] Coherence is arguably constitutive of intuition to the extent that (1) coherence enters implicitly into the process of generation via background knowledge, (2) coherence also enters into the process of generation through a number of marshalling mechanisms and (3) the generation of new elements is sometimes driven by an effort after coherence. Therefore, through intuitive inference, a reasoner can *justify* the 'truth' (or the 'time,' to be precise) of her best explanation.[94]

Generally speaking, in the *process* of crafting or reasoning about lawful relations, intuition plays an important role through judges' perceptual sensitivity.[95] Intuiting the experiences of injustice in a legal case compels

92 Lefebvre, *The Image of Law: Deleuze, Bergson, Spinoza*, 181. (emphasis added)

93 Wright, "The Role of Intuition in Judicial Decisionmaking." Examining judicial coherentism, Wright claims that "If we have no grounds for believing that articulating a judicial coherentism can be achieved merely through inference from principles not intuitively grasped, we should all admit the crucial role of intuition in developing and applying judicial coherentism." 1416.

94 Andreas Glöckner and Irena D. Ebert, "Legal Intuition and Expertise," in *Handbook of Intuition Research*, ed. Marta Sinclair (Cheltenham, UK & Northampton, USA: Edward Elgar, 2011), 157–67. Glockner and Ebert specifically address the significance of the so-called 'constructive intuition' in legal realm insofar as such intuition "constructs consistent interpretations or stories of the evidence." 162. It is suggested that this constructive intuition would be similar with what we term 'intuitive inference' in this study.

95 Jean-Francois Coget and Eugene Keller, "The Critical Decision Vortex: Lessons from the Emergency Room," *Journal of Management Inquiry* 19, no. 1 (2010): 56–67; Jean-Francois Coget, "The Critical Decisions Vortex–Interplay of Intuition, Reason, and Emotion: Comparison of Three Dynamic Industries," in *Handbook of Intuition Research*, ed.

judges' inner capacity to sensitize (or be attentive to) instances of injustice experience through their quality of empathy.[96] Borrowing from Slote, empathy "involves having the feelings of another (involuntarily) aroused in ourselves, as when we see another person in pain."[97] Or, in Nussbaum's words, empathy is "an imaginative reconstruction of another person's experience, whether that experience is happy or sad, pleasant or painful or neutral, and whether the imaginer thinks the other person's situation good, bad, or indifferent."[98] In our context, since empathy is an aspect of intuition, it consequently has temporal characteristics, which makes it slightly distinct from our given definition of it. In other words, we may suggest that empathy is *in* duration in the sense that it conflates the modalities of time to generate (1) temporal encounters as *difference-in-kind*, and (2) legal relations (as the outcome of an inquiry) as *cross-temporal perception*.[99] It is critical to note that empathy is not an intersubjective experience; to wit, legal decision-makers have access to knowledge about historical injustice experiences not through their 'objectified' reason, but rather through their own (internal) experience of empathy. From the Bergsonian lens, the experiences of injustice, as an animate object, cannot be accessible through one's cognitive instruments of intelligence because injustices do not occur in the regime of *repetition*—injustices are rather singular 'events' that each consist of different qualities. The experience of (the time of) injustices exists instead in a regime of *becoming*, based on the fact that memory changes and alters the way one senses reality. In this framework, empathy can guide legal decision-makers to generate a cross-temporal trajectory that is underpinned by (1) the innateness between the actual and the virtual of collective legal responsibility; and (2) the attributability of group's substantive legal responsibility over time.[100]

Marta Sinclair (Cheltenham, UK & Northampton, USA: Edward Elgar Publishing, 2011), 133–44. Suggested by cognitive science experiments, our suggestion about the relationship between reasoning, intuition and empathy can also be framed under Coget and Keller's critical decisions vortex model. This model captures the connections between rational decision making, intuitive decision making and emotion. In Coget's words, "[t]he critical decisions vortex is a meta-process through which experts continually shift among the three processes of thinking, intuiting, and feeling in order to make the right decisions and take action. The metaphor of a 'vortex' attempts to reflect the relentless shifting that occurs among processes, and the lack of apparent order in which the shifts happen." 134.

96 Michael Slote, "Empathy, Law and Justice," in *Law, Virtue and Justice*, ed. Amalia Amaya and Ho Hock Lai (Oxford & Portland, OR: Hart Publishing, 2013), 279–92.

97 Michael Slote, *The Ethics of Care and Empathy* (New York: Routledge, 2007), 13.

98 Martha C. Nussbaum, *Upheavals of Thought: The Intelligence of Emotions* (New York: Cambridge University Press, 2001), 302.

99 See Thomas Schramme, "Empathy with Future Generations?" *Topoi* (2023), https://doi.org/10.1007/s11245-023-09988-1. Relatedly, Schramme argues for two types of interpersonal understanding in the process of empathy, including factive knowledge and concerned attitude.

100 These epistemological underpinnings will be thoroughly analyzed in Chapter 7.

Conclusion

In sum, empathy needs to be seen as part of intuitive-based methodology as it provides a way to access creative minds in crafting lawful relations. Moreover, it is through emphatic intuition that we can fully capture the time and temporalities of injustice. Empathy can fulfill the demands for legal decision-makers to frame time-mindful responsibility. Accordingly, empathy, since it is *in* duration, does not correspond to the traditional counterfactual account of harm, but instead, it is paying attention to the undergoing historical worsening as a truth-maker.[101] Empathy supports the ground for intuitive knowledge about the distinction between, on the one hand, saying someone is guilty (e.g., of past wrongdoing) and, on the other hand, conveying blame responses such as resentment and indignation. Therefore, it is contingent not only on changes on the wrongdoer's part but also on taking into account *how* such changes might take place. Finally, empathic intuition is not exclusively individual (i.e., understanding or analyzing); it is also about social intelligence (i.e., sharing, collaboration)[102]—from which we can comprehend that creativity is an individual task integral to collective tasks pertinent to the crafting of lawful relations.[103]

101 Robin Le Poidevin, *The Images of Time: An Essay on Temporal Representation* (Oxford: Oxford University Press, 2007). It is important to note the way this proposition conforms with philosophical argument about time perception. As we will briefly mention later in Chapter 7 about the modified Causal Truth-Maker Principle, our proposition about the undergoing historical worsening is sufficient to be the truth-maker that has "*some* form of explanatory role in the acquisition of perceptual knowledge" of injustice. 121. Furthermore, borrowing from Poidevin, "Explanation, even of a non-logical kind, is not invariably purely causal. And even in what might ordinarily be called causal explanation, there are non-causal components. Within such explanation, beside reference to the causes themselves, there may also be reference to the properties and relations that structure those causes: their location in space and time, for example. It is a question worth pursuing whether a theory of knowledge based on this more inclusive conception of explanation could more easily accommodate knowledge of abstract objects. In the context of time perception, appeal to what I called chronometric explanation helps us solve the epistemological puzzle while retaining our belief in the mind-independence of order and duration. Thus the fact that psychological models of order and duration perception make such perception indirect does not in itself show that these properties are mind-dependent, any more than the indirect nature of depth perception (involving as it does comparison by the brain of the input from the two eyes) shows depth to be mind-dependent." 121.

102 Picavet, "Bergson and Our Understanding of Interaction, Constraints and Collective Aspirations," 131; Hans Lindahl, "Laws and (Dis) Empowerment," in *Reading Ricoeur Through Law*, ed. Marc de Leeuw, George H. Taylor, and Eileen Brennan (Rowman & Littlefield, 2022), 191. The social nature of judgment can also be seen from Lindahl's reflection on Ricoeur's understanding on the finality of judging, which amounts to collective self-affirmation. Lindahl submits a *restrictive* collective self-formation, in which "[j]udging ought to recognize the other (in ourselves) as one of us and as other than us. More precisely, I submit, the ultimate finality of judging, if judging us to promote public peace." 204.

103 See Amalia Amaya, "Exemplarism and Judicial Virtue," *Law & Literature* 25, no. 3 (2013): 428–45; Amalia Amaya, "Imitation and Analogy," *Analogy and Exemplary Reasoning in Legal Discourse* 13 (2018): 31.

Reference list

Aarnio, Aulis. "On Rational Acceptability: Some Remarks on Legal Justification." In *Law, Interpretation and Reality: Essays in Epistemology, Hermeneutics and Jurisprudence*, edited by Patrick Nerhot, 73–83. Dordrecht: Springer, 1990.

Altamirano, Adriana Alfaro. *The Belief in Intuition: Individuality and Authority in Henri Bergson and Max Scheler*. Philadelphia: University of Pennsylvania Press, 2021.

Amaya, Amalia. "Legal Justification by Optimal Coherence." *Ratio Juris* 24, no. 3 (2011): 304–29.

Amaya, Amalia. "Exemplarism and Judicial Virtue." *Law & Literature* 25, no. 3 (2013): 428–45.

Amaya, Amalia. "The Role of Virtue in Legal Justification." In *Law, Virtue and Justice*, edited by Amalia Amaya and Hock Lai Ho, 51–66. Oxford & Portland, OR: Hart Publishing, 2013.

Amaya, Amalia. *The Tapestry of Reason: An Inquiry into the Nature of Coherence and Its Role in Legal Argument*. Oxford & Portland, OR: Hart Publishing, 2015.

Amaya, Amalia. "Imitation and Analogy." *Analogy and Exemplary Reasoning in Legal Discourse* 13 (2018): 31.

Anderson, Pamela Sue. "Bergsonian Intuition: A Metaphysics of Mystical Life." *Philosophical Topics* 43, no. 1/2 (2015): 239–51.

Basu, Rima. "What We Epistemically Owe to Each Other." *Philosophical Studies* 176 (2019): 915–31.

Berghofer, Philipp. "Motivating and Defending the Phenomenological Conception of Perceptual Justification." *Inquiry* 66, no. 6 (2023): 947–64.

Bergson, Henri. *Matter and Memory*. Translated by N. M. Paul and W. S. Palmer. New York: Zone Books, 1911.

Coget, Jean-Francois. "The Critical Decisions Vortex–Interplay of Intuition, Reason, and Emotion: Comparison of Three Dynamic Industries." In *Handbook of Intuition Research*, edited by Marta Sinclair, 133–44. Cheltenham, UK & Northampton, USA: Edward Elgar Publishing, 2011.

Coget, Jean-Francois, and Eugene Keller. "The Critical Decision Vortex: Lessons from the Emergency Room." *Journal of Management Inquiry* 19, no. 1 (2010): 56–67.

Cox, Courtney M. "The Uncertain Judge." *University of Chicago Law Review* 90, no. 3 (2023): 739–811.

Deleuze, Gilles. *Bergsonism*. Translated by H. Tomlinson and B. Habberjam. New York: Zone Books, 1991.

Deleuze, Gilles. *Difference and Repetition*. Columbia University Press, 1994.

Douzinas, Costas, Ronnie Warrington, and Shaun McVeigh. *Postmodern Jurisprudence: The Law of the Text in the Text of the Law*. Routledge, 1993.

Duggan, William, and Malia Mason. "Strategic Intuition." In *Handbook of Intuition Research*, edited by Marta Sinclair, 79–87. Cheltenham, UK & Northampton, USA: Edward Elgar Publishing, 2011.

Glöckner, Andreas, and Irena D. Ebert. "Legal Intuition and Expertise." In *Handbook of Intuition Research*, edited by Marta Sinclair, 157–67. Cheltenham, UK & Northampton, USA: Edward Elgar, 2011.

Guerlac, Suzanne. "Duration: A Fluid Concept." In *The Bergsonian Mind*, 45–54. Routledge, 2021.

Guthrie, Chris, Jeffrey J. Rachlinski, and Andrew J. Wistrich. "Blinking on the Bench: How Judges Decide Cases." *Cornell Law Review* 93, no. 1 (2007): 1–44.

Harman, Gilbert H. "The Inference to the Best Explanation." *The Philosophical Review* 74, no. 1 (1965): 88–95.

Hutcheson Jr, Joseph C. "Judgment Intuitive The Function of the Hunch in Judicial Decision." *Cornell Law Review* 14, no. 3 (1928): 274–88. http://scholarship.law.cornell.edu/clr/vol14/iss3/2.
Jakubiec, Marek. "Legal Concepts as Mental Representations." *International Journal for the Semiotics of Law-Revue Internationale de Sémiotique Juridique* 35, no. 5 (2022): 1837–55.
Kahneman, Daniel. *Thinking, Fast and Slow*. New York: Farrar, Straus and Giroux, 2011.
Klein, Gary. "Expert Intuition and Naturalistic Decision Making." In *Handbook of Intuition Research*, edited by Marta Sinclair, 69–78. Cheltenham, UK & Northampton, USA: Edward Elgar Publishing, 2011.
Lai, Ho Hock. "Virtuous Deliberation on the Criminal Verdict." In *Law, Virtue and Justice*, edited by A. Amaya and Ho Hock Lai, 241–63. Oxford & Portland, OR: Hart Publishing, 2013.
Lawlor, Leonard. *The Challenge of Bergsonism*. A&C Black, 2003.
Lawlor, Leonard. "Intuition and Duration: An Introduction to Bergson's 'Introduction to Metaphysics'." In *Bergson and Phenomenology*, edited by Michael R. Kelly, 25–41. New York: Palgrave Macmillan, 2010.
Lefebvre, Alexandre. *The Image of Law: Deleuze, Bergson, Spinoza*. Stanford: Stanford University Press, 2008.
Lewinski, Marcin. "Practical Argumentation as Reasoned Advocacy." *Informal Logic* 37, no. 2 (2017): 85–113.
Lindahl, Hans. "Laws and (Dis) Empowerment." In *Reading Ricoeur Through Law*, edited by Marc de Leeuw, George H. Taylor, and Eileen Brennan, 191. Rowman & Littlefield, 2022.
Lipton, Peter. "Inference to the Best Explanation." In *A Companion to the Philosophy of Science*, 184–93. Wiley Online Library, 2017. https://doi.org/10.1002/9781405164481.ch29.
MacCormick, Neil. *Rhetoric and the Rule of Law: A Theory of Legal Reasoning*. Oxford: Oxford University Press, 2005.
MacLean, James. *Rethinking Law as Process: Creativity, Novelty, Change*. Oxon & New York: Routledge, 2012.
Mar, Maksymilian Del. "Judging Virtuously: Developing an Empathic Capacity for Perceptual Sensitivity." *Jurisprudence* 5, no. 1 (2014): 196–208. https://doi.org/10.5235/20403313.5.1.196.
Mar, Maksymilian Del. *Artefacts of Legal Inquiry: The Value of Imagination in Adjudication*. Bloomsbury Publishing, 2020.
McKeon, Matthew William. "Argument, Inference, and Persuasion." *Argumentation* 35, no. 2 (2021): 339–56.
McNeilly, Kathryn. "Are Rights Out of Time? International Human Rights Law, Temporality, and Radical Social Change." *Social & Legal Studies* 28, no. 6 (2019): 817–38. https://doi.org/10.1177/0964663918815729.
Michelon, Claudio. "Practical Wisdom in Legal Decision-Making." In *Law, Virtue and Justice*, edited by Amalia Amaya and Ho Hock Lai, 29–49. Oxford & Portland, OR: Hart Publishing, 2013.
Michelon, Claudio. "Lawfulness and the Perception of Legal Salience." *Jurisprudence* 9, no. 1 (2018): 47–57.
Michelon, Claudio. "The Inference to the Best Legal Explanation." *Oxford Journal of Legal Studies* 39, no. 4 (2019): 878–900.
Modak-Truran, Mark. "A Pragmatic Justification of the Judicial Hunch." *University of Richmond Law Review* 35 (2001): 55.

Nussbaum, Martha C. *Upheavals of Thought: The Intelligence of Emotions.* New York: Cambridge University Press, 2001.
Oberdiek, John. *Imposing Risk: A Normative Framework.* Oxford University Press, 2017.
Osborne, Robert Carry. "What Do We Epistemically Owe to Each Other? A Reply to Basu." *Philosophical Studies* 178, no. 3 (2021): 1005–22.
Palazuelos, Felix Rebolledo, Tania Galli Fonseca, and Andreia Machado Oliveira. "A Philosophical Perspective on Intuition as a Method within Artistic Process." *Studies in Visual Arts and Communication: An International Journal* 5, no. 1 (2018): 1–11.
Picavet, Emmanuel. "Bergson and Our Understanding of Interaction, Constraints and Collective Aspirations." *Bergsoniana*, no. 1 (2021).
Poidevin, Robin Le. *The Images of Time: An Essay on Temporal Representation.* Oxford: Oxford University Press, 2007.
Priel, Dan. "Law Is What the Judge Had for Breakfast: A Brief History of an Unpalat able Idea." *Buffalo Law Review* 68 (2020): 899.
Prosser, Simon. "Why Does Time Seem to Pass?" *Philosophy and Phenomenological Research* 85, no. 1 (2012): 92–116.
Prosser, Simon. *Experiencing Time.* Oxford: Oxford University Press, 2016.
Richards, Diana. "When Judges Have a Hunch: Intuition and Experience in Judicial Decision-Making." *ARSP: Archiv Für Rechts-Und Sozialphilosophie/Archives for Philosophy of Law and Social Philosophy* (2016): 245–60.
Samuel, Geoffrey. *Epistemology and Method in Law.* London & New York: Routledge, 2016.
Sandberg, Joakim, and Niklas Juth. "Ethics and Intuitions: A Reply to Singer." *The Journal of Ethics* 15 (2011): 209–26.
Schramme, Thomas. "Empathy with Future Generations?" *Topoi* (2023). https://doi.org/10.1007/s11245-023-09988-1.
Sinclair, Marta. "Misconceptions about Intuition." *Psychological Inquiry* 21, no. 4 (2010): 378–86.
Singer, Peter. "Ethics and Intuitions." *The Journal of Ethics* 9 (2005): 331–52.
Slote, Michael. *The Ethics of Care and Empathy.* New York: Routledge, 2007.
Slote, Michael. "Empathy, Law and Justice." In *Law, Virtue and Justice*, edited by Amalia Amaya and Ho Hock Lai, 279–92. Oxford & Portland, OR: Hart Publishing, 2013.
Thagard, Paul R. "The Best Explanation: Criteria for Theory Choice." *The Journal of Philosophy* 75, no. 2 (1978): 76–92.
Tushnet, Mark V. "Anti-Formalism in Recent Constitutional Theory." *Michigan Law Review* 83 (1984): 1502.
Urbaniak, Rafał, and Marcello Di Bello. "Legal Probabilism." In *Stanford Encyclopedia of Philosophy.* 2021. https://plato.stanford.edu/entries/legal-probabilism/.
Wheatley, Steven. "Revisiting the Doctrine of Intertemporal Law." *Oxford Journal of Legal Studies* 41, no. 2 (2021): 484–509.
Wright, R. George. "The Role of Intuition in Judicial Decisionmaking." *Houston Law Review* 42 (2006): 1381.
Wüstenberg, Jenny. "Toward Slow Memory Studies." In *Critical Memory Studies: New Approaches*, edited by Brett Ashley Kaplan, 59–67. London, New York & Dublin: Bloomsbury Publishing, 2023.

Chapter 7

Collective responsibility and law's time-mindfulness

The second element of our alternative epistemology of historical injustice is concerned with reevaluating collective legal responsibility. Legal responsibility, seen as one of the fundamental concepts in legal inquiries, draws distinctive boundaries between other equally fundamental concepts, such as right and obligation. Our primordial belief is that when one violates another's legal right or fails to comply with her legal obligations, judges intuitively come up with a set of inquiries as to whether one should be held responsible or accountable for such an event and, importantly, in what way. Our case-studies in Chapters 1-3 have suggested that the judicial inquiry into collective legal responsibility has been pervasive in many historical injustice discourses, up to a point where we can eventually expand it to the Anthropocene.[1] In these contemporary problems, any inquiries into legal responsibility are not only circumscribed by the constant 'who' questions;[2] they also call for a further question regarding responsibility 'on what ground' and 'to what extent'—two matters in which this chapter is interested.

Against such a lawyerly sense of responsibility, Scott Veitch's *Law of Irresponsibility* displays a thought-provoking premise in problematizing collective legal responsibility.[3] Veitch observes that law facilitates irresponsibility rather than ensuring to hold responsibilities for injustices in society over time. Veitch's concern somehow holds that the premise of irresponsibility is basically a symptom of a judge's cognitive dilemma in capturing the multiplicity

1 Iván Darío Vargas Roncancio, "Law as Relation and the Co-Emergence of Beings: Towards a Paradigm Shift in Legal Education," in *Biopolitics and Resistance in Legal Education*, ed. Thomas Giddens and Luca Siliquini-Cinelli (Oxon & New York: Routledge, 2023), 202–14.

2 Maeve McKeown, "Responsibility," in *The Philosopher New Basics: Society*, ed. Anthony Morgan (The Philosopher, 2022), 46–50; Jana Norman, *Posthuman Legal Subjectivity: Reimagining the Human in the Anthropocene* (Oxon & New York: Routledge, 2022); Kathleen Birrell, "Human and Inhuman Subjects and Sediments," in *The Routledge Handbook of Law and the Anthropocene* (Routledge, 2023), 51.

3 Scott Veitch, *Law and Irresponsibility: On the Legitimation of Human Suffering* (Oxon: Routledge-Cavendish, 2007).

DOI: 10.4324/9781003518693-10

of experiences of injustice.[4] The judge's cognitive dilemma yields a possibility for a critique regarding the homogeneity and generality of legal relations that insist judges frame responsibility as a matter of harm and blame *measurement*. Veitch's law of irresponsibility can be read as an urgent call for judges to recognize the complex reality of injustice and to (re-)orient the law of responsibility into multiplicity and heterogeneity.

This chapter's central premise is that collective legal responsibility attribution fundamentally hinges upon its temporal criteria. It is argued that the problem of a judge's cognitive dilemma in historical injustice adjudication can alternatively be resolved through asserting experiential temporality within legal responsibility practices. Here, we focus on understanding the models of temporal inquiry into collective responsibility. Current models, however, are inadequate to generate an alternative epistemology of historical injustice. A 'time-mindful' approach is proposed as an alternative to elucidating collective responsibility. Time-mindful responsibility can be grasped as an active social practice that aims to attain social purposes over time according to the temporal patterns governed by norms of practical coherence. The idea draws from Postema's concept of law's time-mindfulness. Approaching responsibility through this framework engenders the view that collective responsibility practice is fundamentally tied to coherence in a temporally extended social life, which accounts for a reflective engagement between individual, agential and societal time. This approach thereby demands legal decision-makers (1) to frame responsibility as pivotal in the memory of the past and (2) to creatively perceive the direction of responsibility expectations. By propounding time-mindful responsibility, we are developing the conversation beyond the lame contestation about static versus dynamic time, or synchronic versus diachronic models of responsibility, thus providing a clearer epistemology of the judge's cognitive dilemmas.

Law of irresponsibility revisited

Two reflective questions to start with: is law well-equipped with the current responsibility conceptualization to deal with the question of injustice over time? If so, what is the relationship between collectivities and the rules of responsibility attribution in historical injustice discourse?

As a matter of jurisprudential investigation, the concept of responsibility bears distinct characteristics. These characteristics have been widely discussed among theorists who have written about the topic from a legal and moral perspective.[5] While we generally notice the distinctive character of

4 See Introduction.

5 Mathilde Unger and Juliette Roussin, "Frontiers of Responsibility for Global Justice," *Journal of Social Philosophy* 49, no. 3 (2018): 381–92.

legal responsibility from the moral one, an independent or complete separation between the two fields would be less favorable—or even perhaps pointless.[6] In that sense, in searching for a better model of inquiry into historical injustice, our argument will mainly embark on an indicative proposition of legal responsibility. Borrowing from Peter Cane, legal responsibility builds upon two related claims: *first*, responsibility is fundamentally "a set of social practices serving a number of social functions,"[7] and *second*, responsibility is relational in the sense that it is contingent upon "the position of individuals whose conduct attracts responsibility, [and] the impact of that conduct on other individuals and on society more generally."[8]

In this section, it would be rewarding to initially revisit Scott Veitch's *Law and Irresponsibility*.[9] Veitch analyzes law and legal institutions' involvement in organizing what he claims 'irresponsibility.' The idea is that the legal institutions currently practiced have been contributing to the production of large-scale harm globally, including extensive human rights violations, forms of colonialism, environmental damages, or even nuclear devastation. In this sense, legal institutions—understood as law's practices, concepts and categories—"operates to facilitate dispersals and disavowal of responsibility" in rather "consistent and patterned ways."[10] Thus, instead of providing norms that guide society to ascribe responsibility against harmful damages, law and legal institutions contribute to facilitating "the organization of irresponsibility that legitimates" human suffering at large.[11]

The law of irresponsibility, as Veitch calls it, reflects the condition of an asymmetrical relationship between law and responsibility. This asymmetrical relationship is essentially contingent upon the practice of law and legal institutions. In that sense, Veitch argues that there are several fundamental characteristics that explain the capability of legal institutions (norms, practices and reasoning) to organize responsibility (and, of course, irresponsibility). These characteristics include (1) law's claims for its normative correctness (law as rights), (2) law's force (the enforceability of legal standards) and (3) law's priority in normative social hierarchies. Veitch claims that those characteristics have been enabling legal institutions to disavow the question of responsibility, treating human-produced suffering as 'excess' or a mere

6 Brian Leiter, "The Demarcation Problem in Jurisprudence: A New Case for Scepticism," *Oxford Journal of Legal Studies* 31, no. 4 (2011): 663–77; Scott Hershovitz, "The End of Jurisprudence," *Yale Law Journal* 124 (2014): 1160.

7 Peter Cane, *Responsibility in Law and Morality* (Oxford & Portland, OR: Hart Publishing, 2002), 3.

8 Ibid., 4.

9 Scott Veitch, *Law and Irresponsibility: On the Legitimation of Human Suffering* (Oxon: Routledge-Cavendish, 2007).

10 Ibid., 1.

11 Ibid.

departure from the existing legal norm. Therefore, the law of irresponsibility is not an articulation about illegal conduct or activities that imminently generate human suffering, but instead, it emphasizes the need for lawyers to put a perspective on the 'excess-related' activities that already have a strong legal basis, wherein laws simultaneously "allow for and legitimize" the authorization of those 'excesses' of human suffering.[12]

One might ask a follow-up question pertaining to the way in which law, traditionally meant to uphold responsibility, instead organizes its counterpart: irresponsibility. Here, Veitch elucidates a way to understand responsibility—apparently, he treats responsibility applicable diametrically with irresponsibility—beyond its mundane usage and definition in law and philosophy, which understands the notion of *answerability* and *culpability*. Rather, he exhibits responsibility as "a term covering a range of different techniques and purposes, the appearance of which in different social institutions and locations is thus better thought of in the plural."[13] Suggested by Peter Cane's view of responsibility as practices, understanding responsibility through Veitch's viewpoint asserts two vital implications: *first*, responsibility must be seen in the context of social institutions; and *second*, responsibility is malleable, or 'free-floating,' to use Baumann's sociological term, insofar as legal actors could give form and content to it in diverse ways of social practices. From this sociological framework, the proliferation or organization of irresponsibility is allowed to happen because of the combination of social structures and conditions. Central to this mode of proliferation and organization of irresponsibility are the ways in which legal concepts and categories "drive the centrifugal forces" that disaggregate responsibility, which in turn normalize irresponsibility. According to Veitch, these legal concepts and categories include sovereignty, legal personality and techniques of legal reasoning. Relevant to this argument, the asymmetry between law and responsibility might arise due to the limits of language to apprehend "the 'untold' suffering, the 'unspeakable truths, the 'unimaginable' horrors." Veitch assumes that in the midst of such limitations of legal justice to measure the 'excess' of human suffering of injustice, something is "lurking behind the assertion that the asymmetry is one that pushes beyond the boundaries of legal justice and responsibility."[14] According to Veitch, "the excess is not beyond law, but has its roots *within* law, what is *deemed* immeasurable has its roots within the measurable."[15]

While Veitch's law of irresponsibility is invaluable as a critique against traditional law (of responsibility), we will not proceed through a similar

12 Ibid., 58.
13 Ibid., 2.
14 Ibid., 9; Olúfẹ́mi O. Táíwò, *Reconsidering Reparations* (New York: Oxford University Press, 2022).
15 Veitch, *Law and Irresponsibility: On the Legitimation of Human Suffering*, 10. (emphasis original)

'tracing-back' approach about law's institutional defect, so to speak. Rather, building on Veitch, we could point out the limits of law toward the resolution of the excess of human suffering and, from there, try to sketch an alternative orientation in exploring the question of the law of (collective) responsibility. We later elaborate on time-mindfulness as a normative element to elucidate law's capacity of potentially pushing the boundaries of language in understanding the excess of human suffering.[16] Based on these premises, in the next section, we need to pay attention to some questions about the collective personality qualifications and the attributability of a group's substantive responsibility.

Responsibility, personality, temporality

Before we consider the models of inquiry regarding collective responsibility, it would be beneficial to set out a broader view on three related elements to responsibility, namely: personality, attribution and temporality. As a point of departure, we can refer to a common debate regarding the responsibility of people in the present for wrongful acts committed by their ancestors. For such purposes, let us start with the idea of historical responsibility objection (HRO) recently put forward by Thomas Carnes. Carnes chiefly problematizes the inquiry into a compensatory-based historic(al) injustice claim by questioning the compensatory duty-bearers, that is, "whether there is anyone to whom it would be just to ascribe duties of compensation, given that allegedly all the perpetrators—the guilty parties—are dead."[17] In answering the problem, he argues for a claim based on the rejection of HRO. According to Carnes, HRO has two central premises:[18]

(1) one must be guilty of a wrongdoing with respect to a given historic injustice in order to bear a duty to compensate for the injustice, and
(2) no one alive today can be considered so guilty because no one alive today was alive when the historic injustice occurred.

Against these premises, Carnes proposes to accept (1) while refusing to accept (2) on the basis of the nature of collective agency. That is, since such historical injustices might involve the state as the guilty party, it would be difficult to accept (2). Such a rejection of HRO rests on the normative view of states as collective agents who have a point of view of their own. Based on that view, Carnes draws a distinction between: (1) "a state distributing its compensatory duties to constitutive individual agents—which is to say that the

16 This is not to suggest that Veitch is not aware of law's potentials. See ibid., 10–11.
17 Thomas Carnes, "Historic Injustice, Collective Agency, and Compensatory Duties," *Southwest Philosophy Review* 35, no. 1 (2019): 79.
18 Ibid.

state directly assigns second-order compensatory duties to certain identifiable individuals," and (2) "a state discharging its compensatory duties, without directly assigning second-order duties to any individuals, in a way that nevertheless indirectly harms some individuals."[19] Thus, Carnes inferred, HRO should be rejected, and the state, being irreducible to individual citizens, ought to pay compensation against past injustices by any forms of policy that do not impose on innocent citizens a duty for wrongdoings they did not commit. This could be done, among others, through drawing upon savings, diverting foreign aid or delaying infrastructural projects.

Carnes' refutation of HRO is rebuttable from a responsibility analysis framework. As Donelson argues, we could identify two types of responsibility relevant to this framework, namely, attributive and substantive responsibility.[20] The former implies that "A is subject to praise and blame regarding the conduct/attitude," while the latter insists that "A should bear the cost of limiting the negative externalities for the conduct/attitude." According to Donelson, Carnes' premise (1) implies that "substantive responsibility exists only if there is attributive responsibility." However, it is unlikely to be the case. Although the two types of responsibility might coexist, they do not have to be connected to one another. More bluntly, "the lack of attributive responsibility does not settle the question of substantive responsibility."[21] Donelson refers to 'cost-spreading' as an example of justifying the separability of the two, and from there, he argues, "when no one is at fault, the court should assign liability to the party best able to spread the full cost of the injury to society at large."[22] Additionally, he claims that the functionalism approach, as opposed to Carnes's alleged formalism approach, could supplant this idea of cost-spreading. Thus, instead of paying attention to the formal designations of reparation policies, collective (or state's) substantive responsibility against past wrongdoings is justified insofar as the policy redresses the harm efficiently, irrespective of its ability to *spread* the cost.

Although framed hypothetically, such correspondence indicates the multi-dimensional aspect of the discussion about collective responsibility against historical injustice.[23] From the debate, we could surmise two recur-

19 Ibid., 83.

20 Raff Donelson, "Reparations, Responsibility, and Formalism: A Reply to Carnes," *Philosophia* 49, no. 2 (2021): 643–49.

21 Ibid., 648.

22 Ibid., 644.

23 Anthony J. Sebok, "Two Concepts of Injustice in Restitution for Slavery," *Boston University Law Review* 84 (2004): 1405; Jennifer M. Page and Desmond King, "Truth and Reparation for the US Imprisonment and Policing Regime: A Transitional Justice Perspective," *Du Bois Review: Social Science Research on Race* (2021): 1–23; Peter J. Dixon, "Reparations, Assistance and the Experience of Justice: Lessons from Colombia and the Democratic Republic of the Congo," *International Journal of Transitional Justice* 10, no. 1 (2016): 88–107; Peter

ring themes pertaining to *historical responsibility*, which include questions of collective personality qualifications and the attributability of group's substantive responsibility over time. Implicit in the debate are two necessary conditions of collective responsibility at play:

(1) Collective responsibility is not metaphorical or a mere aggregation of several individuals' responsibilities, and
(2) Collective responsibility is not an individual responsibility scale-up, in the sense that it applies to "a collective because it satisfies one or more of the metaphysical conditions required for moral responsibility."[24]

Scrutinizing the intricate relationship between the two themes is significant in two ways: *first*, it enables us to identify both the abstractness and fluidity of legal personality forms, and *second*, it later provides a route for us to bring the temporal element of the epistemology of responsibility.

Collective responsibility and legal personality

Most theories of responsibility are built upon the 'humanistic approach,' which focuses on a modern view of human agency.[25] This means that our underlying paradigm of responsibility is to assign it to *human* personality or personhood. Humans, in this sense, hold a sort of superiority over anything else, such as animals, on the basis of their possession of mind and body. This is a claim that makes legal theorists, such as H.L.A. Hart,[26] argue for capacity responsibility, which insists on modern legal system recognizing and incorporating both criteria of human personhood in framing legal responsibility. Nonetheless, given the lack of a human mind and body, collectivities are seen as non-human entities and thus fail to be seen as morally capable of bearing responsibility. In that humanistic sense, as Cane claimed, the relationship between collective responsibility and personality is approached by

J. Dixon, "Reparations and the Politics of Recognition," *Contested Justice* (2015): 326–51, https://doi.org/10.1017/cbo9781139924528.016.

24 Alberto Giubilini and Neil Levy, "What in the World Is Collective Responsibility?" *Dialectica* 72, no. 2 (2018): 193.

25 Christian List and Philip Pettit, *Group Agency: The Possibility, Design, and Status of Corporate Agents* (Oxford: Oxford University Press, 2011). It is important to note at this point what agency commonly means. List and Pettit drew three features of agency as a system: (1) It has representational states that depict how things are in the environment. (2) It has motivational states that specify how it requires things to be in the environment. (3) It has the capacity to process its representational and motivational states, leading it to intervene suitably in the environment whenever that environment fails to match a motivating specification. (20)

26 H. L. A. Hart, *Punishment and Responsibility: Essays in the Philosophy of Law* (Oxford University Press, 2008).

exclusively treating "moral responsibility as a function of personality, and personality as a function of human agency."[27]

Such a performative-humanistic approach appears to be at odds with both the law and established social practices. The approach, says Cane,

> seems to rule out vicarious liability because it limits a person's responsibility to their own intentional conduct . . . . In everyday life, for instance, people frequently attribute responsibility to groups; and many people have no difficulty with the idea that employers should accept responsibility to repair harm done by their employees in the course of employment.[28]

On many law-related occasions, other than states and companies, the forms of collectives are reflected in the forms of, for instance, non-governmental organizations, nations, indigenous people, political parties and so on.[29] Against this practical backdrop, to understand collective (legal) responsibility, we should reject the performative-humanistic approach for two reasons: (1) it focuses exclusively on human agents, and (2) it leaves untouched the reality of functions and the relational nature of legal responsibility practices. That said, the fact that collectivities are not *naturally* human does not mean that they are not legal persons who bear legal rights and obligations.

Reading from List and Pettit's theory of agents, a group has three features: (1) representational states, (2) motivational states and (3) a capacity to process them and to act on that basis in the manner of an agent.[30] These features could be seen as essential conditions for responsibility, in which "the group is organized so as to seek the realization of certain motivations in the world and to do so on the basis of certain representations about what that world is like."[31] In line with this premise, we could argue that collectivities (or groups, to be more appropriate) are first a juridical person, and, by virtue of that social fact, they are capable of bearing legal responsibility. Thus, in law, unlike the humanistic approach, collective responsibility could be understood as the *cause* of legal personality, whereas the former treats responsibility as a function of legal personality.[32]

27 Cane, *Responsibility in Law and Morality*, 180.
28 Ibid., 144.
29 Susana Aires de Sousa and William S. Laufer, "The State's Responsibility for Corporate Criminal Justice," *The Journal of Corporation Law* 47, no. 4 (2022): 1109–25; Rashwet Shrinkhal, "'Indigenous Sovereignty' and Right to Self-Determination in International Law: A Critical Appraisal," *AlterNative: An International Journal of Indigenous Peoples* 17, no. 1 (2021): 71–82; Richard Vernon, "Punishing Collectives: States or Nations," in *Accountability for Collective Wrongdoing*, ed. Tracy Isaacs and Richard Vernon (New York: Cambridge University Press, 2011), 287–306.
30 List and Pettit, *Group Agency: The Possibility, Design, and Status of Corporate Agents*, 32.
31 Ibid.
32 Cane, *Responsibility in Law and Morality*, 146.

According to Feinberg, collective responsibility—Feinberg rather used the term *liability*—roots in an organized group with "a high degree of *de facto* solidarity." Feinberg claims that,

> [c]ollective responsibility not only expresses the solidarity, it also strengthens it, and thus is a good thing to whatever extent the preexistent solidarity was a good thing. A group has solidarity to the degree that its members have mutual interests, bonds of affection, and a "common lot." The mutual interest may be a specific overlap of shared interest, or it may be a community of interest of the sort that exists when each member's integrated set of interests contains the integrated interest set of each of the others. Such "community" is often associated with bonds of sentiment directed toward common objects or with reciprocal affection between the parties. Finally, the parties share a common lot insofar as their goods and harms are necessarily collective and indivisible. Where there is solidarity there is no hurting one member without hurting them all; and because of the way their interests are related, the successes and satisfactions of one radiate their benefits to the others.[33]

Slightly different from Feinberg, Giubilini and Levy nonetheless found that the so-called bonds of solidarity were rather unconvincing. They argue that such a view treats collective responsibility as a metaphor for individual responsibility because they maintain that "the identities, intentions and actions involved are merely the identities, intentions and actions of the individuals who form bonds of solidarity with each other."[34] To be regarded as a collective from their viewpoint, a group agent must be distinct from its members in a way that "it is defined by the (shared) intention to perform a certain action rather than by the fact that it is constituted by certain specific individuals or by a certain number of individuals."[35] Giubilini and Levy furthermore maintain that

> [b]ecause, exactly like an acting, functioning body, a collective engaging in a joint action is not reducible to a mere aggregation of individual identities—or, to stick to the metaphor, a mere aggregation of body parts—the collective that engages in a joint action meets in this respect the first condition for attribution of genuinely collective moral responsibility: the identity of the group is not a mere aggregation of individual identities.[36]

33 Joel Feinberg, "Collective Responsibility," *The Journal of Philosophy* 65, no. 21 (1968): 677.
34 Giubilini and Levy, "What in the World Is Collective Responsibility?" 202.
35 Ibid., 214.
36 Ibid.

That being the case, we can submit that the relationship between collective responsibility and legal personality in law is essentially functional; that is, the responsibility of a group *causes* its legal personality, which makes the latter functional to the former. If read in that way, legal personality is by all means not a natural artifact in which a collective entity is an extension of human person. It rather signifies a legal artifact since the law recognizes abstract entities for the purpose of responsible practices in social life. But, even if we try to escape the humanistic individuation approach to group personality, we are left with two problematic recurring themes of the group's continuity and change.[37] As Cane asserts, groups or corporations operate in two dimensions:

> On the one hand, there is contemporaneous conduct of a group of human beings, and on the other a corporation has a continuity of existence over time despite changes in the composition of the group of human beings whose conduct constitutes the activities of the corporation at any one time.[38]

Since we understand legal personhood as law's artifact, we may therefore argue that law's recognition of the groups' existence over time and their conduct constituting activities is essentially "a function of holding them responsible."[39] A group's 'continuity and change' over time is therefore *not* a natural thing, but rather, it is made of and produced by legal rules.[40] In that sense, to fulfill responsibility functions, one must maintain the three conditions of representational states, motivational states and a capacity to process them and to act on that basis in the manner of an agent. Accordingly, List and Pettit claim,

> [w]hat makes an agent a person, then, is that he or she is capable of contracting obligations by entering into legal and other conventional arrangements with others. And what makes an agent the same person over time is that obligations and entitlements contracted earlier are inherited later.[41]

Collective legal responsibility, which is equally applicable to individual responsibility, is a conclusion rather than a premise.[42] Such a conclusion can

37 See August Faller, "How Groups Persist," *Synthese* 198, no. 8 (2021): 7149–63.
38 Cane, *Responsibility in Law and Morality*, 146.
39 Ibid., 148.
40 Foluke I. Adebisi, "Educating for the End of a Necropolitical World What Happens Beyond Decolonisation in Legal Education? Foluke I. Adebisi," in *Biopolitics and Resistance in Legal Education*, ed. Thomas Giddens and Luca Siliquini-Cinelli (Oxon & New York: Routledge, 2023), 20.
41 List and Pettit, *Group Agency: The Possibility, Design, and Status of Corporate Agents*, 173.
42 Eric A. Posner and Adrian Vermeule, "Reparations for Slavery and Other Historical Injustices," *Columbia Law Review* 103 (2003): 689. It is interesting to highlight Posner and

be reached by a range of techniques and technologies of law employed as a mode to *express* the reality of established social practices.[43] Practically, in Cane's words,

> [b]ecause of the law's institutional geography, because legal sanctions are severe and underwritten by state coercion, and because issues of responsibility that enter the legal domain cannot be left unresolved, legal concepts and practices of group responsibility provide a detailed and highly developed model for this approach to the relationship between responsibility and personality.[44]

Collective responsibility and the rules of attribution

The conventional way to describe responsibility is by outlining it as part of a sequential process that involves psychological reactions toward a particular adverse event. This so-called motivational sequence is usually depicted as: Outcome Causal determination Responsibility Blame Punishment. Meanwhile, in the context of collective legal responsibility, according to Cane, "[t]he key feature of the legal model of corporate responsibility is a set of rules and principles for attributing human conduct and mental states to abstract entities."[45] Based on our previous observation, the attribution of collective responsibility could only work through 'reciprocal affection' amongst members of a group. Reciprocal affection is seemingly construed upon interests that appear to be a natural arrangement. This sort of natural arrangement, in Feinberg's words, is composed of "parties who are largely of one mind to begin with are led (or forced) by circumstances to act in concert and share the risk of common failure or the fruits of an indivisible success."[46] In such a moral sense, Feinberg maintains that collective responsibility is a form of *liability without fault*, which is often referred to by most people as liability with noncontributory fault, contributory group fault that is collective and distributive and contributory group fault that is collective but not distributive.[47] That said, we could affirm that collective responsibility is simply not a scaled-up individual responsibility.

Vermeule's insight on the issue of historical injustice reparations seen from a policy design perspective.

43 This argument will be thoroughly discussed in case studies in Chapters 6 to 8.

44 Cane, *Responsibility in Law and Morality*, 148.

45 Ibid., 163.

46 Feinberg, "Collective Responsibility," 677.

47 Björn Petersson, "Collective Guilt Feelings," in *The Routledge Handbook of Collective Responsibility*, ed. Saba Bazargan-Forward and Deborah Tollefsen (New York & London: Routledge, 2020), 228–42.

The rules of attribution for collective responsibility could be grounded on two basic assumptions: individualist and division of labor. In the former assumption, there are five basic legal rules of attribution of responsibility, namely: the constitution (e.g., of a corporation), agency, vicarious liability, delegation and identification. The latter assumption, instead of regarding groups as mere additions of various individuals, allocates groups as divisions of individuals' activities. As we will observe later, these two basic assumptions are fundamental to understanding the temporalities of collective legal responsibility. At this point, it would suffice to say that collective responsibility deals with a special role undertaken by a certain group's identity (e.g., citizens) against particular (harmful) actions.[48] As one might be aware, we are here taking scale into consideration: Groups are no longer seen as a unified meaning of collectivity since they should fall into some *scaled* categories according to which special role is determined. As suggested by List and Pettit, the scale could be reflected in what they call a *shortage of enactor responsibility* among group members.[49] Practically, the lesser the shortfall or shortage of enactor responsibility, the wider the responsibility we could ascribe to the group. The main reason why one would be persistent in pursuing, for instance, a nation's or corporate's responsibility is based on such a developmental rationale. In this sense, List and Pettit argued that

> [t]o refuse to ascribe responsibility to the group as a whole, on the grounds that the evil done was done entirely by the spokesbody, would be to miss the opportunity to put in place an incentive for members of the group to challenge what the spokesbody does, transforming the organizational structure under which they operate: making it into a structure under which similar misdeeds are less likely. By finding the group responsible, we make clear to members that unless they develop routines for keeping their government or episcopacy in check, they will share in member responsibility for what is done by the group and may also have a negative form of enactor responsibility for allowing it to be done. We may also make clear to the members of other similar groupings that they too are liable to be found guilty in parallel cases, should their collective body bring about one or another ill.[50]

Collective responsibility of this kind is always considerably (publicly) political. In this context, attributing collective responsibility implies the

48 Amy Sepinwall, "Citizen Responsibility and the Reactive Attitudes: Blaming Americans for War Crimes in Iraq," in *Accountability for Collective Wrongdoing*, ed. Tracy Isaacs and Richard Vernon (New York: Cambridge University Press, 2011), 231–60.
49 List and Pettit, *Group Agency: The Possibility, Design, and Status of Corporate Agents*, 168.
50 Ibid., 168–69.

involvement of public accountability in the purported wrongdoings. Arendt once wrote that this kind of responsibility appears in the older form of the community and in the actions taken under the community's name.[51] In general, this sense of public accountability comprises the following hallmarks:

(1) public responses to wrongdoing relate to or belong to some group of people, in the sense that the response is made by members of that group (rather than merely being made by the victim);
(2) public responses to wrongdoing affect or concern an entire community in the sense that the response is made in the interests of the community (rather than merely in the interests of the victim);
(3) public responses to wrongdoing are made in such a way that they are open to general observation by those within the community.[52]

From these propositions, the public nature of collective responsibility makes it critical for us to further examine the ways in which the concept of experiential time affects collective responsibility practices.

Collective responsibility and temporalities

How, then, can our temporal frame instantiate a just measure in coming to terms with the experiences of suffering? Recall this chapter's main premise: that the underlying framework of our understanding of collective responsibility would be its temporal criteria. Accordingly, these temporal criteria play a critical role in addressing both legal personality and rules of responsibility attribution, although some adjustments might be necessary to differentiate collective responsibility from individual responsibility.

In displaying the legal personality criteria, Feinberg's *de facto* solidarity of a group or Giubilini and Levy's agential shared intention is fundamentally determined by the passage of time—i.e., is the group in T_2 similar to the group in T_1? Is the company now the same as the company of the distant past? Meanwhile, in establishing the rules of attribution criteria, the passage of time could, for instance, affect the way we grasp the entanglement between temporalities of harm and blameworthiness.[53] Critical to this examination is that "[t]he moderate reasons responsiveness condition for membership in

51 Hannah Arendt, *Responsibility and Judgment* (New York: Schocken, 2003), 149.
52 Michelle Madden Dempsey, "Coercion, Consent, and Time," *Ethics* 131, no. 2 (2021): 359.
53 Jules Coleman and Alexander Sarch, "Blameworthiness and Time," *Legal Theory* 18, no. 2 (2012): 101–37; Yan Kai Zhou, "What It Means to Suffer Harm," *Jurisprudence* (2021): 1–26.

the moral community is an internal condition that connects the motivational mechanism of the subject to an action." That said,

> [m]oral responsibility ascriptions focus on a subject's internal decision states, including what it intended, not on events that may have a direct causal relationship to its actions though were not captured in the scope of the operations of its neuro-psychological mechanism or its decision processes.[54]

In general, we have two models for understanding the temporalities of collective responsibility. The first is the synchronic model, which concerns collective agent's responsibility for an action at a particular time in the past. The second is the diachronic model, which concerns the transfer of a collective agent's responsibility for an action later in the future. In the context of historical injustice, as we have discussed in Chapter 5, we may understand that the diachronic model suffuses the debate between Waldron's supersession theory (i.e., which highlights the difference between a group's action in T_1 and a group's responsibility in T_2) and Thompson's transgenerational reparation theory (i.e., which treats an ancestor's responsibility for wrongdoings in the past as transferable to the present generation). The following sub-sections will describe these temporal models of drawing responsibility.

Synchronic model

Legal responsibility is commonly understood through a linear view of time. This model treats time as static and symmetric. In this context, responsibility is construed upon the causes of events, which are traditionally divided into two symmetric modalities of time, that is, the past and the future. Two distinct views are important to note in framing the temporalities of collective responsibility within this model, namely backward- and forward-looking.

The first synchronic model of responsibility is a backward-looking approach in the form of answerability, liability or accountability.[55] Cane labeled this kind of approach historic responsibility. This system of legal responsibility is based on lawyers' common intuition that the law of responsibility is applicable only to events that happened in the past. Said to be the dominant practice of responsibility-based legal liability, in this approach, "the harm or circumstance for which we seek to hold agents responsible is

54 Peter A. French, "Types of Collectives and Responsibility," in *The Routledge Handbook of Collective Responsibility* (Routledge, 2020), 12.

55 Maeve McKeown, "Backward-Looking Reparations and Structural Injustice," *Contemporary Political Theory* (2021): 1–24.

usually an isolatable action or event that has reached a terminus."[56] Historic responsibility, as Cane suggests, is the pathological form of legal responsibility.[57] In practice, to determine the existence of harm liability, this kind of temporal orientation is generated from causal responsibility, as previously discussed. Furthermore, speaking of responsibility of historical injustices, as Nuti observes,

> backward-looking approaches argue that the past still has claims on the present; however, they also reiterate that the past (and the considerations of justice stemming from it) should not be theoretically and normatively confused with what present injustices are. The past and the present cannot be regarded as the same.[58]

The second synchronic model is a forward-looking view of responsibility, or what we may call prospective responsibility. This model lays upon the expected futuristic nature of duties and obligations, in which we may expect a claim for either productive (good things produced) or preventive (bad outcomes hindered) responsibilities. In contrast to the backward-looking responsibility, "the basis of and the justification for imposition of liability is forward-looking, and the fact that the person held liable was historically responsible is incidental."[59] In practice, to name a few, the forward-looking approach is reflected in the prolific application of economic analysis of law in determining responsibility account.[60]

Outside the backward and forward approaches, we may also find a sort of mixed approach within the synchronic model. Relying on consequentialist grounds of responsibility, some theorists advocate what they call role responsibility. In Hart's taxonomy, role responsibility is

> whenever a person occupies a distinctive place or office in a social organization, to which specific duties are attached to provide for the welfare of others or to advance in some specific way the aims or purposes of the organization, he is properly said to be responsible for the performance of these duties, or for doing what is necessary to fulfil them.[61]

56 Iris Marion Young, "Responsibility and Global Justice: A Social Connection Model," *Social Philosophy and Policy* 23, no. 1 (2006): 121.
57 Cane, *Responsibility in Law and Morality*, 35.
58 Alasia Nuti, *Injustice and the Reproduction of History: Structural Inequalities, Gender and Redress* (Cambridge: Cambridge University Press, 2019), 22.
59 Cane, *Responsibility in Law and Morality*, 61.
60 Eric A. Posner and Cass R. Sunstein, "Climate Change Justice," *Georgetown Law Journal* 96 (2008): 1565.
61 Hart, *Punishment and Responsibility: Essays in the Philosophy of Law*, 212.

According to Cane, role responsibility is fundamentally a concept of authority rather than capacity. By taking the English doctrine of ministerial responsibility as an instantiation of role responsibility, Cane perceives it as

> responsibility for the (non-) exercise of normative power and authority, not responsibility for the (non-) exercise of physical and mental capacities and control. Authority and power are intrinsically social and institutional phenomena that attach to human beings as office-holders, not to human beings as possessors of physical and mental capacities.[62]

Furthermore, another line of thought is from Iris Marion Young, who professes a social connection model in advocating for collective responsibility. Young asserts that this model is distinct from a legal-based liability approach to justice. Instead of individuating justice, Young brings responsibility for injustice in a structural sense, in which "responsibility is essentially shared and cannot be discharged by oneself alone."[63]

Nevertheless, without needing to further elaborate on these mixed concepts, it suffices to say at the moment that they employ a linear view of temporality in explaining responsibility. They assert that the time for responsibility is a sort of compartment that can be instrumentalized in determining the temporal orientation of responsibility practices.

Diachronic model

The diachronic model of collective legal responsibility takes the passage of time into account. It does not posit responsibility at a particular point in time; rather, it understands the temporalities of responsibility as alterable. This model perceives time as both dynamic and asymmetric. That said, while the synchronic model is seemingly inadequate in explaining the current challenge of persistent historical injustices, some scholars have advocated a kind of approach that accommodates the flux and multiplicity of historical time—some also juxtapose this with structural injustice.[64]

The diachronic model somehow fills the gap that fails to be seen through the synchronic one. In that sense, it has been suggested that the backward- and forward-looking approaches division is somehow subtle since both could overlap and be interchangeable in any court's decisions. However, we may highlight the importance of backward-looking and puts forward-looking

62 Peter Cane, "Role Responsibility," *The Journal of Ethics* 20, no. 1 (2016): 286.

63 Iris Marion Young, *Responsibility for Justice* (New York: Oxford University Press, 2011), 181; Maeve McKeown, "Iris Marion Young's 'Social Connection Model' of Responsibility: Clarifying the Meaning of Connection," *Journal of Social Philosophy* 49, no. 3 (2018).

64 Young, "Responsibility and Global Justice: A Social Connection Model"; Maeve McKeown, "Structural Injustice," *Philosophy Compass* 16, no. 7 (2021): e12757.

inside the political representation authority box (however, we do not speak about authority at this point because the important point is the ways in which responsibility reasoning can in fact shift, alter, and emphasize one temporal frame over another).[65] This alternative model lays upon the idea of dynamic temporalities that correspond to the concept of social time. In this perspective, time is understood as socially constructed, meaning that it has its origins in society. This model treats time as both dynamic and instrumental.

Several responsibility theorists have instantiated the dynamic-time model. Building upon the growing discourse of global trends of public apology, Janna Thompson outlines what she calls 'transgenerational responsibility' against past wrongdoings. Thompson has worked on this theme mostly in the context of the United States' legacy of slavery. In her theory, Thompson contends that the separation of backward- and forward-looking responsibility cannot sufficiently provide a complete description of the necessity of transgenerational obligations and entitlements. Hence, she claims that reparation for past wrongdoings should be based on transgenerational responsibility that is construed upon the relationship between today's generation with their ancestors and future predecessors, or between the dead and the not-yet.

In legal discourse, dynamic-time implies diachronic interests pursuing interactive justice. This, for instance, can be shown in Knop and Riles' work, which grounds legal challenges of historical injustice adjudication on conflict of laws techniques.[66] What is important to highlight from Knop and Riles' anthropological approach is that they argue that sequencing is a style of legal reasoning that sees moments of injustice in totality. By problematizing the contested issue of Japanese reparation for sexual enslavement during the Second World War, they advance the technique of *sequencing* that recognizes the spatiotemporal diffusion of injustices. In this sense, sequencing involves several steps: (1) attention to the individual's experience; (2) comparison of the affected states' general domestic interests and laws; (3) consideration of the interstate's diplomatically negotiated interests, which in turn invokes imaginary time of the international system of states; and (4) a loopback reconsidering the present day's fundamental rights between the defendant and court. We may argue that sequencing is a methodological example of dynamic time because it is, as the authors suggest, "not a causal pathway, linking one position to another, like a flowchart or a logic tree. Rather, it is a temporal experience of taking on one framework, and then trading it for another."[67]

65 Niklas Luhmann, "The Future Cannot Begin: Temporal Structures in Modern Society," *Social Research* (1976): 130–52.

66 Karen Knop and Annelise Riles, "Space, Time, and Historical Injustice: A Feminist Conflict-of-Laws Approach to the Comfort Women Agreement," *Cornell Law Review* 102 (2017): 853.

67 Ibid., 921.

Dualistic character of temporalities

The two models provide building blocks for us to generate a plausible response to judges' cognitive dilemmas. In this context, the building blocks refer to our recognition of the *dualistic* character of temporal elements in determining collective legal responsibility.[68] Such dualistic character could be seen in two matters: types of temporal framework in understanding responsibility and the distinction of the roles of time.

First, from our previous observations, we may identify a dualistic character of the temporal frame applied in each model. The first is time in a chronological frame. This frame simply refers to the so-called clock time, time that is ticking and measurable, which is also the primary sense of the word 'time' in Ancient Greek, *Chronos*.[69] Time as chronology brings us to the understanding that temporality is composed of and flows linearly from the future to the present and from the present to the past. In this approach, judges do not separate time from space, or, to be precise, time is essentially framed in terms of space. As explained in Chapter 1, the chronological approach works appropriately with the logic of propositional knowledge in legal reasoning. In this mode of knowledge, time and temporality are universal to all legal events, and they are simply reducible units or measurable metrics. The primary method of reasoning that is 'to treat similar cases alike' is arguably based on this mode of knowledge, since we can simply individuate and contain events and locate past cases analogous to similar present ones. Evidently, a chronological approach fits better with formalist judges with an inclination toward mechanical legal reasoning. To a certain degree, the chronological approach to time has become the source of subsumption in legal adjudication. In this sense, instead of delivering judgment, judges are basically subsuming their perception through memory recollection; they make decisions based on what is already known from the past.

The second type is an experiential frame. It approaches time as experience, as depth or intensity in terms of quality. It is another sense of the word 'time' in Ancient Greek, *Kairos*.[70] While experiential time shares the same feature with chronological frame—which sees time as modalities of the future, present and past—it treats each modality as a continuity of different events. Under this temporal frame, one should *prima facie* reject the idea of similar cases, as it treats each case as singularity. To recall, this examination of experiential time embarks from Bergson's theory of duration. According to Bergson, time is *la durée* or duration, meaning that time is lived experience

68 Theodore T. Bergsma, "'Both Directions at Once': Chronos, Aion and the Timelessness of the Unconscious," *Deleuze and Guattari Studies* 16, no. 1 (2022): 73–88.

69 François Hartog, *Chronos: The West Confronts* (New York: Columbia University Press, 2022).

70 François Hartog, *Regimes of Historicity: Presentism and Experiences of Time* (New York: Columbia University Press, 2015); Carlo Rovelli, *The Order of Time* (Penguin, 2019).

construed upon the juxtaposition between perception and memory. Time is in its pure form through this lens, disconnected from our spatial configuration—in a way we may claim that the chronological view explained here is our way to understand time in terms of space, not time itself.

We need to understand two characteristics of this approach: (1) time is multiplicity, in which we are experiencing time in a rather dynamic flux. The multiplicity of time implies that time is variegated and sedimented—it rejects the idea of linear or static time as the sole reality, and (2) time is singularity, meaning that there is a single back-and-forth process of recollection of the virtual past that leaps to the actual present.[71] It also implies that there are no two identical moments in life—it is always a singularity. Based on these two characteristics, we can argue that people experience events (e.g., continuity, persistence, discontinuity, etc.) within which their perception and memory are embedded. This perception/memory can assist us in making meaning of the present reality with respect to the difference (in kind) between the reality of the past and future.

Second, the two models insist on distinguishing the dualistic role of time, that is, time as orientation and justification. As suggested by Radzik, we could argue that the distinction between backward and forward-looking is a matter of contestation between orientation versus justification.[72] By orientation, we are suggesting that time, or points in time to be exact, is a matter of focus that judges make in enforcing or ascribing responsibility. Responsibility that is backward-looking in orientation focuses on a certain act or event at a particular moment in time, whereas responsibility that is forward-looking involves acceptance of a role in the future. To give a simple example, the former is shown by a contract that was concluded in the past and subsequently breached sometime in the present, in which holding one's responsibility focuses on her conclusion to the contract. The latter is shown by one's failure to do a role *based on* her acceptance of doing it; for instance, one would be held responsible for failing to do duties as a lifeguard in a swimming pool based on the expectation of her acceptance of doing the job. Justification, on the other hand, involves responsive (or blaming) attitudes such as resentment, blame and indignation—these are what we commonly call reasons for responsibility. This kind of Strawsonian view of responsibility may be backward in a way that responsibility is "supported by desert-based or justice-based claims rather than by the good consequences that might be brought about by the enforcement or satisfaction of such responsibilities."[73]

71 Gilles Deleuze, *Bergsonism*, trans. H. Tomlinson and B. Habberjam (New York: Zone Books, 1991).

72 Linda Radzik, "Historical Memory as Forward-and Backward-Looking Collective Responsibility," *Midwest Studies in Philosophy* 38 (2014): 26–39.

73 Ibid., 33.

At the same time, justified responsibility can also be forward-looking in the sense that the reason for doing a certain role (or job) is to result in the good of the role.

Time-mindful responsibility

Instead of laying down collective responsibility as a concept that focuses solely on the agential inquiry, it must also be comprehended as a relational practice set in a wider agential community. In that sense, collective responsibility comprises a three-way relationship between the individual agent, the victim or one's adversary and the wider society.[74] Following Cane, we could portray this relationship from three paradigms. The first is the criminal law paradigm, which places emphasis on agents' conduct. Since criminal law's sanction regime is inclined to be offender-oriented, responsibility assertion depends on the agent's action or failure to act. The second is the civil law paradigm that puts a balance of rights and obligations between parties, or, we could say, between the agent and her victim. This paradigm demands the "objective standard of the ideal reasonable or prudent person" in assessing responsibility.[75] The third is the public law paradigm, which focuses on the consequences of conduct. While private law, as opposed to public law, emphasizes identifying rights and obligations in framing responsibility, public law rather

> focuses primarily on the rights, powers and obligations of governments and on the performance of what might be called "public functions". [And,] [o]ne concern of public law is whether and how rules of private law (such as the law of contract) should be modified in their application to governmental bodies and the performance of public functions.[76]

Thus, it does not focus only on protecting individuals or citizens' legal interests but also on protecting them from the state's illegal conduct. Under this paradigm, our spectrum of collectivity could be far-fetched as it treats

74 Cane, *Responsibility in Law and Morality*, 56; Benjamin C. Zipursky and John C. P. Goldberg, "Unrealized Torts," *Virginia Law Review* 88 (2002): 1625; Scott Hershovitz, "Corrective Justice for Civil Recourse Theorists," *Florida State University Law Review* 39 (2011): 107.

75 Richard W. Wright, "The Grounds and Extent of Legal Responsibility," *San Diego Law Review* 40 (2003): 1433. In this sense, Wright infers that "[t]o have sufficient security, each individual's person and property must be secured not merely against harm caused by the subjectively blameworthy conduct of others, but also against harm caused by objectively specifiable conduct by others that, if generally allowed to occur, would (contrary to the supreme principle of Right) foreseeably reduce, rather than enlarge, everyone's equal external freedom. (1433)

76 Cane, *Responsibility in Law and Morality*, 51.

companies, states and even groups of citizens' representation as forms of legal persons that have legal standing before the court of law.

Arguably, it is under the public law paradigm that time-mindful collective legal responsibility finds its plausible tapestry.[77] This idea of a time-mindful model is widely informed by emerging socio-legal studies on legal temporalities that have been incorporating memory, emotion and phenomenology into legal study—specifically in theories of adjudicative decision. As fields of study, memory, emotion and phenomenology have expanded the traditional dogmatic view of law and the legal system. In the area of legal reasoning, those fields of study have helped legal scholars understand the intersection between judicial and non-judicial truths about the past, the implications of judicial reasoning and decisions for inter- and transgenerational remembrance, and also the intricate relationship between emotion and experiences and the way judges justify their arguments and decisions—as we have demonstrated in Chapters 1-3.[78]

Immeasurable responsibility

The current law of responsibility persistently insists on measuring the degree to which we should ascribe responsibility, in our case, to collective entities. We have observed in Chapter 5 that temporal legal inquiry is a reflective inquiry that insists lawyers (i.e., judges) to be attentive to law's potential or possibilities in any given historical injustice case. There are two steps to an alternative argument. First, the problem of measuring responsibility logic in law and legal institutions. Second, the temporal elements of responsibility are borrowed from the Deleuzian philosophical concept of qualitative difference and repetition.

Measuring responsibility eludes us from the temporal inquiry since we are moving our inquiry toward the question of space. But why is this the case? Because by measuring responsibility, we are in fact treating responsibility (or a responsible person)[79] as a difference in degree, while it (and case law in general) can also be about differences in kind. To make the claim clear, let us refer once again to Veitch's laws of irresponsibility stated at the outset of this chapter. Veitch argues that there is a discrepancy in measuring responsibility in such a way that legal language has been limited in proportionately balancing responsibility ascription and harmful suffering. It seems that legal institutions have been determined to be capable of measuring responsibility,

77 For a general explanation of the relational structure in private and public laws, see Zhong Xing Tan, "Rethinking Relational Architecture: Interpersonal Justice beyond Private Law," *University of Toronto Law Journal* 73, no. 3 (2023): 293–347.

78 Addie C. Rolnick, "Indigenous Subjects," *Yale Law Journal* 131 (2021): 2652.

79 Scott Hershovitz, *Nasty, Brutish, and Short: Adventures in Philosophy with My Kids* (Penguin, 2022).

and such a measurement results in an outcome imposing liability on certain parties. The rationale behind responsibility measurement, henceforth, is to elucidate the degree of responsibility. As a matter of degree, responsibility is to be posited under a certain spectrum, indicating that parties addressed are less or more responsible. That is, in a temporal situation T, A is less (or more) responsible than B. Or it is also equal to say that in temporal situation T_1, A is less (or more) responsible than A in situation T_2. Consequently, it seems plausible for Veitch to justify such a demand for a symmetrical equation in law between responsibility and harms suffered.

In this context, as suggested by Wright, we may identify three limitations that hardly match with such a space-based harm-risk approximation: (1) the "no-worse-off" limitation, which is "when the harm would have occurred anyway in the absence of any tortious conduct or condition"; (2) the "superseding cause" limitation, which is "when there was a superseding cause of the harm" or (3) the "risk playout" limitation, which is "when the harm did not occur as part of the realization and playing out of one of the foreseeable risks that made the person's conduct tortious, before the hazards created by the realization of that risk had dissipated."[80] Following from Wright, it is common among legal theorists to account for causation measurement in determining actions that one should be held responsible for.[81] There are two common ideas (or tests) that underpin our intuition in declaring the essence of causation: necessary and sufficient criteria.[82] The former claims that "a cause is *necessary* for its effect; that in the absence of the cause, the effect would not be happened."[83] The latter indicates that "a cause is *sufficient* for its effect; the cause is whatever it takes to bring the effect about."[84] Arguably, the two tests have been applied heuristically since the court could use them in indiscriminate types of cases. Holton, however, argues for the defeasibility of necessary and sufficiency criteria of causation, saying that in cases of overdetermination and preemption, we apparently cannot determine the causes of action.[85] Overdetermination deals with redundancy of causes and preemp-

80 Wright, "The Grounds and Extent of Legal Responsibility," 1427.
81 Richard A. Epstein, "The Temporal Dimension in Tort Law," *The University of Chicago Law Review* 53, no. 4 (1986): 1175–218.
82 For recent discussion about the relationship between responsibility and causation in philosophy, see Justin Sytsma, "Causation, Responsibility, and Typicality," *Review of Philosophy and Psychology* 12 (2021): 699–719; Justin Sytsma, Pascale Willemsen, and Kevin Reuter, "Mutual Entailment between Causation and Responsibility," *Philosophical Studies* (2023): 1–22.
83 Richard Holton, "Causation and Responsibility," in *The Cambridge Companion to the Philosophy of Law*, ed. John Tasioulas (Cambridge: Cambridge University Press, 2020), 239. (emphasis original)
84 Ibid.
85 Ibid., 245–46.

tion simply deals with a clear factor of cause, while there is another factor that brings equal effects should the preemptive one not occur.

In practice, nonetheless, the application of responsibility measurement is not as significant as it may seem. Holton specifically mentions two doctrines against the practice of measurement. *First*, in criminal law, sometimes some crimes of aiding and abetting are treated similarly to those of the principal offender. *Second*, in tort law, we recognize the doctrine of joint and several liabilities of the defendants, which means that "the plaintiff may recover damages from any one of the defendants, leaving it up to that defendant to recover the due share from the others."[86] Therefore, in line with Holton's arguments, we could say that approximating causation is not *necessarily* relevant in accounting for both criminal and tort responsibility, at least in some peculiar cases.[87]

Let us consider once again our suggestion in Chapter 5 about the untimeliness of inquiry. Under such an untimely framework, legal responsibility should be understood in a qualitative rather than quantitative tone. Measuring legal responsibility in its 'qualitative intensity' provides us with a temporally nuanced inquiry about responsibility. So, what do we mean by qualitative intensity? Here, the logic is borrowed from Deleuzian jurisprudence. Specifically, the suggestion for arguing against measuring responsibility is inspired by Deleuze's philosophy of difference.[88] Deleuze's philosophy of difference generates two kinds of difference, namely difference in degree and difference in kind. The former depicts quantitative, measurable differences, while the latter is about qualitative, immeasurable differences. The difference in degree reflects the spatial dimension of difference, focusing on the externalities to each other and indicated by numerical (physical) measurement. Meanwhile, the difference in kind reflects the temporal dimension of difference, focusing on continuity and heterogeneity, and cannot be measured or reduced in terms of their relation to each other.[89]

86 Ibid., 246.

87 For a discussion on future injury and inchoate torts, see Zipursky and Goldberg, "Unrealized Torts."

88 Gilles Deleuze, *Difference and Repetition* (Columbia University Press, 1994).

89 See Diego M. Papayannis, "The Morality of Compensation through Tort Law," *Ratio Juris* 36, no. 1 (2023): 3–25. Implementing an interpersonal justice within law of responsibility is a risky business, especially in tort law, claims Papayannis. It is argued that "because failing to find someone responsible for the harm suffered means failing to obtain compensation. By contrast, other mechanisms in which compensation and liability are addressed separately allows for the possibility that the state will fail to find someone responsible, without this necessarily frustrating the victim's right to be compensated. The nonbilateral mechanism provides much wider protection for victims in matters relating to their welfare, at a cost of renouncing the remedy that deals with the lack of respect expressed in the unjust interaction. The extent to which sacrificing interpersonal justice is justified is a contingent matter." 21.

Measuring responsibility, as Veitch has suggested and one that pervades in responsibility practices, in fact reflects differences in degree. The logic of generalizing the law of responsibility is seen as unable to provide a clear reality, and this has been the underpinning structure of Veitch's law of irresponsibility. The rationale behind the law of irresponsibility has been to measure a fixed comparison, which tends to think of responsibility in terms of space. Measuring responsibility, therefore, hides or conceals the qualitative dimension of it in the pursuit of generalization and homogeneity. Veitch's argument for the law of irresponsibility is basically weighing the degree of responsibility, whereas what is actually happening is a concealment of the qualitative dimension of responsibility—hence, it is not irresponsibility itself. In a way, Veitch, in that sense, has actually tried to measure responsibility up to the point of the *lowest degree* of responsibility norm.

To supplant—rather than to completely negate—responsibility measurement, we could argue that legal responsibility practice is primarily different in kind rather than exclusively in degree. In that way, responsibility should be framed as an immeasurable experience, a sensation rather than an objectified incident that separates subject from object. Borrowing from Bergson's theory of duration, the *virtual* past responsibility lives and coexists with the *actual* present responsibility.

Two things are of significance from this claim. *First*, suggested by the philosophy of difference, we can argue that (the time of) responsibility should be understood in terms of difference in kind. The essence of responsibility is therefore construed as "internal or constitutive difference, continuous, heterogeneous, interpenetrated, without clear-cut outlines or boundaries, and incomparable with each other or with a common measure."[90] It can be measured by law (as a measuring term), which then reduces it to harm and blame that act as external differences. These external differences are interacting in such a way that they are "produc[*ing*] a flux that is not without some order or organization, but whose structure fluctuates and transforms itself over time."[91] Under this frame, legal responsibility can be seen as sensation and affect rather than as an object matter that can be measured, repeated or regulated. As in *Time and Free Will*, Bergson wrote that,

> [w]hen we speak of material objects, we refer to the possibility of seeing and touching them; we localize them in space. In that case, no effort of inventive faculty of symbolical representation is necessary in order to count them; we have only to think them, at first separately, and then simultaneously, within the very medium in which they come under our

90 Elizabeth Grosz, *The Nick of Time: Politics, Evolution, and the Untimely* (Durham & London: Duke University Press, 2004), 159.

91 Ibid.

> observation. The case is no longer the same when we consider purely affective psychic states, or even mental images. Here, the terms being no longer given in space, it seems *a priori*, that *we can hardly count them except by some process of symbolic representation.*[92]

Second, situating the theory of *duration* in our temporal frame suggests singularity and multiplicity of responsibility. Seen through this lens, responsibility would be symbolically represented (or expressed, to be precise) by the interaction between perception and memory; that is, responsibility sustains both singularity and multiplicity. Such an immeasurable responsibility *posits* the present as the sole actual: "[t]he present, then, is not an instant, a measurable and regulated moment; it is a dynamic concept that extends itself to include the fringes that touch both past and present."[93] At the same time, the past and the future remain virtual. The extent of legal responsibility is assessed through mental images, which somewhat resembles Stapelton's 'historical involvement' or 'historical role.'[94] The image of backward responsibility, however, is in a state of latency, and judges can only access it through a leap from the actual into the virtual. Recalling the backward-looking justification and orientation, the former resides in the actuality of the present, whereas the latter is in the past. Therefore, it is through the expansion of the past that we can exert the potential for the justification in determining the just dessert of wrongdoings.

This proposition implicitly negates both the synchronic and diachronic approaches. It is because in both approaches, the past and the future, as modalities or parts of temporality, appear to be all-actual; that is, they are fixed at some point in time which we then put in a rather static *position*. Meanwhile, what is being suggested from Bergson-Deleuze's philosophy of difference is that (legal) responsibility is always in flux and always takes part in the process of (law's) becoming.

Law's time-mindfulness and collective responsibility

One can reasonably ask: what does the immeasurable responsibility proposition tell us about the temporalities of legal responsibility? It is our main claim in this chapter that the problem of temporal discrepancy can alternatively be resolved through asserting experiential temporality within the law

92 Henri Bergson, *Time and Free Will: An Essay on the Immediate Data of Consciousness* (Routledge, 2014), 85–86. (emphasis added)

93 Grosz, *The Nick of Time: Politics, Evolution, and the Untimely*, 177.

94 Jane Stapleton, "Legal Cause: Cause-in-Fact and the Scope of Liability for Consequences," *Vanderbilt Law Review* 54 (2001): 941; Richard W. Wright, "Once More into the Bramble Bush: Duty, Causal Contribution, and the Extent of Legal Responsibility," *Vanderbilt Law Review* 54 (2001): 1071.

of responsibility in order to activate the potential of the past. At this point, we need to refer again to Postema's jurisprudence, from which we can formulate *time-mindful collective responsibility*. To wit, this kind of responsibility is a re-formulation of the two recurring themes addressed in this chapter's introduction—i.e., collective personality qualifications and the attributability of a group's substantive responsibility over time—which can accommodate the temporalities of injustice.

First, collective personality qualification is an extrapolation subjective to agential and social time. The time-mindful responsibility is informed by Postema's legal time-mindfulness, which exerts time's essential position in law's normativity. Postema outlines the concept of law's time-mindfulness by initially observing law's normative force. In that sense, as Postema argues,

> law seeks to guide the practical reasoning and the actions of self-directing, intelligent agents, and it provides these agents with a framework within which they can publicly justify their actions and demand justification from others, especially from those who exercise political power over them.[95]

As a normative enterprise, law must be able to act as a mode of guidance, enabling what Postema calls 'rational self-directing agents.' These agents, argued Postema, "not only can follow norms, but they can also take (at least some of) these norms as standards for evaluation and vindication of their actions and the actions of others."[96] Time-mindfulness requires agents' (judges', citizens', lawyers') attention, memory and anticipation in a way that the three actions reflect their grasps or senses toward the past, present and future. Considering the weight of temporal dimension of law's normativity would give us an understanding of the way law structures judicial reasoning—from which Postema later claimed that "law orders time in its distinctive way because it can normatively guide practically rational human agents only if it enables rational agents to integrate its proposed ordering into their own cross-temporal practical perspectives."[97]

To support this temporal underpinning, we need to outline three 'types' of time. The first is subjective time, which is essentially personal, experienced time. The second is person time, which is an extension of an individual's experienced time. The extension could be reflected in two levels: (1) at the

95 Gerald J. Postema, "Melody and Law's Mindfulness of Time," *Ratio Juris* 17, no. 2 (2004): 206.
96 Ibid., 220.
97 Gerald J. Postema, "Time in Law's Domain," *Ratio Juris* 31, no. 2 (2018): 173; Casey Rebecca Johnson, *Epistemic Care: Vulnerability, Inquiry, and Social Epistemology* (New York & Oxford: Taylor & Francis, 2023). Casey Johnson's epistemic care seems to be relevant in understanding law ordering time in ways that we acknowledge the ethics of epistemic interdependence in which we are shifting from individualistic to social knowers.

conscious level, involving "the processes of synthesis and organization operating at the sub-personal level of immediate perceptual experience,"[98] and (2) at the sub-personal level, involving memories and experiences that no longer belong to one's personal experience but rather "internally *related to* and *bearing on each other*."[99] In Postema's words,

> [a] fundamental fact about the moral life is that what we have done and what has happened to us in the past not only shape the circumstances and options we face in the present, but they also engage us as persons and agents; they cast us into a future already populated by our incomplete selves. Our promises, projects, and commitments to persons, colleagues, congregations, and communities engage the selves that were, are, and will continue to be. Likewise, the temporally extended values we care about, to which we find ourselves attached, engage our temporally extended selves. We bear responsibility, and we must take responsibility, for that past and that future. It is a responsibility owed to ourselves and to others. Moreover, it is not only a responsibility to them, but crucially in many cases a responsibility borne together with them.[100]

The third type is agent time, which takes place when such person time is deliberated or acted upon in the world of agents, involving both *ex ante* formation and *medias res* deliberation of one's or a group's plan or project. Agent time indicates the collective process of making sense, where responsibility gets its meaning amongst temporally extended selves.[101] Read in that way, the practical meaning of collective legal responsibility is not only within the domain of 'planned' *ex ante* formation, since as a part of practical deliberation, it is mostly engaged *in medias res*. Therefore, through the agential time lens, the way legal decision-makers understand collective responsibility exerts a recognition of "the intersection of one's own cross-temporal practical histories with those of many others."[102]

The existing approaches, both synchronic and diachronic, have been focusing on the *actuality* of collective responsibility, thus leaving the *virtual* account of responsibility to the past. Sketching from the law's time-mindfulness

98 Postema, "Time in Law's Domain," 168.
99 Ibid. (emphasis original)
100 Ibid., 170.
101 Simon Prosser, *Experiencing Time* (Oxford: Oxford University Press, 2016), Chap. 5.
102 Postema, "Time in Law's Domain," 173; Paul Faulkner, "Collective and Extended Knowledge," *Philosophical Issues* (2022): 1–14, https://doi.org/10.1111/phis.12231. In addition, the agent time somehow reflects the concept of collective knowledge. To be understood as collective knowledge, two cases are necessarily observed: *first*, there must be a certain kind of evidence or argument for a certain knowledge is discovered, and *second*, such an evidence or argument is created collectively.

approach, both approaches are inclined to treat the past and future as 'temporal parts' rather than as 'Janus-ordered' responsibility. Unlike the models under the diachronic approach umbrella, this kind of Janus-ordered responsibility integrates temporalities—both in terms of orientation and justification—within practical legal reasoning in order to attain *a degree of coherence in temporally extended social lives.*[103] It is, according to Postema,

> [l]ike melody, action is essentially temporal. This is as true of our interactions with others as it is true of purely private actions. To pursue purposes in our social lives is to pursue them in the company of and in complex interaction with others. The patterns of interaction must provide us with the resources for achieving coherence in our actions and interactions over time. Rational self-directing human agents find cross-temporal meaning in their actions in part as a function of the devices and structures made available in the community for this purpose.[104]

Borrowing from the concept of coherence in extended social lives, time-mindful responsibility can therefore be grasped as an active social practice that aims to attain social purposes over time according to the temporal patterns governed by norms of practical coherence. In a similar vein, collective legal responsibility should now be framed by legal decision-makers in terms of agential cross-temporal trajectory to the extent that such a legal concept may enable them "to orient their deliberation to it [law of responsibility] and integrate it into their own temporally mindful deliberations."[105] The cross-temporal trajectory is plausibly in line with our reading of Bergson's philosophy of duration in two senses: (1) duration could assist judges in understanding the temporalities of collective legal responsibility in a way that the innateness between the actual and the virtual of responsibility is the essential part of the argument, and (2) the attributability of a group's substantive responsibility over time. Through this approach, we could argue that the limits of language claimed by Veitch earlier should be seen as potential rather than defects.[106] The language of responsibility has been seen as *limited* because causal responsibility is *absent* in most cases of harmful suffering. To wit, A is deemed irresponsible for Ø-ing that results μ to C, because Ø-ing by A does not necessarily cause μ to C. As such, this incident is drawn under the logic of the outcome μ suffered by C, which is understood as a single, linear situation. Meanwhile, using the Bergson-Deleuzian lens, the incident should be seen as *duration*, meaning that the untold suffering, unspeakable truth and

103 Postema, "Melody and Law's Mindfulness of Time," 220–21.
104 Ibid., 220.
105 Postema, "Time in Law's Domain," 175.
106 Infra (4).

so on are actually *expressions* of a judge's cognitive dilemma because of her limitation to capture the multiplicity of time—time that is seen as experience. As a consequence, this limitation, using Bergsonian singularity and multiplicity, maintains that judges need to conflate or even dissolve the Strawsonian triad of responsibility. That is to say, they need to dissolve guilt, resentment and indignation (it is, in fact, a singularity) in attributing responsibility, and thereby, they can now regard the triad as, in fact, merely analytical: "[t]o have negative desert just is to be *to blame* for something, *to be guilty* for it, and *to deserve punishment* for it."[107]

Consequently, the time-mindful model of responsibility practice demands that legal decision-makers (1) frame the memory of the past pivotal onto responsibility ascription and (2) creatively perceive the direction of responsibility expectation. In this respect, time-mindful responsibility is by nature a relational practice that requires two creative incidents under the following concepts: *First*, a temporal comparative account of harm or, simply, historical worsening is to be the *object* of collective responsibility. Since time-mindful responsibility accepts the innate relations between the actual and the virtual, this attitude could eventually shape the way judges understand what they mean by suffering harm. Time-mindful responsibility is underpinned by the temporal comparative account of harm, according to which one suffers harm if and only if one undergoes historical worsening.[108] This approach suggests that "what it means to suffer harm is for a person to come to be in a state in which they are worse off than they were before."[109] Thus, we can argue that the object of time-mindful responsibility is *when* one is suffering harm based on the event in time. It is somehow pivoted on a *chronotopic* explanation that appeals to "the temporal location and extent of things, or to the rate of change."[110] Arguably, while suffering harm is *relational*, it is not *relative* to other situations in time insofar as it can feature in any non-causal explanations.[111] That being the case, this approach represents a rejection of the common causal-based comparative counterfactual account of harm. *Second*,

107 Radzik, "Historical Memory as Forward-and Backward-Looking Collective Responsibility," 37.

108 Stephen Perry, "Harm, History, and Counterfactuals," *San Diego Law Review* 40 (2003): 1283.

109 Zhou, "What It Means to Suffer Harm," 3.

110 Robin Le Poidevin, "A Puzzle Concerning Time Perception," *Synthese* 142 (2004): 130.

111 Poidevin, "A Puzzle Concerning Time Perception." In this article, Poidevin asserts an important point of view about causal theory of knowledge. Poidevin offers an alternative approach to modify the causal truth-maker principle. The argument is that "[i]nstead of making causal relations between truth-maker and belief bear alone the burden of conferring the status of knowledge, we should require instead that *the truth-makers play some form of explanatory role in the acquisition of perceptual knowledge*. Explanation, even of a non-logical kind, is not invariably purely causal. And even in what might ordinarily be called causal explanation, there are non-causal components. Within such explanation, beside references to the causes themselves, there may also be reference to the properties and

a 'modified' perpetual blameworthiness is needed as the *ground* of collective responsibility. In this sense, we may argue that there is a distinction between blameworthiness and reactive emotion accounts.[112] That is, there is an intuitive distinction in the judges' minds between saying someone is guilty (e.g., of a wrongdoing) and conveying a blame response, such as resentment and indignation. It depends not only on changes on the wrongdoer's part, but it also takes into account *how* such changes took place. From this point of view, attentiveness to the process over time is crucial for judges in determining the perpetuity of the blaming practice.[113]

Conclusion

This final chapter has argued for time-mindful collective responsibility as an approach that enables legal decision-makers to narrow their limited capacity to represent the reality of injustice and its corresponding lawful relations. As we have noted, the major challenge for lawyers in contemporary legal encounters is presented by Veitch's law of irresponsibility. Based on Veitch's view, we have identified that lawyers are often, if not always, positioned to measure responsibility—i.e., perceiving responsibility in more-or-less terms. Borrowing from the idea of the philosophy of difference, we have come to the view that such a difference in degree conceals (or hides) another type of reality, that is, difference in kind. As our case studies in Chapters 1-3 have described, we can confirm that intuitive judicial reasoning requires legal decision-makers to reason about collective responsibility in terms of difference in kind. In such a framework, time-mindful collective legal responsibility ought to be construed upon two elements: (1) temporal comparative account of harm as the object of collective responsibility and (2) modified perpetual blameworthiness as the ground of collective responsibility. This sort of framing of collective responsibility can be seen as one possible theoretical rejoinder to an alternative epistemology of historical injustice adjudication from the lens of judicial temporalities.

Reference list

Adebisi, Foluke I. "Educating for the End of a Necropolitical World What Happens Beyond Decolonisation in Legal Education? Foluke I Adebisi." In *Biopolitics and Resistance in Legal Education*, edited by Thomas Giddens and Luca Siliquini-Cinelli, 9–23. Oxon & New York: Routledge, 2023.

Arendt, Hannah. *Responsibility and Judgment*. New York: Schocken, 2003.

relations that structure those causes: their location in space and time, for example." 137. (emphasis added) See also Chapter 6 on judicial intuition.

112 Coleman and Sarch, "Blameworthiness and Time."

113 Stefan Riedener, "Forgiveness and the Significance of Wrongs," *Journal of Ethics and Social Philosophy* 21 (2022): 82.

Bergsma, Theodore T. "'Both Directions at Once': Chronos, Aion and the Timelessness of the Unconscious." *Deleuze and Guattari Studies* 16, no. 1 (2022): 73–88.

Bergson, Henri. *Time and Free Will: An Essay on the Immediate Data of Consciousness*. Routledge, 2014.

Birrell, Kathleen. "Human and Inhuman Subjects and Sediments." In *The Routledge Handbook of Law and the Anthropocene*, 51. Routledge, 2023.

Cane, Peter. *Responsibility in Law and Morality*. Oxford & Portland, OR: Hart Publishing, 2002.

Cane, Peter. "Role Responsibility." *The Journal of Ethics* 20, no. 1 (2016): 279–98.

Carnes, Thomas. "Historic Injustice, Collective Agency, and Compensatory Duties." *Southwest Philosophy Review* 35, no. 1 (2019): 79–89.

Coleman, Jules, and Alexander Sarch. "Blameworthiness and Time." *Legal Theory* 18, no. 2 (2012): 101–37.

Deleuze, Gilles. *Bergsonism*. Translated by H. Tomlinson and B. Habberjam. New York: Zone Books, 1991.

Deleuze, Gilles. *Difference and Repetition*. Columbia University Press, 1994.

Dempsey, Michelle Madden. "Coercion, Consent, and Time." *Ethics* 131, no. 2 (2021): 345–68.

Dixon, Peter J. "Reparations and the Politics of Recognition." *Contested Justice* (2015): 326–51. https://doi.org/10.1017/cbo9781139924528.016.

Dixon, Peter J. "Reparations, Assistance and the Experience of Justice: Lessons from Colombia and the Democratic Republic of the Congo." *International Journal of Transitional Justice* 10, no. 1 (2016): 88–107.

Donelson, Raff. "Reparations, Responsibility, and Formalism: A Reply to Carnes." *Philosophia* 49, no. 2 (2021): 643–49.

Epstein, Richard A. "The Temporal Dimension in Tort Law." *The University of Chicago Law Review* 53, no. 4 (1986): 1175–218.

Faller, August. "How Groups Persist." *Synthese* 198, no. 8 (2021): 7149–63.

Faulkner, Paul. "Collective and Extended Knowledge." *Philosophical Issues* (2022): 1–14. https://doi.org/10.1111/phis.12231.

Feinberg, Joel. "Collective Responsibility." *The Journal of Philosophy* 65, no. 21 (1968): 674–88.

French, Peter A. "Types of Collectives and Responsibility." In *The Routledge Handbook of Collective Responsibility*, 9–22. Routledge, 2020.

Giubilini, Alberto, and Neil Levy. "What in the World Is Collective Responsibility?" *Dialectica* 72, no. 2 (2018): 191–217.

Grosz, Elizabeth. *The Nick of Time: Politics, Evolution, and the Untimely*. Durham & London: Duke University Press, 2004.

Hart, H. L. A. *Punishment and Responsibility: Essays in the Philosophy of Law*. Oxford University Press, 2008.

Hartog, François. *Regimes of Historicity: Presentism and Experiences of Time*. New York: Columbia University Press, 2015.

Hartog, François. *Chronos: The West Confronts*. New York: Columbia University Press, 2022.

Hershovitz, Scott. "Corrective Justice for Civil Recourse Theorists." *Florida State University Law Review* 39 (2011): 107.

Hershovitz, Scott. "The End of Jurisprudence." *Yale Law Journal* 124 (2014): 1160.

Hershovitz, Scott. *Nasty, Brutish, and Short: Adventures in Philosophy with My Kids*. Penguin, 2022.

Holton, Richard. "Causation and Responsibility." In *The Cambridge Companion to the Philosophy of Law*, edited by John Tasioulas, 237–52. Cambridge: Cambridge University Press, 2020.

Johnson, Casey Rebecca. *Epistemic Care: Vulnerability, Inquiry, and Social Epistemology*. New York & Oxford: Taylor & Francis, 2023.
Knop, Karen, and Annelise Riles. "Space, Time, and Historical Injustice: A Feminist Conflict-of-Laws Approach to the Comfort Women Agreement." *Cornell Law Review* 102 (2017): 853.
Leiter, Brian. "The Demarcation Problem in Jurisprudence: A New Case for Scepticism." *Oxford Journal of Legal Studies* 31, no. 4 (2011): 663–77.
List, Christian, and Philip Pettit. *Group Agency: The Possibility, Design, and Status of Corporate Agents*. Oxford: Oxford University Press, 2011.
Luhmann, Niklas. "The Future Cannot Begin: Temporal Structures in Modern Society." *Social Research* (1976): 130–52.
McKeown, Maeve. "Iris Marion Young's 'Social Connection Model' of Responsibility: Clarifying the Meaning of Connection." *Journal of Social Philosophy* 49, no. 3 (2018).
McKeown, Maeve. "Backward-Looking Reparations and Structural Injustice." *Contemporary Political Theory* (2021): 1–24.
McKeown, Maeve. "Structural Injustice." *Philosophy Compass* 16, no. 7 (2021): e12757.
McKeown, Maeve. "Responsibility." In *The Philosopher New Basics: Society*, edited by Anthony Morgan, 46–50. The Philosopher, 2022.
Norman, Jana. *Posthuman Legal Subjectivity: Reimagining the Human in the Anthropocene*. Oxon & New York: Routledge, 2022.
Nuti, Alasia. *Injustice and the Reproduction of History: Structural Inequalities, Gender and Redress*. Cambridge: Cambridge University Press, 2019.
Page, Jennifer M., and Desmond King. "Truth and Reparation for the US Imprisonment and Policing Regime: A Transitional Justice Perspective." *Du Bois Review: Social Science Research on Race* (2021): 1–23.
Papayannis, Diego M. "The Morality of Compensation through Tort Law." *Ratio Juris* 36, no. 1 (2023): 3–25.
Perry, Stephen. "Harm, History, and Counterfactuals." *San Diego Law Review* 40 (2003): 1283.
Petersson, Björn. "Collective Guilt Feelings." In *The Routledge Handbook of Collective Responsibility*, edited by Saba Bazargan-Forward and Deborah Tollefsen, 228–42. New York & London: Routledge, 2020.
Poidevin, Robin Le. "A Puzzle Concerning Time Perception." *Synthese* 142 (2004): 109–42.
Posner, Eric A., and Cass R. Sunstein. "Climate Change Justice." *Georgetown Law Journal* 96 (2008): 1565.
Posner, Eric A., and Adrian Vermeule. "Reparations for Slavery and Other Historical Injustices." *Columbia Law Review* 103 (2003): 689.
Postema, Gerald J. "Melody and Law's Mindfulness of Time." *Ratio Juris* 17, no. 2 (2004): 203–26.
Postema, Gerald. J. "Time in Law's Domain." *Ratio Juris* 31, no. 2 (2018): 160–82.
Prosser, Simon. *Experiencing Time*. Oxford: Oxford University Press, 2016.
Radzik, Linda. "Historical Memory as Forward-and Backward-Looking Collective Responsibility." *Midwest Studies in Philosophy* 38 (2014): 26–39.
Riedener, Stefan. "Forgiveness and the Significance of Wrongs." *Journal of Ethics and Social Philosophy* 21 (2022): 82.
Rolnick, Addie C. "Indigenous Subjects." *Yale Law Journal* 131 (2021): 2652.
Roncancio, Iván Darío Vargas. "Law as Relation and the Co-Emergence of Beings: Towards a Paradigm Shift in Legal Education." In *Biopolitics and Resistance in Legal Education*, edited by Thomas Giddens and Luca Siliquini-Cinelli, 202–14. Oxon & New York: Routledge, 2023.

Rovelli, Carlo. *The Order of Time*. Penguin, 2019.
Sebok, Anthony J. "Two Concepts of Injustice in Restitution for Slavery." *Boston University Law Review* 84 (2004): 1405.
Sepinwall, Amy. "Citizen Responsibility and the Reactive Attitudes: Blaming Americans for War Crimes in Iraq." In *Accountability for Collective Wrongdoing*, edited by Tracy Isaacs and Richard Vernon, 231–60. New York: Cambridge University Press, 2011.
Shrinkhal, Rashwet. "'Indigenous Sovereignty' and Right to Self-Determination in International Law: A Critical Appraisal." *AlterNative: An International Journal of Indigenous Peoples* 17, no. 1 (2021): 71–82.
Sousa, Susana Aires de, and William S. Laufer. "The State's Responsibility for Corporate Criminal Justice." *The Journal of Corporation Law* 47, no. 4 (2022): 1109–25.
Stapleton, Jane. "Legal Cause: Cause-in-Fact and the Scope of Liability for Consequences." *Vanderbilt Law Review* 54 (2001): 941.
Sytsma, Justin. "Causation, Responsibility, and Typicality." *Review of Philosophy and Psychology* 12 (2021): 699–719.
Sytsma, Justin, Pascale Willemsen, and Kevin Reuter. "Mutual Entailment between Causation and Responsibility." *Philosophical Studies* (2023): 1–22.
Táíwò, Olúfẹ́mi O. *Reconsidering Reparations*. New York: Oxford University Press, 2022.
Unger, Mathilde, and Juliette Roussin. "Frontiers of Responsibility for Global Justice." *Journal of Social Philosophy* 49, no. 3 (2018): 381–92.
Veitch, Scott. *Law and Irresponsibility: On the Legitimation of Human Suffering*. Oxon: Routledge-Cavendish, 2007.
Vernon, Richard. "Punishing Collectives: States or Nations." In *Accountability for Collective Wrongdoing*, edited by Tracy Isaacs and Richard Vernon, 287–306. New York: Cambridge University Press, 2011.
Wright, Richard W. "Once More into the Bramble Bush: Duty, Causal Contribution, and the Extent of Legal Responsibility." *Vanderbilt Law Review* 54 (2001): 1071.
Wright, Richard W. "The Grounds and Extent of Legal Responsibility." *San Diego Law Review* 40 (2003): 1425–531.
Xing Tan, Zhong. "Rethinking Relational Architecture: Interpersonal Justice beyond Private Law." *University of Toronto Law Journal* 73, no. 3 (2023): 293–347.
Young, Iris Marion. "Responsibility and Global Justice: A Social Connection Model." *Social Philosophy and Policy* 23, no. 1 (2006): 102–30.
Young, Iris Marion. *Responsibility for Justice*. New York: Oxford University Press, 2011.
Zhou, Yan Kai. "What It Means to Suffer Harm." *Jurisprudence* (2021): 1–26.
Zipursky, Benjamin C., and John C. P. Goldberg. "Unrealized Torts." *Virginia Law Review* 88 (2002): 1625.

Conclusion

Throughout this study, sound and robust arguments about the relationship between law, time and historical injustice have been presented through a critical examination of intuitive judicial reasonings. To recall, this book's central argument is that historical injustice adjudication is essentially built upon an interplay between how judicial reasoning is shaped by any given temporal presuppositions and how it enacts temporal ordering. Chapters in this book have unfolded the fundamental role of time and temporality in shaping the ways legal decision-makers (i.e., judges) conceptualize their reasoning process, which guide them in shaping the legal inquiry of historical injustice adjudication and, hence, justifying legal responsibility. In this context, we have notably established the value of judicial intuition in the legal reasoning process. Judicial intuition is valuable for legal decision-makers in finding justifying reasons for cases involving historical injustice insofar as it allows them to signal creative and experimental legal inquiries into the multiplicity of experiences of injustice. To wit, judges' intuition enables them to recognize the transition from the regularity and expediency of adjudication to a form of creative and experimental judgment—deemed to be necessary in navigating judges' cognitive dilemmas of historical injustice adjudication.

Working along the strands of doctrinal study, legal philosophy and epistemology, this study concludes several important findings about the epistemology of historical injustice adjudication. Our first finding is that, based on the case-studies in Part I, the structure of judicial reasoning in historical injustice adjudication is internally comprised of three constructive elements, namely plurality of *schemes* of intelligibility, epistemic *representation* of rules and facts and *justification* of outcomes in the form of lawful relations. Such an understanding of the legal reasoning structure has helped us situate the concept of time and temporalities within the process of justification in historical injustice adjudication.

Our second important finding is an extrapolation of the concept of law's time-mindfulness to the law-as-process approach. From such an extrapolation, we can claim that historical injustices adjudication is contingent upon

DOI: 10.4324/9781003518693-11

the Encounter of legal norms and fact-patterns.[1] Arguably, it is against such Encounters that judges alter their structure of reasoning—since the Encounter creates doubts and hesitation. Based on our case-studies—of transition, trauma and uncertainty—intuitive judges, due to the Encounter, then resist the plain application of proximate causality because intuition stimulates them to be sensitive toward, for instance, any non-causal explanations.

The third finding is that the idea of legal temporalities brings a discussion about historical injustice adjudication into a philosophical engagement with intuition in legal decision-making process. Here, intuition is considered a judicial method performed by legal decision-makers to express justifying reasons in historical injustice adjudications. It is therefore an *access* to legal argument stemming from virtue argument. This claim somehow confirms Valverde's assertion that in understanding creativity and experimental in law, "[a] lawyer, a judge, or a plaintiff using a term in a novel manner is unlikely to have done so out of a well-designed creative plan to reform language in general or law in general."[2] Experimentations or "innovations," said Valverde, "often (probably most often) arise from tactical decisions to borrow a term that intuitively seems to work for one's pragmatic purpose."[3] Intuition in this sense is a kind of judicial practice or judges' mode of thinking that enables them to create and justify forms of lawful relations, considering their epistemic capacity to represent the reality of injustice and to express the law in historical injustice adjudication.

Our last notable finding is that having critically examined three narratives related to historical injustice—transitory racial discrimination, traumatic colonial extractivism and uncertain climate injustice—we have been able to conceptualize an epistemology of historical injustice adjudication that builds upon an interaction between legal temporalities and theories of responsibility practice. This kind of interaction can be seen as a processual change that operates *within* the judge's intuition in order to find and select justifying reasons. In this regard, our contemporary theories of law of responsibility have been focused on *measuring* quantitative harm, risk and, by implication, responsibility practice. In fact, our case-studies have shown that responsibility practices are generated from the *immeasurable*, that is, (1) untimely inquiry, in a way that the courts' narratives do not necessarily follow progressively from the past or present, and (2) coherence that governs temporal patterns, based on which the justification for collective legal responsibility may attain social purposes over time.

1 See Amalia Amaya, "Exemplarism and Judicial Virtue," *Law & Literature* 25, no. 3 (2013): 428–45. Or perhaps we might want to refer to this extrapolation as a 'model' that emulates reasoning.

2 Mariana Valverde, *Chronotopes of Law: Jurisdiction, Scale and Governance* (Oxon & New York: Routledge, 2015), 26.

3 Ibid.

Thus far, this study has engaged with several areas of legal study, particularly in the three interrelated subjects of legal theory, legal reasoning and legal epistemology. It is now important to highlight some of the study's contributions in the field of legal studies.

First, in the field of legal theory, this study contributes to the larger theoretical conversation about legal reasoning. It particularly asserts the potential of judicial creativity in representing law's virtuality into the actual case. This topic has spanned from the use of imagination processes to the examination of legal perception and memory in legal adjudication. Building primarily on Del Mar's *Artefacts on Legal Inquiry*[4] and Alex Lefebvre's *The Image of Law*,[5] this book makes its contribution by expanding the theoretical apprehension about the ways judges gain access to knowledge in finding and selecting justifying reasons. From Del Mar's, we have learned about the process of legal imagination being exercised by the court of law in their decision, from which we can trace synchronous, social and multiple characters of imagination. These processes, claimed Del Mar, then help judges shape their inquiry in a legal case. Meanwhile from Lefebvre, the idea of law *in* duration sparks a novel perspective on how judicial decision is experienced and thereby takes into account a movement within the judge's memory and perception. Putting the two authors into our conversation has generated a novel outlook regarding judicial reasoning. Specifically, this study contributes to the epistemological conversation by synthesizing grounds for a temporal approach to legal reasoning. It is then fair to say that the theoretical orientation towards law's time and legal reasoning crafted in this study is fundamental in recognizing the judicial creative and transformative capacity.

Second, this study has cast an explanation about time as an inherent part of judicial attitude in legal proceedings. In this understanding, time will no longer be seen as a separate dimension of law but rather part of law's ontology. In the context of historical injustice adjudication, judges are doing law *in* time, and their epistemic attitude is translated into what we call judicial techné or technology. The way judges apply norms and principles is fundamentally a reflection of their epistemic attitude toward the framing of time and temporality. While existing studies have eruditely tried to examine law's temporality in judges' reasoning, this study has extended those findings into a larger dimension of human suffering (i.e., racial discrimination, post-colonial extractivism and climate injustice) captured by judicial decisions. For instance, one may register Chowdhury's work, *Time, Temporality*

4 Maksymilian Del Mar, *Artefacts of Legal Inquiry: The Value of Imagination in Adjudication* (Bloomsbury Publishing, 2020).

5 Alexandre Lefebvre, *The Image of Law: Deleuze, Bergson, Spinoza* (Stanford: Stanford University Press, 2008).

and Legal Judgment,[6] which is critical in the field, from which we can grasp the concept of concrete legal judgment. Extending such a conceptualization to a broader contemporary collective human suffering is essential to justify the transformative effect of experiential temporal frame through legal judgment, or, borrowing from Chowdhury's argument, to show legal judgment as a form of transformative adjudication.[7] In so doing, our examination of the legal techniques crafted by intuitive judges in the case-studies suggests that these techniques can be understood as a result of judicial intuition, a method through which legal decision-makers reason about the temporalities of injustice.

Third, in terms of methodology, this book provides some methodological alternatives, particularly for comparativists-at-law. The case-studies examined in this study move forward the conversation surrounding the concepts of comparative jurisprudence. To recall, comparative jurisprudence refers to Ewald's term that highlights comparative law as a comparison of minds that examines "the intellectual conceptions that underlie the principal institutions of one or more foreign legal system."[8] As we have noted in Part II, our theoretical underpinning of law's ontology propounds time as the 'principal institution' of law and legal system.[9] Current methodology in comparative judicial attitude has notably highlighted judges' intuition as an internal factor in legal reasoning. Nonetheless, this study has tried to move forward the methodological conversation in three senses:

(1) a legal case should be seen *intuitively*, through the lens of legal decision-makers, as an amalgamation of rules and fact-patterns. In adjudicating a case, judges do not separate rules from facts. Rather, it is a singular process that involves memory recollection and perception. This type of intuition is a mode of 'methodological individualism' so to speak, trying to seek personal experience as explanans of justice. From this methodological stance, legal reasoning in comparative research is better read as reasoning about a case that *mediates* rules and factual patterns. Instead of treating rules separately from fact-pattern in adjudicative decisions, our focus needs to shift to legal cases understood as a mediated form

6 Tanzil Chowdhury, *Time, Temporality and Legal Judgment* (Oxon & New York: Routledge, 2020).

7 Ibid., 14.

8 William Ewald, "Comparative Jurisprudence (I): What Was It Like to Try a Rat," *University of Pennsylvania Law Review* 143 (1994): 1889–2149.

9 Gerald J. Postema, "Time in Law's Domain," *Ratio Juris* 31, no. 2 (2018): 160–82; Dan Priel, "Analytic Jurisprudence in Time," in *Philosophy of Law as an Integral Part of Philosophy: Essays on the Jurisprudence of Gerald J. Postema*, ed. Thomas Bustamante and Thiago Lopes Decat (Oxford: Hart Publishing, 2020), 213–41; Gerald J. Postema, "Melody and Law's Mindfulness of Time," *Ratio Juris* 17, no. 2 (2004): 203–26.

between rules and fact-patters through a variety of schemes, concepts and taxonomies.[10] Read in that way, a case is part of the 'casuistry of relations' from which it creates rights and legal principles.[11] A case in this sense is distinct in itself, a pure actual case rather than a represented one, which might somehow create dispute or disagreement about generality, objectivity and determinacy in law—a discussion that we have observed as a confusion between time and space.[12] Consequently, a comparative judicial attitude in a legal case needs to be understood primarily as a comparison within certain categorical temporalities. It is not necessarily similar to the idea of temporal contextualization of a case, but rather a case is grasped as an account to appreciate the judges' shifting from the regularity and expediency of adjudication into a creative and experimental judgment;

(2) comparing forms of intuition alters our attention from adjudicative practices that see difference-in-degree as the sole reality toward experiencing difference-in-kind. With the difference in degree, we will end up in the lame debate about chronology versus dynamic temporality of legal responsibility of past injustices (i.e., timeliness or timelessness of a claim for legal responsibility). Meanwhile, difference in kind, as we have noted in Chapter 5, engenders us to the untimely, suggesting that legal decision-makers (i.e., judges) look into the pure reality (in a temporal sense) of injustice—that is, a qualitative reality of suffering that is not containable and measurable. In this sense, the time of injustice is seen as lived experience construed upon the juxtaposition between legal decision-makers' perception and memory. Through this lens, time is in its pure form, disconnected from our spatial configuration (in a way, we may claim that the chronological view is merely our way to understand time in terms of space, not time in itself). For comparativists-at-law and legal theorists, we can now understand two characteristics of legal temporalities by using this approach: (a) time is multiplicity, which understands that humans are experiencing time in a rather dynamic flux. The multiplicity implies that time is variegated and sedimented—it rejects the idea of linear or static time as the sole reality; and (b) time is homogeneity, meaning that there is a single back-and-forth process of recollection of the virtual past

10 Geoffrey Samuel, *Epistemology and Method in Law* (London & New York: Routledge, 2016); Geoffrey Samuel, *An Introduction to Comparative Law Theory and Method*, vol. 11 (Bloomsbury Publishing, 2014).

11 Edward Mussawir, *Jurisdiction in Deleuze: The Expression and Representation of Law* (London: Routledge, 2011).

12 Alexandre Lefebvre, "A New Image of Law: Deleuze and Jurisprudence," *Telos* 130 (2005): 103–26.

that leaps to the actual present.[13] Based on the two characteristics, we can argue that legal decision-makers experience events (e.g., continuity, persistence, discontinuity, etc.) within which their perception and memory are embedded.[14] This perception-memory leap assists legal decision-makers in making sense of the present reality with respect to the *difference* between the reality of past and future;

(3) the untimely yields the possibility for comparativists and legal theorists to appreciate judicial creativity in the face of the Encounter. This contribution extends Ewald's philosophical criticism of 'traditional' comparative law methodology.[15] In this sense, we could highlight two prongs of judicial creativity regarding historical inquiries. First, such inquiries put past events in the realm of a trajectory that is full of possibilities.[16] This methodological stance is arguably close to Legrand's negative comparison.[17] In line with this proposition, borrowing from Seo, history then is "not to prescribe those choices, but to liberate us from the past, illuminate paths not taken, and perhaps even inspire new directions."[18] Second, the law's time ordering is reflected by its cross-temporally projectable shape that purports adjudicative decision as a sub-species of duration: to anticipate the unknown and to understand the case as unique in itself. Creativity in this sense fits well with the coherence principle in legal reasoning, specifically in the context of *universalizable* particular reasoning. That said, to think of creativity in law and legal practice is to suggest that, quoting from Wu, "the justification rules of particular reasoning only articulate the *salient feature(s)* that make the case sufficiently particular to be excluded or allowed to deviate from universal rules or principles."[19]

13 Gilles Deleuze, *Bergsonism*, trans. H. Tomlinson and B. Habberjam (New York: Zone Books, 1991).

14 Joy Twemlow, "Critical Phenomenology as a Good Friend," *Critical Legal Thinking*, 2023, https://criticallegalthinking.com/2023/02/02/critical-phenomenology-as-a-good-friend/.

15 Ewald, "Comparative Jurisprudence (I): What Was It Like to Try a Rat," 2138.

16 Karen Knop and Annelise Riles, "Space, Time, and Historical Injustice: A Feminist Conflict-of-Laws Approach to the Comfort Women Agreement," *Cornell Law Review* 102 (2017): 853; Elizabeth Grosz, "Bergson, Deleuze and the Becoming of Unbecoming," *Parallax* 11, no. 2 (2005): 4–13.

17 Pierre Legrand, *Comparative Law and the Task of Negative Critique* (Oxford & New York: Routledge, 2023).

18 Sarah A. Seo, "Users Guide to History," in *Research Handbook on Modern Legal Realism* (Edward Elgar Publishing, 2021), 475. Seo's argument in this context is that "The historian's métier is storytelling; by explaining how things came to be, historians identify problems and their origins, which is a crucial first step to figuring out what to do next." (476)

19 Jingjing Wu, "Justifying Particular Reasoning in a Legal Context," *Informal Logic* 40, no. 3 (2020): 432. (emphasis added)

Reference list

Amaya, Amalia. "Exemplarism and Judicial Virtue." *Law & Literature* 25, no. 3 (2013): 428–45.

Chowdhury, Tanzil. *Time, Temporality and Legal Judgment.* Oxon & New York: Routledge, 2020.

Deleuze, Gilles. *Bergsonism.* Translated by H. Tomlinson and B. Habberjam. New York: Zone Books, 1991.

Ewald, William. "Comparative Jurisprudence (I): What Was It Like to Try a Rat." *University of Pennsylvania Law Review* 143 (1994): 1889–2149.

Grosz, Elizabeth. "Bergson, Deleuze and the Becoming of Unbecoming." *Parallax* 11, no. 2 (2005): 4–13.

Knop, Karen, and Annelise Riles. "Space, Time, and Historical Injustice: A Feminist Conflict-of-Laws Approach to the Comfort Women Agreement." *Cornell Law Review* 102 (2017): 853.

Lefebvre, Alexandre. "A New Image of Law: Deleuze and Jurisprudence." *Telos* 130 (2005): 103–26.

Lefebvre, Alexandre. *The Image of Law: Deleuze, Bergson, Spinoza.* Stanford: Stanford University Press, 2008.

Legrand, Pierre. *Comparative Law and the Task of Negative Critique.* Oxford & New York: Routledge, 2023.

Mar, Maksymilian Del. *Artefacts of Legal Inquiry: The Value of Imagination in Adjudication.* Bloomsbury Publishing, 2020.

Mussawir, Edward. *Jurisdiction in Deleuze: The Expression and Representation of Law.* London: Routledge, 2011.

Postema, Gerald J. "Melody and Law's Mindfulness of Time." *Ratio Juris* 17, no. 2 (2004): 203–26.

Postema, Gerald J. "Time in Law's Domain." *Ratio Juris* 31, no. 2 (2018): 160–82.

Priel, Dan. "Analytic Jurisprudence in Time." In *Philosophy of Law as an Integral Part of Philosophy: Essays on the Jurisprudence of Gerald J. Postema*, edited by Thomas Bustamante and Thiago Lopes Decat, 213–41. Oxford: Hart Publishing, 2020.

Samuel, Geoffrey. *An Introduction to Comparative Law Theory and Method.* Vol. 11. Bloomsbury Publishing, 2014.

Samuel, Geoffrey. *Epistemology and Method in Law.* London & New York: Routledge, 2016.

Seo, Sarah A. "Users Guide to History." In *Research Handbook on Modern Legal Realism*, 464–78. Edward Elgar Publishing, 2021.

Twemlow, Joy. "Critical Phenomenology as a Good Friend." *Critical Legal Thinking*, 2023. https://criticallegalthinking.com/2023/02/02/critical-phenomenology-as-a-good-friend/.

Valverde, Mariana. *Chronotopes of Law: Jurisdiction, Scale and Governance.* Oxon & New York: Routledge, 2015.

Wu, Jingjing. "Justifying Particular Reasoning in a Legal Context." *Informal Logic* 40, no. 3 (2020): 423–41.

Index

Note: Page numbers in **bold** indicate a table on the corresponding page.

FSC
www.fsc.org
MIX
Papier | Fördert
gute Waldnutzung
FSC® C083411

Kolibri 360 GmbH
Ferdinand-Jühlke-Straße 7
99095 Erfurt, Deutschland
produktsicherheit@kolibri360.de